ADVANCE PRAISE FOR *SHADOWS OF THE CROSS*

Shadows of the Cross beautifully displays the healing aspects of prayer, meditation, and Bible study while in the early stages of recovery from sex addiction. The authors expertly weave in modern day stories that capture the essence of classic Biblical stories that are sure to inspire and strengthen faith. Christians new to recovery will treasure the message shared in *Shadows of the Cross* that God is the ultimate supporter of their recovery.

Stefanie Carnes, PhD, author of *Mending a Shattered Heart: A Guide for Partners of Sex Addicts, Facing Addiction: Starting Recovery from Alcohol and Drugs,* and *Facing Heartbreak: Steps to Recovery for Partners of Sex Addicts*

One of the passions of my professional life has been to integrate sound theology and biblical truths with treating addictions. *Shadows of the Cross* does this extremely well. As a Christian minister, psychologist, and certified sex addiction therapist, I am grateful for this new resource which can be helpful to therapists, clients, and to anyone who is open to a faith based foundation for therapy. The suggestions are very practical, therapeutically intuitive, and "doable."

Ralph H. Earle, M.Div., PhD, ABPP, CSAT

After providing Christian based treatment for sexual addiction since the mid 1990s, I believe that sex addiction is the addiction of choice among Christians. For years Christian clients and clinicians alike have begged for clinically sound materials that speak from their spiritual belief system. *Shadows of the Cross* combines the proven worth of the Thirty Task Model with the truth and language of scripture. Using the parables of Jesus and other passages, this much needed resource is a treasure that multiplies the blessings of both clinical excellence and the healing of the Great Physician. I'm thrilled to recommend Shadows of the Cross to every Christian client and counselor.

Marnie C. Ferree, MA, LMFT, CSAT, director of Bethesda Workshops in Nashville, TN and author of *No Stones—Women Redeemed from Sexual Addiction*

Shadows of the Cross is a treasure chock full of biblical gems that will give Christians the confidence to embark on a path of recovery. The authors have masterfully woven the Twelve Steps into theological precepts illuminating a path for how to achieve a healthy sexuality while in recovery from sex addiction. Therapists who read this book will learn how to implement new ways of working with the process of recovery or risk trying interventions they had previously been unsure of. I highly recommend this book.

Alexandra Katehakis, Founder & Clinical Director, Center for Healthy Sex and author of *Mirror of Intimacy: Daily Meditations on Emotional and Erotic Intelligence* and *Erotic Intelligence: Igniting Hot, Healthy Sex While in Recovery From Sex Addiction*

Shadows of the Cross does an incredible job of blending biblical truth and Bible stories with Patrick Carnes' Thirty Task Model for sexual addiction recovery. As a result, readers will be able to integrate their faith in Christ with recovery thus empowering them to live in freedom from enslaving behavior. I am very excited to have this recovery tool and will use it to help my clients deepen their recovery as they walk with God. This is a "must read" for Christians struggling with sexual addiction as well as the helping professionals who work with them.

N. Ben Licata, MSW, LCSW, CSAT-S, Lighthouse Counseling Center

So many Christians ask if the Twelve Steps can be considered biblical. *Shadows of the Cross* shows how you can utilize scripture with the Twelve Steps as part of your comprehensive approach toward healing and wholeness. The authors have broken new ground while providing a much needed pathway of healing for Christian sex addicts. Having worked with sex addicts in both the civilian and military environment, *Shadows of the Cross* is a much needed resource. Chaplains, pastors, Christian counselors, and others now have a tool and roadmap for Christian sex addicts on their journey to wholeness and faith formation.

John O Lundin, Chaplain, Colonel USAF (Ret)/Reverend John O Lundin, Senior Pastor, Hope Lutheran Church, ELCA

SHADOWS
of the CROSS

A Christian Companion to *Facing the Shadow*

SHADOWS
of the CROSS

A Christian Companion to *Facing the Shadow*

CRAIG S. CASHWELL, PhD, PENNIE K. JOHNSON, LPC,
AND PATRICK J. CARNES, PhD

Gentle Path Press
P.O. Box 3172
Carefree, AZ 85377
www.gentlepath.com
Copyright © 2015 by Gentle Path Press

For more information regarding our publications,
please contact Gentle Path Press at
1-800-708-1796 (toll-free U.S. only).
ISBN: 978-0-9832713-3-8

Editor's note:
All the stories in this book are based on actual experiences.
The names and details have been changed to protect the privacy of the
people involved. In some cases, composites have been created.

Contents

Preface

Getting the Most from This Book

"For I know the plans I have for you," declares the Lord, "plans to prosper you and not to harm you, plans to give you hope and a future."
JEREMIAH 29:11

We do not presume to know with any detail what God's plan is for you today and the remaining days of your life. If you have started to read this book, however, we assume you are struggling with your sexual behavior. As a Christian, you may feel a great deal of shame and be weighed down by regrets of what you have done and the consequences experienced by you and those you love. You may be in emotional turmoil, struggling to make sense of what this means and where to turn next. While we admit that we do not know God's plan for your life, we know what it is *not*. You should *not* spend the rest of your days ensnared in the trap of addictive sexual behavior. Jeremiah 29:11 promises that God has plans for your life that will give you hope and a future.

The Blessings of Recovery—Psychological and Spiritual

Whether you feel hope in this moment or whether your thoughts about the future leave you terrified, take comfort in knowing that God desires that you live a sexually healthy life. The most common word used to describe the process you are now undertaking is "recovery." As you go through this process, you will grow to realize the importance of this word. What will you recover? Besides a sexually healthy life, expect

- a more intimate connection to God
- full contact with reality by breaking through any remaining denial about your addiction
- clarity about God's plan for your life
- clarity about how to handle the struggles inherent in recovery

- clarity about what you can manage and, more important, what you cannot manage on your own
- new skills to help you deal with the challenges of recovery
- integrity gained through confession and making amends to those you have wronged
- compassion for others who struggle with sexual addiction

Shadows of the Cross is a Christian companion to Dr. Patrick Carnes's book *Facing the Shadow*. Dr. Carnes has developed a thirty-task model for recovery that includes specific tasks to complete. Each task includes activities called "performables." *Facing the Shadow* highlights the first seven tasks of recovery from sexual addiction (see Appendix A) and helps you understand your addiction and develop a recovery plan. For many of you, this may raise the question of whether recovery from sexual addiction is primarily psychological or spiritual. We believe it is both. God has inspired researchers, therapists, and scholars to develop and refine the skills that support recovery and help people live lives of sexual and spiritual integrity according to God's will.

The spiritual life of people in recovery is an important part of Carnes's task model. Some people who are not religious may focus on the psychological aspects of recovery first. Since you are a Christian, your spiritual life is so foundational to who you are, it is important to incorporate your faith into the early tasks of recovery. *Shadows of the Cross* will give you a Christian perspective on what it means to be sexually addicted and will help you use your faith, beliefs, and spiritual practices to support you in your recovery.

Going Deep—One Task at a Time

Beyond this, *Shadows of the Cross* is intended to give you an *experience* of your relationship with God as the ultimate supporter of your recovery. As such, there are many experiential activities and tasks to complete throughout the book. Some of you may be inclined to move through this book quickly to "hurry up" the recovery process. Encountering God, however, involves slowing down enough to hear the "still small voice" (I Kings 19:12). Similarly, the psalmist tells us that "Deep calls to deep" (Psalm 42:7).

The call to recover from sexual addiction also is a call to deeper, fuller, and more authentic living in communion with God, something that you already know in the depths of your being. So, deep calls to deep. We encourage you to work slowly and carefully through the materials in this book. Some experiences may speak to you more than others, and there may be activities that you want to do more than once. Take your time. God is unfolding a recovery plan for you that will continue for the rest of your life.

To get the most out of your recovery experience, read the first three chapters of this book before beginning your work in *Facing the Shadow*. Chapters 1–7 in *Facing the Shadow* parallel the work in chapters 3–10 of this book.

You will notice four icons throughout the book. These guide you on how to sequence your work using both books. You'll be prompted to:

 read and do exercises in *Facing the Shadow*

 read and study particular Bible passages

 pray

 journal your responses

Use the Activity Checklist in Appendix E. This is a map of the ways you interact with the material. Return to it once each week and check off the activities in each chapter that you've done. In the process, you will give yourself the gift of regularly celebrating your recovery. You will also create a visible record of your progress.

In short, this is a book to read and *do*. Take your time—and take the gentle path—by moving through the text one section and one activity at a time. The final chapter of this book in particular will help you explore long-term recovery within a Christian framework.

We recommend simultaneously working through the tasks in *Facing the Shadow* and the material in this book. In that way, you will address both the spiritual and psychological aspects of your addiction. This combination will best support your recovery.

Ask for Help

We all need help during the early stages of recovery. This may come in the form of a spiritually sensitive and competent therapist. Support may also come from others in a recovery group, a sponsor, or a non-shaming clergyperson. Regardless of what help you need, finding a compassionate person to support you through this journey will be vital to your continued growth and success.

Walking the Path with Support and Guidance

Each of us authors have been affected by addiction. We have also each experienced the power of recovery and the importance of our spirituality in the recovery process. We believe the relationship between our spiritual lives and recovery is a two-way street. That is, our spiritual lives, including our faith in a loving God and our spiritual practices, greatly enhance the recovery process. At the same time, the process of recovery deepens our spiritual communion with a loving God.

We also believe that you may need support and guidance throughout this process. One of the hallmarks of addiction is an inner voice that whispers, "I can handle this by myself." This voice is not the voice of Truth.

The spiritual component of recovery for Christians is captured aptly in Step Eleven of the Twelve Steps, which states, in part, that we should pray "only for knowledge of [God's] will for us and the power to carry that out." Broadly speaking, we already know God's will for us:

> *He has shown you, O mortal, what is good. And what does the Lord require of you? To act justly and to love mercy and to walk humbly with your God.*
>
> MICAH 6:8

In the end, our prayer is that *Shadows of the Cross* will offer you the structure you need to act justly, love mercy, and walk humbly with God. How amazing to know that as you walk through this process of recovery, you do not walk alone.

Craig
Pennie
Pat

Chapter One
Understanding Sex Addiction

Blessings to the seekers of healing in the name of God the Most Merciful and the Most Compassionate! As you begin this adventure, we pray that you find a path leading toward freedom, a journey filled with peace and serenity. We know from experience, however, that it will also include pain, tears, and grief. Prepare yourself as if you were taking a trip into an unknown territory. Keep your heart open and your eyes looking up to the heavens. Know, without doubt, that you do not travel this journey alone. God is with you and you will find love, forgiveness, acceptance, and guidance on your recovery journey. Within yourself you will find joy for the spirit and health for the body. Renew connection with your soul and rest from the difficulties.

Why should I seek? I am the same as he.
His essence speaks through me.
I have been looking for myself!
RUMI

May you find the peace for which your soul is searching.

Each chapter in this book offers a series of meditations, reflections, teachings, and spiritual practices designed to help you reflect on your life as a recovering sex addict and Christian. We encourage you to move through the material slowly, thoughtfully, and prayerfully, allowing God to work in you through the structure of this book.

Begin by reading the following meditation slowly and prayerfully, reflecting on its application to your life in recovery.

Meditation: Samantha's Story

Samantha grew up in a Christian home with all the comforts any girl could hope for, but she continually felt out of place. She believed she was not as pretty, smart, or popular as her older sister. As much as she wanted to fit in with the crowd, her adolescent years were filled with anguish.

After high school graduation, her restless heart and need to "fit in" could no longer be contained and she announced to her parents that she was moving out. Begrudgingly, her father relinquished the savings account meant for her college education and allowed her to go out into the world "to find herself."

As she bought her train ticket to New York City, her heart pounded with excitement. She was ready to leave behind the days of small-town quietness and her small home church congregation where the hymns sung had become monotonous and the people had become too common for her pleasure. Samantha wanted to see the world, not be stuck in the same ordinary routine.

As the train pulled into "the Big Apple" her wide eyes were filled with anticipation of the good times yet to come. Her first stop was a restaurant/bar filled with loud music, drinking, and the sound of people laughing, talking, and dancing. In her mind, she congratulated herself, "I have arrived." Soon, she made friends with some women at the bar who offered Samantha her first alcoholic drink. The drink gave her instant comfort. In her new circle of friends, she found acceptance and the man they introduced her to became her first lover.

Weekly, her father wrote to her. His letters contained news from home, prayers for her safety, and words of love and appeals to "come home when you can." Home? She was home. Life was good. Making living arrangements was easier than she thought it would be. She rented a room above the bar she frequented. Making money was easy when all she had to do was dance, laugh with the patrons, and, on occasion, give herself away to the desires of the paying guest.

But what to tell her family?

Of course, this life was not one they could understand or appreciate. So, she created an imaginary world. In this life, she was an administrative assistant working at a large corporation on Fifth Avenue. She had met a friend and she became her roommate. There was a church around the corner that she attended every Sunday. At this time, her letters back to her dad were upbeat, peaceful, and confident. And her double life began.

One day, as she awoke from a drunken sleep, she turned over in bed to find her lover gone. Standing at the mirror, she discovered that makeup could not cover the bruises left from the fight the night before. Her nails and teeth were becoming dark and yellow from the nicotine and red wine. No longer recognizing the woman returning her gaze in the mirror, she cried. Through her tears, she glimpsed the small blue box decorated in trinkets and charms from her childhood underneath her bed, the box filled with her father's letters. Sinking into her cushioned chair, she reread his words. Every letter contained the same basic news from home, including comments from her youth director asking about her and her church friends sending their love and prayers. Each letter ended with "Baby, I love you. Come home when you can." Her sobs became uncontrollable as reality began to sink into her soul. Her new life was out of control and unmanageable.

As Samantha began packing her bags, she noticed how much weight she had lost. The clothes she arrived with no longer fit and her new clothes were much too slinky and tight to wear in her small town. Finding a few things to fit into one small bag, she walked out of this life and hoped to return to the familiarity of her family and friends.

At the train depot, she called her home phone number. Three attempts and each time, no answer. The last call she made, she left a message: "Daddy, I want to come home. I have messed up my life. I have no money left and my heart, mind, and soul are in such a dark place. I understand if you are ashamed of me and do not want me to return in this shape and, if so, I will continue on until I can find other help. I now understand that it is the prayers of you and the church that have brought me back to some kind of sanity. For that I am eternally grateful."

In quiet despair, she allowed the rhythm of the train to rock her to sleep. She awakened as the train pulled into the depot she had walked through two years ago. Would anyone be there to receive her? And if so, would they notice her weight loss, unclean hair, and nicotine-stained fingers? Would she be able to withstand the shame and the guilt?

Suddenly, through the crowd, she saw her dad standing with his arms open wide and his eyes filled with tears. Racing off the train, she fell into his arms and wept. "Daddy, Daddy, I am so sorry." Looking deep into her eyes, he held her by the shoulders and said, "No need to apologize, my precious child. Forgiveness was given long before you left. Now let's hurry, you have a reception at the church waiting for you. People have been preparing for your return. Welcome home, sweetheart."

Walking into the church, Samantha could hear the choir rehearsing for the Sunday morning service. Her heart opened as she listened to "Amazing Grace"; the familiar hymn now had comforting sentiment. Tears flowed again. Never had she felt the words of the song as strongly as she did that day. In her heart, the words rang true…

Amazing Grace, how sweet the sound
that saved a wretch like me.
I once was lost, but now am found,
was blind, but now I see.

Samantha and the Prodigal Son

Self-destructive behavior can put us on the path to a miserable life. It takes real spiritual maturity to admit we have gone down the wrong path.

Review the Parable of the Prodigal Son (Luke 15:11–32), a story that reminds us that God *always* wants us to come back to Him, *no matter where we have gone or what we have done.*

 Comparing your story to that of Samantha and the Prodigal Son, reflect on the following questions:

- How do these stories relate to your personal situation?
- Where are you in your desire to change? Are you willing to "return home"?
- Are you willing to walk through the painful steps of recovery before you can find the "peace that surpasses all understanding" (Philippians 4:7)?

Quote for Today

Author Anaïs Nin wrote, "The day came when the risk to remain tight in a bud was more painful than the risk it took to blossom." Recovery begins when you realize that the pain of staying the same is greater than the pain to change.

 Read this quote several times slowly. If possible, read it aloud. Allow the words to *really* sink in. Now take a few minutes to reflect.

Prayer for Today

Lord, help me to find you in my brokenness. I need to feel your arms comforting me. I want to begin the journey of a life without the chaos I create. I ask that you bring people across my path to guide me back to sanity. It is Your Mercy and Your Grace that will carry me through. For that and all you provide for me, I am eternally grateful for Your Goodness. Amen.

Journal

We listen to music differently when we close our eyes and open our ears and hearts to listen, closing out the distractions of the outer world. Locate and listen to the song "Amazing Grace" and reflect on the lyrics as they pertain to your current reality.

Focus on a particular line or phrase to "emerge" and journal about what this means to you at this point in your recovery.

A Christian "Lens" on Sex Addiction

Consider for a moment a passage from Paul's second letter to the church at Corinth:

Therefore, in order to keep me from becoming conceited, I was given a thorn in my flesh, a messenger of Satan, to torment me. Three times I pleaded with the Lord to take it away from me. But he said to me, "My grace is sufficient for you, for my power is made perfect in weakness." Therefore, I will boast all the more gladly about my weaknesses, so that Christ's power may rest on me. That is why, for Christ's sake, I delight in weaknesses, in insults, in hardships, in persecution, in difficulties. For when I am weak, then I am strong.
II Corinthians 12:7b–10

In this passage, Paul was writing, in letters that predated the writing of the four Gospels, about being humbled by a "thorn in the flesh." He recognized that it was only through this humbling experience that the Lord was made perfect to him.

What was the "thorn in the flesh"? Great theologians and biblical scholars have offered many possibilities, including a physical ailment, a speech impediment, or a personality/angel/demon sent to tempt him. What if Paul's thorn in the flesh was some type of addiction? The reality is we simply do not know what it was that made Paul weak and led him to rely more fully on God.

What we do know is that it caused torment and difficulties, experiences with which any addict is familiar. We also know that Saul, before his conversion experience, traveled around speaking out against the teachings of Jesus. On the road to Damascus, Saul had a mystical experience that transformed him into the man we have come to know as Saint Paul. Perhaps this was his "rock bottom." The experience left him temporarily blind and unable to eat or drink. Through his days as a missionary, he continued to be mindful of the "thorn in his flesh" that forced him to rely on the grace of God.

 Take some time to reflect on II Corinthians 12:7b–10.

Read this passage several times slowly. If possible, read it aloud. As you do this, breathe deeply and allow the words to *really* sink in. After doing that, reflect on the following questions:

- How has your addiction to sexual behavior become a thorn in your flesh?
- In what ways has your addiction tormented you?
- What does the phrase "my grace is sufficient" mean to you?
- Paul says, "For when I am weak, then I am strong." In your recovery, what does this mean to you?

Can I Be a Christian and a Sex Addict?

Acknowledging your addiction may cause you to ask the following questions:

- If I am really a Christian, how can I be a sex addict?
- If I am really a sex addict, how can I be a Christian?

The creation story (Genesis 1) provides a good backdrop for these questions. Adam and Eve were living in Eden, in Paradise, which we might equate with living fully in accord with God's will. Based on certain choices and behaviors, however, they soon found themselves "East of Eden" and yearning to return home to a paradise of full communion with God.

What, then, can we call these two people in exile? If our Christian beliefs tell us anything, it is that they continued to be children of God.

No matter what you have done as a sex addict, you are a child of God.

Pause for a moment to think about that phrase.... You are a child of God.

Let's rephrase that statement.... I am a child of God.

Now read the sentences below aloud several times, reading slowly, breathing deeply, and, in turn, emphasizing each of the **bolded** words of the sentence. Pay attention to any experiences in your body as God speaks to you as you read these words.

I am a child of God.

I **am** a child of God.

I am a **child** of God.

I am a child of **God**.

 Journal your reflections and reactions to this activity.

Shadows of the Cross: A Christian Companion to *Facing the Shadow*

Often, we encounter Christian men and women in recovery who believe they are beyond redemption and that they simply cannot and will not be forgiven for their past behaviors. God's word is clear on this issue. The psalmist writes, "As far as the east is from the west, so far has He removed our transgressions from us" (Psalm 103:12). We will discuss forgiveness (including self-forgiveness) later. For now, we simply encourage forgiveness and compassion toward others and ourselves. This is the model offered to us by Jesus. As we read in the Promises of Alcoholics Anonymous (AA), found in the Big Book, "We will not regret the past nor wish to shut the door on it" (Promise 2 of *Alcoholics Anonymous*).

While we, in our humanness, do not forget the past (that is, shut the door on it), it seems that God can forgive our transgressions. What does God do with memories of our past as we begin the journey of recovery and work at changing our thoughts and deeds? Simply put, He forgets them:

> *"I will put my laws in their hearts, and I will write them on their minds.*
> *Then he adds: "Their sins and lawless acts I will remember no more."*
> HEBREWS 10:16B–17

Most of us struggle to understand the immense depth of God's love, forgiveness, and mercy. Can you begin to believe the words of Hebrews 10:16b–17? Not only does God forgive, but God forgets what you have done in the past.

Perhaps this is a moment to remember that God is a good and loving God.

In early recovery, many addicts stumble over the phrase "We will not regret the past nor wish to shut the door on it." This encouragement to forgive yourself but not forget your past struggles rings hollow to many addicts in early recovery who are filled with deep regret. If you find yourself in a place of overwhelming remorse at this point in your recovery, take heart. Most of us do. Know that in time, the healing journey of recovery will help you begin to forgive yourself and others so you can finally own the memories of the past without them owning you.

The God-Shaped Hole

Over 350 years ago, Pascal, a philosopher and mathematician, recognized how often we try to fill the emptiness within us with "things" (substances, food, relationships, sex, prestige) that simply will not last nor sustain us. If you are working through this book, you have been trying in vain, perhaps for a long time, to fill this void with sexual behavior.

Sex in itself is not bad. In fact, it is beautiful and a gift from our Creator. Healthy sexuality is not a problem. When sex is compulsive, however, it becomes a problem. Pascal referred to this emptiness within us—this void, this vacuum that yearns to be filled—as a "God-shaped hole" because he recognized that only God could fill this hole.

As a Christian, you probably experienced a great deal of shame over your compulsive sexual behaviors. This shame likely led you to be even more profoundly aware of your God-shaped hole. You may have felt even more empty inside. Often, this leads to changes in frequency, type, or risk of sexual behaviors, a phenomenon that addiction specialists refer to as tolerance. Over time, your soul became increasingly disconnected from God as the God-shaped hole grew. Meanwhile, your attempts to fill this void also escalated.

An important task of early recovery is recognizing the futility of trying to fill the God-shaped hole with compulsive sexual behavior. At this point, you likely are realizing that for some time, perhaps for many years, you have been unsuccessful in trying to manage your sexual behaviors. Your compulsive sexual behaviors are an attempt to put a "square peg in a round hole." No matter how hard you have tried to force the issue, these sexual behaviors simply cannot fill the vacuum inside of you. Only God can.

In some respects, the process of recovery is a combination of both emptying yourself of thoughts, behaviors, and feelings that compromise your recovery and filling this void with new thoughts, behaviors, and feelings that support your recovery. As you acknowledge the God-shaped hole within you, you begin to work collaboratively with God to empty that which does not feed your soul. By doing so, you consciously fill the void in ways that feed your soul and support your recovery.

Scripturally, this is captured in Paul's first letter to the church of Corinth when he wrote, *When I was a child, I talked like a child, I thought like a child, I reasoned like a child. When I became a man, I put the ways of childhood behind me* (I Corinthians 13:11). If you have ever parented or watched young children, you know that there is a period of development where children are selfish. The words "me," "no," and "mine" form the foundation of their vocabulary. They simply want what they want and can be quite adamant in their attempts to get it. In all likelihood, when you were active in your addiction, this described you. Most addicts become very self-centered and are unable to see how their behaviors are negatively impacting those around them. This leads to self-centered behaviors that are entitled ("me"), rigid ("no"), and controlling ("mine").

In recovery, you are putting away childish things.

Even as you are committing to change, you will find some residuals of your addictive sexual behavior. These may include

- memories of previous sexual experiences that may trigger you sexually

- flashes of pornographic images or themes of images that you have looked at frequently in the past
- an "out of nowhere" sexual fantasy
- sexualizing others in nonsexual situations (for example, looking at sexual "parts" of others without seeing the whole person)
- sexualizing conversations or using sexual humor

Many of these behaviors are normal reactions to the process of "detoxing" from your sexual addiction. While you want to mindfully stop these experiences as soon as you realize they are occurring, do not beat yourself up for them and thereby exacerbate your shame, as this can become fuel for further addictive sexual behavior.

Shame Solver

When you engage in addictive sexual behaviors, do the following:

1. Make instant amends to yourself and to God by stopping the behavior.
2. Say a brief prayer asking for forgiveness. When you pray for forgiveness, remember what Jesus said about forgiveness. When asked by Peter whether he should forgive someone up to seven times, Jesus responded that forgiveness should be offered not seven times, but seventy times seven (Matthew 18:22). We think that Jesus' point here was *not* that forgiveness should be offered 490 times (70 x 7) but rather should be given freely. If we ask God earnestly for forgiveness, it will be freely given.

The good news is that, over time, these residual thoughts, feelings, and behaviors will begin to decrease and living a life in recovery will become easier.

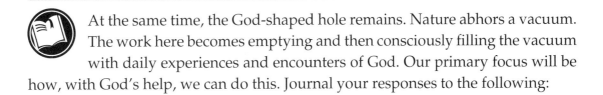 At the same time, the God-shaped hole remains. Nature abhors a vacuum. The work here becomes emptying and then consciously filling the vacuum with daily experiences and encounters of God. Our primary focus will be how, with God's help, we can do this. Journal your responses to the following:

Emptying

- What is one **thought** (about yourself, others, or God) that you sometimes have that does not support your recovery?
- What is one **behavior** that you still do that does *not* support your recovery?
- Describe one **emotion** that triggers you sexually.

Filling

- What is one **thought** (about yourself, others, or God) that will support your recovery?
- What is one **behavior** that supports your healing and recovery?
- What is one **emotion** that supports your healing and recovery?

In early recovery, it may be difficult to be clear about thoughts, behaviors, and emotions that support recovery. If you are unclear about your reflections, take time to consult with your safe counsel to make your list more complete.

 Look back over the lists you have just created in your journal. Now pray for God's guidance as you make these changes.

Attachment to God

Your views about God may have been formed as you grew up. A person's relationship with God is far more complex than simply believing whether or not He exists. Since God can be experienced but not seen, each of us develops two types of representations of God. Researchers call these doctrinal and experiential.

Doctrinal Representations of God

Doctrinal representations, also called "head knowledge," characterize what you have been told about God by church leaders, family members, and others. This may be what you think you *should* believe about God.

 What have you been taught to believe as true about God?

Experiential Representations of God

Each of us has our personal experiences and representations of God, sometimes referred to as "heart knowledge." To identify what you truly believe, try to:

- Let go of what you have been taught, your "head knowledge" of God.
- Take a few minutes to prepare yourself by closing your eyes, breathing deeply and asking God to lead you into the internal places (thoughts, feelings) that you need to access for this activity to be beneficial.

As you respond to each of the following questions, continue to breathe deeply and access the "heart" of your experiences rather than how you think you "should" respond. In your journal, elaborate on your responses.

- Do you believe in your heart that God is available to you?
- Do you believe that God is responsive to you?
- Do you believe that God is engaged with you in your sexual addiction recovery?
- In your heart, do you believe that God has, at some point, abandoned you either in your addiction or in your recovery process? Do you fear that God might abandon you in the future?
- Do you worry at times that you may not be good enough to be loved by God?

 Now, take a few minutes to prayerfully consider any differences between your "head knowledge," or what you think you *should* believe about God, and your "heart knowledge," which represents your actual experience of God. Journal any differences that you perceive.

It's important to remember that we all have some disparities between our "head knowledge" (what we believe or have been told about God) and our "heart knowledge" (our experience of God).

This is *not* an exercise to shame you about how you experience God. Instead, it is intended to help you see where you struggle in your relationship with God. You may have found you are insecure about your attachment to God.

If you feel that God has or might abandon you, you most likely experience anxiety. If this describes you, you might meditate on the words of Deuteronomy 31:6:

> *Be strong and courageous. Do not be afraid or terrified because of them,*
> *for the Lord your God goes with you; he will never leave you nor forsake you.*

If you fear that you are not good enough for God to love you, you may be avoiding your relationship with God. If this describes you, meditate on Romans 3:23–24:

> *For all have sinned and fall short of the glory of God, and all are justified freely by his grace through the redemption that came by Christ Jesus.*

You may even find that you experience both anxiety *and* avoidance in your relationship with God. The activities and experiences suggested in this book are designed to help you develop a more secure connection with God in Christ. This is vital and will lead to either a decrease in anxiety, avoidance, or both as you find the secure resting place in which, like a baby, you are always cradled in the arms of God.

"Progress Not Perfection"

In Twelve Step communities, recovery is said to be about "progress not perfection." In the Gospel of Matthew, however, Jesus is quoted as saying, "Be perfect, therefore, as your heavenly Father is perfect" (Matthew 5:48). How, then, as a Christian in recovery can you possibly make sense of this?

From a spiritual perspective, we know that truly being "perfect" is not possible (see Romans 3:23). Perfect is defined as being without flaw or defect. And from a psychological perspective, perfectionism is not something we should even strive for; doing so is problematic. Consistently, researchers have found that perfectionism is fueled by shame and that attempts to be perfect (or at least present ourselves that way) are actually attempts not to feel shame. Thus, when addicts present themselves as "perfect," they are trying to mask their shame over their addictive behavior. Unfortunately, portraying oneself as perfect is the very opposite of the behaviors that support recovery (such as relying on a supportive community and accountability partners, and being fearlessly honest with yourself and others).

From a psychological perspective, then, perfectionism is an enemy. While we have encouraged humility, humility is not the same thing as inadequacy. Humility supports recovery; a pervasive sense of being inadequate does not. Humility is correlated with mental health while inadequacy correlates with a lack of mental health. How, then, can we reconcile this?

Read the following passage from Matthew 5:45b–48:

> *He causes his sun to rise on the evil and the good, and sends rain on the righteous and the unrighteous. If you love those who love you, what reward will you get? Are not even the tax collectors doing that? And if you greet only your own people, what are you doing more than others? Do not even pagans do that? Be perfect, therefore, as your heavenly Father is perfect.*

A key to this passage is translation. Jesus would have spoken these words in Aramaic, an ancient Middle Eastern language. The Aramaic words that are translated as good and evil in verse 45 do not correspond to what we typically think of as morally right or wrong but have an agricultural meaning and refer to fruit that is ripe (good) and unripe (evil). Alternatively, the words could be translated as "mature" and "immature." This fits with other teachings of Jesus where he speaks of good trees bearing good fruit and evil trees bearing evil fruit (see Matthew 7:17). It is possible, then, that Jesus spoke more of our maturity/immaturity in verse 45 than of being good and evil. With this interpretation, God is encouraging us to love all people as He loves those whose lives are balanced and those, like you in your addiction, whose lives were out of balance, "unripe" as it were.

This brings us back to verse 48. While reading this verse, it is easy to skip over the word "therefore," but it is a vital word in this verse. The word "therefore" tells us that Jesus was speaking in reference to what he had just said. This verse does not stand alone; we cannot simply lift this one verse out of its surrounding text.

Within the context of what he was saying, Jesus then used the Aramaic word *gmar* for "perfect" in verse 48. The root of *gmar* means to accomplish or be complete. *Gmar* was originally translated into the Greek *telios*, which carries a parallel meaning of complete or mature. "Mature" is an interesting translation given the context (ripe and unripe fruit, mature and immature trees and fruit) within which Jesus was talking.

It is possible, then, that Jesus was not laying upon us the burden of perfection, but rather calling us to be complete, to be mature in a way that is godlike. In the context of calling us to love all people, not only our friends and family, Jesus asks us to be complete or mature, but not perfect. Jesus simply calls us here to "mature" into loving all people. This is very different from calling us to be perfect, an unattainable goal that has left many Christians feeling inadequate and ashamed. This is not just semantics. It is very important, especially for you as a recovering addict. Shame is one of the most potent fuels for the addictive cycle and, for many addicts, is at the very core of the repetitive cycle of addictive behavior. You are not yoked with the task of being perfect in Matthew 5:48. What you are called to do, though, is to mature, to ripen so that you might bear good fruit.

When you were active in your addiction, you were neither mature nor complete. That is, the immature tree was not bearing good fruit. As you may already realize, recovery is not simply about getting sober from your addictive sexual behavior; that is simply the beginning. The process of recovery is about growing spiritually, becoming a good tree that bears good fruit, and becoming more complete through Christ.

Being in recovery is not about being perfect. It is about being more mature in our relationship with God through Christ, with ourselves, and with those we love.

Perhaps similar to Paul's encouragement to the church (I Corinthians 13:11), Jesus is asking us to put away childish things, including addictive sexual behavior.

Perhaps, then, God's call, revealed to us through the teachings of Christ and Paul's letters, is one of maturity and completion. If you are complete, you must embrace and accept all of your "parts." This includes the part of you that has done things you deeply regret and have likely hidden from others in shame.

The good news is that there is a big difference between being mature and being perfect. Indeed, you are already taking steps in the direction of being more mature as a Christian and as a recovering person.

Immature/Unripe	Mature/Ripe
You see yourself as separate, both from God and from other people.	You recognize that you are connected, both to God and to healthy people in healthy ways.
Viewing yourself as separate, you struggle to be unique and special.	You know, without doubt, that you are created in the image of a Divine Creator.
You vacillate between shame and disavowing your shortcomings, presenting yourself as "special" in some way to counter the shame.	Without shame, you acknowledge your shortcomings to yourself and to others who offer safe and wise counsel.
You deny experiences and emotions that are uncomfortable.	You "own" all of your experiences. You acknowledge that all of your experiences and emotions, indeed all that you are, is from God.
You distort the truth through denial, justification, minimization, and rationalization.	You are fearless in being honest with yourself, with God, and with safe others.
You deny responsibility for your thoughts, emotions, and behaviors.	You take responsibility for your thoughts, emotions, and behaviors.
You strive to be special by feeding your own ego, including sexual conquests and fantasies.	You affirm and accept that you are loved by God just as you are.
Your inner critic often is quite loud.	You experience self-compassion even as you acknowledge your responsibility for past addictive behaviors.
As you disavow your own struggles, you are quick to judge others.	Experiencing less harsh self-judgment and judgment of others, and finding this replaced with compassion and empathy, you *selflessly* long to support others in their healing journey.

The path to perfection is unattainable and, in fact, potentially leads to more destructive behavior as you will never "be enough." On the other hand, the path to maturity, that of "progress not perfection," is quite attainable. You may already have experienced some of this transformation. How are you already becoming more complete?

 Just as it takes a tree (and the fruit from that tree) time to mature and ripen, it also will take you time to fully "ripen." By continuing the healing spiritual and psychological work you are doing in recovery, you will become more complete over time. Envision the fully "ripe" version of yourself after completing three to five years of recovery work. What will be different about you?

In Matthew 7:20, Jesus has just been talking of trees bearing good and bad fruit and says, "Thus, by their fruit you will recognize them." In sustained recovery, you will begin to bear good fruit. With God's help, positive changes will continue to occur (that is, you will bear more and more good fruit). What will those close to you see that will tell them you are bearing good fruit?

 Reflect on your responses, and then pray for a few minutes, specifically praying for

- God's forgiveness for those ways in which you were "unripe" in your addiction
- God's presence in your "ripening"
- your openness to hear God's plan for your healing process
- you to have the courage to carry out God's plan

A Self-Directed Vision of Maturity

 First, take a few moments to close your eyes, take a few deep breaths, and offer a prayer asking God to direct your heart and mind in this process.

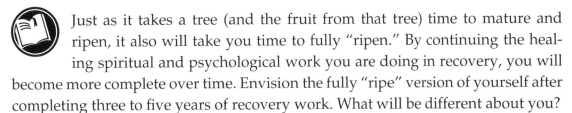 Now, in each of the following areas, take some time to reflect and journal about times and ways in which you have been *immature*, as defined above, throughout your addictive process. Be as thorough and honest with yourself as possible. When and how have you shown

- spiritual immaturity
- relational immaturity

- moral immaturity
- sexual immaturity
- vocational/work immaturity
- behavioral immaturity
- emotional immaturity
- cognitive immaturity (that is, how have you distorted the truth?)

 Now, develop a similar list in your journal of what *maturity* will look like for you as you continue to grow in each of the areas listed above.

Review the bulleted list provided and

1. Put a star by any category that is already present or growing in your life of recovery.
2. Put two stars by a few items (two to four) that seem most important to you *in this moment* in becoming more mature in your walk with Christ and your recovery.

To finish this activity, review what you've written in your journal. This is, in part, a map of where you have been, where you currently are, and where you intend to go with God's help.

 Finally, look at the items on the list with one and two stars. Pray about the changes that already are present and growing in your life and for those parts of your life that remain incomplete, asking God to guide your steps in a way that will help you become more complete and more mature.

Collaboration with God

Ken Pargament, a clinical psychologist who studies religious coping, has noted that people tend to have one of three primary coping styles. The first, a *deferring style*, is characterized by the belief that God will deliver you from your struggles and that you need not do anything other than trust this to be true. In this framework, God is the sole problem solver. The second, which Pargament called a *self-directing style*, is characterized by the belief that God has given you what you need to handle the problem on your own. This is essentially the "God helps those who help them-selves" approach. Grounded in extensive research, Pargament has found the third type of coping, which he termed *collaborative coping*, to be related to the best psychological outcomes. We see references to collaborative coping on car bumper stickers and front license plates that read "God is my copilot." In essence, collaborative coping is thinking of God as a teammate in the problem-solving process consider the following examples.

Jasmine used a deferring style of coping unsuccessfully:

Jasmine is a young Christian woman who has a long history of one-night stands and occasional swinger parties, both of which leave her feeling a deep sense of shame and regret. She repeatedly prays that God will deliver her from her behavior and vows to God that she will never do such things again, only to break this promise shortly after. At the request of her pastor, she attends a Christian Twelve Step meeting and tells the group that she refuses to call her behavior an addiction because "that sounds so permanent and I know that God will deliver me from this." She refuses to work the Twelve Steps or get a sponsor, stating, "If I do all of that, I am acting like this is in my control. God is in control and will save me from this." Jasmine continues to act counter to her values and soon drops out of the Twelve Step group because she fears judgment from others in the group.

Paul used a self-directing coping style unsuccessfully:

Paul is a highly religious man who served as a deacon in his church. Paul's wife discovered he was using pornography after he had promised twice before to discontinue this behavior. Each of the first two times, Paul went through the motions of couples therapy with his wife "to get her to calm down and get her off my back." Paul was in a profession where he managed other people and situations. He also worked hard to control his image and "manage" his wife's emotional responses. He acknowledged to his wife that he had a problem but continued to assure her that he was serious about stopping and did not need a therapist or a support group because "I can handle this myself." Yet, without the support and coping resources provided in therapy and support groups, Paul was soon secretly using pornography again.

James used collaborative coping successfully for long-term sobriety:

James, age fifty-eight, has served in his church in many capacities. He has also struggled with pornography use and one-night stands for much of his adult life. He feels great shame over his behavior and has questioned whether he can truly be a Christian with his long history of sexually acting out. He reached his "rock bottom" after going to an adult bookstore and masturbating while he knew he was being watched. As he walked out of the bookstore, he saw one of his church members walking along the street. Although the church member did not see him, this raised James's awareness of how bad his problem was. He started going to therapy and a Twelve Step group his therapist recommended. He soon found a sponsor and began to work the Steps as well as continuing to see his therapist. He was deeply moved by the words of the Serenity Prayer and began to meditate on it. Each day, he now prays for wisdom to discern what he can control in his recovery process and what he cannot. He prays for courage to change what he can and serenity for those things he cannot change.

 Reflect on the following questions to understand how you can better collaborate with God in your recovery:

1. Do you ever find yourself praying to stop your addictive behaviors but failing to follow through on recovery-related behaviors?
2. Does someone in your life supply you with verses and prayers believing that God will "take this sin" from you? How does this affect your personal recovery program?
3. Do you ever find yourself in an "I've got this" mentality where you believe you can control or manage your addiction without the help of God and other people?

There are some active tasks you can do to help you in your recovery. There are other things, however, that are beyond your control. To distinguish between these two takes wisdom. This process of collaborating with God is captured eloquently in the Serenity Prayer.

Serenity Prayer

Begin your study of the Serenity Prayer. The short version of the Serenity Prayer is perhaps the most important twenty-seven words written for people in recovery from any addiction. There is much wisdom in the Serenity Prayer. As an act of faith, commit to memorizing the short version of the prayer so that you can quote it silently or aloud at any time. Written by the American theologian Reinhold Niebuhr, this prayer provides critical guidance for recovery:

> *God, grant me the serenity to accept the things I cannot change,*
> *The courage to change the things I can,*
> *And the wisdom to know the difference.*

Many are familiar with these words. What many do not know is that this is an abbreviated version of a longer prayer written by Niebuhr. The full version states:

> *God, give me grace to accept with serenity*

the things that cannot be changed,
Courage to change the things
which should be changed,
and the Wisdom to distinguish
the one from the other.
Living one day at a time,
Enjoying one moment at a time,
Accepting hardship as a pathway to peace,
Taking, as Jesus did,
This sinful world as it is,
Not as I would have it,
Trusting that You will make all things right,
If I surrender to Your will,
So that I may be reasonably happy in this life,
And supremely happy with You forever in the next.
Amen.

Read this longer version of the Serenity Prayer several times. If possible, read it out loud. As you read this prayer, breathe deeply, and allow the words to permeate not only your mind but also your heart.

 In this moment, allow one word or phrase from the Serenity Prayer to reveal itself as most important to you *right now*. Respond to the following questions in your journal:

- What word or phrase emerges as most important for you at this point in your recovery journey?
- What makes this word or phrase so important to you *right now*? That is, what is the personal meaning of this word or phrase?

 Offer a short prayer to thank God for what you have learned from this short activity. Now, take time to reflect on the passages below from the full version of this prayer.

God, grant me the serenity

With these beginning words, we acknowledge that our serenity will come from God and it is on Him that we must rely. "And the peace of God, which transcends all understanding, will guard your hearts and your minds in Christ Jesus" (Philippians 4:7).

. . . to accept the things that cannot be changed

With these words, we admit that there are parts of our addiction over which we are powerless. Our attempts to change that which is beyond our control can become a flash point for our addiction. We attempt to change the unchangeable when we are not at peace with our limitations, when we refuse reality. With these words, however, we agree to accept life on life's terms, including recognizing that there are some aspects of our lives that we cannot change.

. . . courage to change the things which should be changed

While there is assuredly an act of surrender in admitting and confessing our addiction and finding the peace that comes with accepting aspects of our lives that we cannot change, other aspects of recovery require action, some of which are difficult and painful, and easy to avoid. This is why it is so important to pray for courage to take action where it is needed.

. . . taking, as Jesus did, this sinful world as it is, not as I would have it

Again, with these words, we are called to the act of acceptance. Even as we engage in an active process of recovery, we recognize that harboring resentments about our struggles and what we do not have or did not get in our early lives will not serve our recovery in any way. Our judgments of others and our resentments toward what is and what is not will actually make recovery far more difficult.

. . . if I surrender to Your will

Step Eleven encourages us to deepen our conscious contact with God, "praying only for knowledge of His will for us and the power to carry that out." With these words, we are reminded that when we were active in our addiction, we were not submitting to God's will. The call to recovery also is a call to discern and surrender to God's will for us.

. . . reasonably happy in this life

With these words, Niebuhr offers a reality check that is more relevant now than when he wrote the words in the 1940s. We live in a society that all too often promotes immediate gratification. Ever desiring happiness and being averse to difficulty, we seek a life of constant pleasure that, simply stated, is not realistic. We face hard and difficult days. At times, we are sad. At other times, we are fearful. This is the human condition. By practicing acceptance and surrendering to God's will for our lives, though, we can be "reasonably happy," which is a far more realistic and sustainable goal!

. . . supremely happy with You forever

While we are offered the promise of being realistically happy in this life, God has promised an eternity that no human can fathom (Ecclesiastes 3:10–12).

Hope for Recovery

Many Christian men and women have come to us seeking guidance for recovery from sexual addiction. They report past behaviors counter to the very essence of who they are as Christians. Many question whether they even are Christians, exclaiming, "How can I really be a Christian given all of my sin?"

This is complex. Some hold fast to a core belief that they are hopelessly flawed, that somehow they don't deserve to be forgiven. Others believe that God is limited in His capacity to forgive.

Either way, whether this belief is more about yourself or about God, you have likely subscribed to this belief for some time and will not easily adopt a new way of thinking.

But you can change these beliefs—and you should—because scripture tells us time and again that neither of these beliefs is true. By relying on scripture and the support of important people around you, you can slowly take on new beliefs and, indeed, must do so in order to fully embrace recovery.

If you are questioning whether you can truly be a follower of Jesus given your history and current struggles, remember the stories of the Samaritan woman in the Gospel of John and the prodigal son in the Gospel of Luke.

The Samaritan Woman

 Read John's account of the Samaritan woman at the well (John 4:3–42). Read the story slowly and imagine that you are the Samaritan woman. Where scripture refers to the woman, substitute the word "I" to help you imagine what an encounter might be like with Jesus.

 Now, respond to the following questions:

- What does Jesus offer to you?
- What does he ask of you?

Jesus broke several cultural taboos of his day in this passage. He not only spoke to a woman in public; he spoke to a Samaritan woman! As a Jewish man, he should never have asked her for a drink because any water vessel she carried would have been considered unclean and the passage specifically tells us that Jesus carried no vessel for water. Biblical scholars disagree about what it means that the woman had five husbands (4:16–18).

Nonetheless, it is clear that Jesus was reaching out to someone with whom, for many reasons, he should not even have been talking. Yet, it was to this very woman that Jesus first revealed he was the Messiah. Also, this passage is the longest account of a private conversation between Jesus and anyone in the New Testament. Whatever her past, she mattered to Jesus. So do you.

The Parable of the Prodigal Son

Jesus was a storyteller. Often, he communicated his message through stories. One of his most famous parables is the story of the prodigal son. The word "prodigal" means wasteful, reckless, and dissolute (engaging in vices or overindulging in physical pleasures to a point that is considered immoral or harmful). Sound familiar?

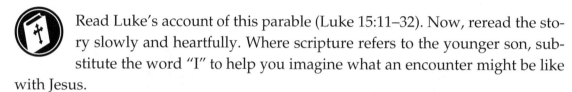 Read Luke's account of this parable (Luke 15:11–32). Now, reread the story slowly and heartfully. Where scripture refers to the younger son, substitute the word "I" to help you imagine what an encounter might be like with Jesus.

Now, reread verse 20 from this first-person perspective: "So I got up and went to my Father. But while I was still a long way off, my Father saw me and was filled with compassion for me; He ran to me, threw his arms around me, and kissed me."

Read these words of the first-person perspective several times, out loud if possible. Read slowly and breathe as if you could literally breathe these words right into your heart.

If you are questioning whether you can still be a Christian and be forgiven, remember that God's love, compassion, mercy, grace, and forgiveness are all far deeper than we can fathom.

You are a child of God, cleansed by the blood of Christ and, accordingly, you are far better than the worst thing you have ever done. In recovery, you can begin to acknowledge that this is the Truth, directly from God's word. In this profound knowing, there will be a deepening of your inner peace and contentment. You will learn that you are drawing upon a Life that is bigger than you could have realized. No longer must you question whether you have enough or whether you are enough.

You are a child of God.

Chapter Two
The Importance of Spiritual Disciplines

There is an old joke that comes with a life message:

Q: How do you get to Carnegie Hall?
A: Practice, practice, practice.

The cleverness of this joke is in the wordplay, yet it also offers a principal expression for your life as a recovering Christian. The same answer can be applied to the following questions: "How do I enter into a deeper relationship with God?" and "How do I discern God's will for my life now that I am in recovery?" Practice, practice, practice.

For many people, living as a Christian is primarily about holding certain beliefs. We say, "I am a Christian because I believe that Jesus is the Son of God and that he was crucified for our sins, was buried, and on the third day arose from the dead and ascended into heaven to the right hand of God." We agree that beliefs are very important. *That* you believe in God and *what* you believe about God are essential to your recovery.

Beliefs, however, are not what bring you into personal communion with God through the Holy Spirit. Rather, your spiritual practices allow you to personally encounter the living Christ that is, in fact, beyond beliefs, but deeper and richer. You cannot "believe" or "think" your way into knowing God's will for your life. You must *surrender* to the still small voice that will lead you home to a right relationship with God. To surrender, you must learn to trust the process that God is putting into place.

Reflect on the following questions:

- What is this process?
- What parts of the process do you need to let go and trust God to take over?
- What will you have to sacrifice in order to surrender to God's will?

Q: How do you surrender to this still small voice?
A: Practice, practice, practice.

In your addiction, you most likely practiced the opposite of surrender through willfulness and control. To do this, you likely used the addiction trinity:

- **Minimization** ("It's not that bad")—you minimized the magnitude of your bondage to addictive sexual behavior.

- **Justification** ("All I want is a little relief")—you justified your sexual acting out in a way that often was self-pitying and manipulative of others.

- **Rationalization** ("It's not my fault")—you justified your addictive sexual behavior by explaining it in a logical manner to avoid the true reasons for the behavior.

Addictions are "cunning, baffling, powerful" and, throughout recovery, you must watch for ways that you subtly use the addiction trinity in attempts to control your situation. Instead, continue to practice surrender. Even as you struggle to turn over your addiction to God, remember that your heartfelt desire to do the will of God is, in fact, the truest will of God.

Beliefs, Practices, and Experiences

Beliefs, practices, and experiences are all related. The spiritual disciplines that you ultimately select for daily practice will be influenced by your beliefs about what is important. For example, if you want to grow in knowledge of God's word, you might select reading and meditating on a passage from the Bible. If you want to hear the still small voice of God, you might practice some form of contemplative prayer or Christian meditation.

There may be some spiritual disciplines in this chapter that do not fit with your personal beliefs. As the Twelve Step adage goes, "Take what you like and leave the rest." Some people in early recovery avoid contemplative practices, not because of their beliefs, but because in the quiet space of contemplation they encounter the emotional and psychological pain that they previously avoided through addictive sexual behavior. Rather than directly deal with this pain, they distract themselves with work and other activities. While this may be acceptable in the earliest stages of recovery, such avoidance will not, in all likelihood, support long-term recovery. Quite simply, avoidance is another attempt to control recovery and *is* not an act of surrender. Avoiding your emotional and psychological pain is another type of denial and minimization, and likely will sabotage your recovery.

Making yourself overly busy to avoid what matters is captured in scripture in the story of Mary and Martha.

 Read Luke 10:38–42:

As Jesus and his disciples were on their way, he came to a village where a woman named Martha opened her home to him. She had a sister called Mary, who sat at the Lord's feet listening to what he said. But Martha was distracted by all the preparations that had to be made. She came to him and asked, "Lord, don't you care that my sister has left me to do the work by myself? Tell her to help me!"
"Martha, Martha," the Lord answered, "you are worried and upset about many things, but few things are needed—or indeed only one. Mary has chosen what is better, and it will not be taken away from her."

 Reflect on ways in which you are like Martha; that is, ways in which you are so "distracted by all the preparations" that you do not focus on what is most important.

General Guidelines for Spiritual Practice

- Any practice is better than no practice.

- Develop a *daily* practice.

- Do not overdo things; many people develop an unrealistic spiritual practice (for example, they plan to meditate and pray for three hours each day) and are then discouraged when they do not follow through. This can create shame and do more harm than good in your recovery.

- Watch out for your inner critic to shame you for missing a day or not doing a practice "right."

- Develop a discipline that involves at least two practices.

- Develop a discipline that involves some depth of experience. For example, although some people read the Bible each day, they do so in a way that stays intellectual and emotionally detached from a personal encounter with God. Strive for a personal encounter with God.

The focus of this chapter is on spiritual disciplines that have been well established. We will review and describe a large number of spiritual disciplines that you may choose to adopt. Think of it as a spiritual discipline buffet. We ask that you try each of the disciplines described here unless it runs counter to your personal beliefs. The goal is to develop a manageable and meaningful *daily* spiritual practice that supports recovery and a closer walk with God. Developing a daily spiritual practice is important. Create non-negotiable routines of positive behavior, with spiritual disciplines as a cornerstone of this plan.

Ultimately, the spiritual disciplines you use must be of your choosing. Develop a meaningful plan for your spiritual practice that works *for you* and evolves over time. Be consistent, but not rigid, with this plan. For example:

- Carlos found that doing his spiritual practice first thing in the morning worked best for him. He would wake up thirty minutes early, get a cup of coffee, and read a short scripture passage and a daily meditation for people in recovery and then reflect on each reading. He would conclude by saying the Serenity Prayer, read a silent prayer, and then say the Lord's Prayer.

- Sharon decided that when she fed her body three times each day, she would feed her soul as well. Each morning she read from a Twelve Step devotional book and read a passage of scripture. She then prayed for God's presence as she moved through her day. During lunch she read a Christian meditation for about ten minutes. This calmed her anxiety and helped her through the remainder of her workday. Each evening she examined her consciousness to see if she had wronged anyone or acted out of accord with God's will. This helped her take a personal inventory and continually admit her wrongdoings (Step Ten). When Sharon discerned that she had wronged another, she journaled about this and committed to making amends to the individual as soon as possible. When she felt she had acted out of accord with God's will, she prayed for forgiveness without shaming herself.

- Daniel used technology to support his spiritual practice. He signed up to receive a daily email devotional, which he read before going to work and journaled about how the devotion spoke to his recovery. Daniel set daily alerts so that his smartphone prompted him to pray twice during his workday. Daniel also spent time in prayer during the evening.

These are simply examples of what worked for Carlos, Sharon, and Daniel. Remember, there is no *right* or *wrong* way to begin a spiritual practice.

It is a *personal* encounter with God that is at the heart of spiritual disciplines. Your goal here is not to know *about God* but to *know God* and to *develop a personal relationship* with Him. Intellectual study is good and important but, in and of itself, it will only lead us to know more *about God*. Spiritual practices increase our relational depth with God, with others, and with ourselves. Create a practice that brings you into daily contact with God, not just a detached process like the following people:

- Debbie, a woman in early recovery from love and sex addiction, struggled with anxiety and depression, which she had long masked with her addictive sexual behavior. She believed in the transformative power of prayer and committed to praying each day. Because she had not begun to work through the shame around her sexual behavior, though, her prayers were "detached." Although she spoke her prayers daily, she was not opening herself to God. In fact, she would shut down emotionally because of an unconscious fear that God would judge her. As a result, her prayers felt like an exercise in futility and she soon became sporadic in her practice.

- Juan, a man in his early fifties who grew up in the church, had long struggled with addictive sexual behavior until three months ago, when his wife discovered his "stash" of pornography on his computer. Juan told his therapist that he still read the Bible each day but that he had stopped praying and was not open to any other spiritual practices than reading the Bible. When his therapist gently probed for the reason behind Juan's hesitation to pray, Juan cited from memory, "For the eyes of the Lord are on the righteous and his ears are attentive to their prayer, but the face of the Lord is against those who do evil" (1 Peter 3:12). In the depth of his shame, Juan believed that God would not hear his prayers because of all of the sins he had committed, so he stopped praying. Juan's therapist worked with him to address the shame that separated Juan from God's love and grace. Over time, Juan accepted the forgiveness and began to pray again in earnest.

As you develop your own spiritual discipline, seek wise counsel to ensure that you are developing a spiritual practices plan that supports your sexual health and spiritual growth. Another way to think of this is to remember the "God-shaped hole" discussed in chapter 1. Spiritual disciplines will

- make you more aware of your deep longing to be in a right relationship with God

- provide you with a way to begin to fill the void within you with the love of God

- help you begin to more clearly discern God's will for your life

Augustine once wrote that the hearts of Christians are restless until they find their rest in God. As a sex addict, you are likely quite familiar with that feeling of restlessness. Spiritual practices can provide you with a structured discipline that allows you to find rest in God.

Finally, as you think about establishing a spiritual discipline, think "map" versus "GPS." With a GPS, we plug in an address and are told exactly how to reach that destination turn by turn. This is not the way of spiritual disciplines. Instead, spiritual disciplines can be better understood as a map, though even this analogy is imperfect. Maps show us there are many different paths to any given destination. It is up to you (with the support of wise counsel) to determine the best "path" (spiritual practices) to help you move closer to your ultimate destination, which is a deeper and fuller communion with God. The map is not the territory, though, so even a map may leave you feeling lost and unsure at times. Seek wise counsel and trust that God longs for a relationship with you, so in His time He will help you find your way.

Patience.

And practice.

Preliminary Plan

Before we look at specific disciplines you might use, develop a plan for incorporating such disciplines into your life. As you create a preliminary plan, remember to

- Be realistic.
- Be specific.
- Be flexible.

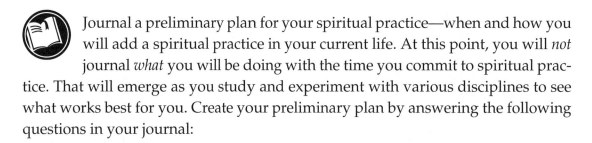 Journal a preliminary plan for your spiritual practice—when and how you will add a spiritual practice in your current life. At this point, you will *not* journal *what* you will be doing with the time you commit to spiritual practice. That will emerge as you study and experiment with various disciplines to see what works best for you. Create your preliminary plan by answering the following questions in your journal:

- *Duration:* Given what you know about the time commitments you already have at this point in your life, what is a *realistic and sustainable* amount of time to commit to your spiritual practice? We recommend at least fifteen minutes per day to start.
- *Location:* Where will you practice? Locate a physical space to minimize interruptions and distractions.
- *When:* Choose a time that will support your commitment to practice each

day. For now, choose a single time to practice, though this may need to be modified as your specific plan emerges.

- *Accountability:* Reflect on how you can make yourself accountable to another person to increase your commitment.

The following are specific spiritual disciplines to consider for your daily practice. Again, we emphasize that there is no *right* practice, only the one that is right for you.

Prayer

Prayer is far and away the most common spiritual practice within Christian communities and with good reason. Prayer invokes a personal dialogue with God and is a powerful spiritual practice.

Christian communities often practice prayer with heads bowed and eyes closed. These are a ways of humbling oneself before God (heads bowed) and removing external distractions (eyes closed). There is nothing sacred about this, though. Experiment with what helps you most in prayer. Many people report that sitting upright supports them in breathing more deeply, which deepens their openness and encounter with the Holy Spirit. In the end, exactly how you pray is between you and God, and no one else. There is power in prayer and in feeling God's reach toward us.

Unfortunately, religious communities often engage in and teach very limited forms of prayer. Prayers of petition and intercession are the most common forms of prayer.

Prayer is really an invocation. The word "invocation" comes from the Latin verb *invocare* which means "to call on." Prayer, then, is the opening of a conversation. It is like picking up the phone and making a call. As with any conversation, though, there is a give-and-take, a time to talk and a time to listen, and choices to be made about what to say and when to listen. Accordingly, we organize this section into prayers where we are primarily talking to God and prayers where we are mostly listening. To some extent, this dichotomy is artificial as God can speak to us at any point, but it may help you organize your practice of prayer. Danish theologian Søren Kierkegaard stated, "A man prayed, and at first he thought that prayer was talking. But he became more and more quiet until in the end he realized that prayer is listening."[1]

Because prayer is the beginning of a conversation, God wants heartful prayers, not eloquent prayers. We encourage you to let go of thoughts of "getting it right" and saying it perfectly. This misses the point. If you struggle to find the right words and stumble in the way you say them, you are more likely being heartful in your prayers.

In actual practice, you might combine many of these prayer types into a single prayer. For now, though, we will separate out each type so that you can become more conscious about *how* you are praying. Over time, your prayers likely will incorporate many of these types into a single prayer.

Also, as you begin trying out the various types of prayers, find a private quiet place to more fully explore your prayer life. You might create a special place to pray by hanging up inspiring pictures, sayings, quotes, or scriptures in the space and setting up a comfortable spot to sit or kneel. However you choose to arrange your environment to pray, make it meaningful for you.

But when you pray, go into your room, close the door and pray to your Father, who is unseen. Then your Father, who sees what is done in secret, will reward you.
MATTHEW 6:6

To begin your exploration of prayer, we encourage you to read about the following types of prayer and then take a few minutes to practice each way of praying. We will then ask you to reflect on your experience.

Speaking Prayers

Type of Speaking Prayer	Description
Intercessory	Prayer that asks God to intercede on another's behalf
Petitionary	Prayer requests for God to do something
Adoration	Prayer where we have the opportunity to worship God
Thanksgiving/Gratitude	Prayer where we tell God what we are grateful for
Repentance/Forgiveness	Prayer that is a self-review of our past deeds where we feel remorse or sorrow but not shame
Deliverance	Prayer that asks God to deliver us from the bondage of addiction
Jesus	Short one-line prayer where we pray to Jesus to cultivate a quiet mind and an open heart
Submission	Prayer that surrenders us to God's will

Type of Speaking Prayer	Description
Eleventh Step	Prayer that reminds us that God is in charge
Breath	Prayer that uses a favorite scripture passages or phrase of our choosing that helps us communicate with God in a way that brings us peace

A more detailed description of each speaking prayer follows.

Intercessory prayer. This is a common form of prayer asking God to intercede on another's behalf. When we pray for family, friends, and even enemies, we engage in intercessory prayer.

 Take a few minutes to pray using intercessory prayer. Allow yourself to pray for whoever comes to mind but focus solely on others and not yourself.

 After finishing your prayer, reflect and then journal about your experience of lifting up others in prayer to God.

Petitionary prayer. Prayers of petition are requests we make for God to do something.

 Take a few minutes to pray. Petitions may be made on your own behalf or on the behalf of others. Try to focus primarily on petitions for yourself today.

 After finishing your prayer, reflect and then journal about your experience of lifting up your petitions to God in prayer.

Prayers of adoration. A prayer of adoration worships God through prayer. In this type of prayer, you simply breathe deeply and allow yourself to connect with the depth of the Father's love, grace, and mercy. The words that flow from this experience are simply words of adoration, adulation, and worship.

 Take a few minutes to pray. Do not "overthink" the words, but rather allow the adoration to flow spontaneously from whatever is in your heart.

 After finishing your prayer, reflect and then journal on your experience of communicating through prayer your adoration of God.

Prayers of thanksgiving/gratitude.
Amidst all the pain and struggles of recovery, remember to take time to pray with thanksgiving and gratitude for all that you have been given. For one thing, you still have life, which is more than some addicts can say. Lifting up your prayers of thanksgiving/gratitude to God shows that you adore God and are grateful for what you have (including recovery).

 Take a few minutes to pray. In your prayer, express your gratitude for whatever comes to mind. If you are in a place of resentment right now, simply skip this practice and come back to it later.

After finishing your time of prayer, reflect and journal on this experience.

Prayers of repentance/forgiveness.
The idea of repentance is ubiquitous in scripture. It literally involves a self-review of one's past deeds and feeling contrition *but not shame.* We will distinguish between guilt and shame more fully in chapter 4. For now, simply think of guilt as a negative feeling about something you have done and shame as a negative feeling about who you are. The voice of guilt says, "I am saddened by what I have done." The voice of shame says, "I am saddened by who I am." As we have discussed, you are a child of God. Period. God does not ask you to come to Him ashamed of your past:

Caveats about Prayers of Thanksgiving/ Gratitude

1. At points in your recovery, you will most likely struggle with anger and resentments. Holding on to resentments and being unforgiving will not support your recovery. You might think that offering prayers of gratitude would help decrease feelings of resentment, but we believe the opposite can be true. Instead, we recommend practicing prayers of thanksgiving/gratitude when you are not in a place of acute resentment to anyone or anything. Over time, you will discern the best times to practice forgiveness and when to offer prayers of gratitude or adoration.

2. People sometimes use prayers of thanksgiving/gratitude to distance themselves from their psychological and emotional pain. In times of acute distress, this may be a way to calm yourself down. However, as a chronic coping strategy, prayers of thanksgiving/gratitude should not be used to avoid the painful experiences that inevitably accompany recovery.

And hope does not put us to shame, because God's love has been poured out into our hearts through the Holy Spirit, who has been given to us.

ROMANS 5:5

Prayers of repentance/forgiveness are expressions of remorse for what you have done and how this has affected your relationship with God, yourself, and others. Because such prayers focus on what you have done, they also involve a commitment to change these behaviors and to make amends for what has happened.

The first documented command of Jesus in the New Testament was:

"Repent, for the kingdom of heaven has come near."

MATTHEW 4:17

In saying this, Jesus is repeating the words of John the Baptist (Matthew 3:2) Similarly, in his Pentecost sermon, Peter challenged people to repent and described the gift this would bring:

Peter replied, "Repent and be baptized, every one of you, in the name of Jesus Christ for the forgiveness of your sins. And you will receive the gift of the Holy Spirit.

ACTS 2:38

In Twelve Step programs, Step Five states "Admitted to God, to ourselves, and to another human being the exact nature of our wrongs." Unfortunately, many people think that they have already "admitted to God" during the process of writing out their Fourth Step, as He assuredly was present and aware of their Fourth Step. Yet there is a reason that the wisdom of the Twelve Steps specifically calls us to admit to God the exact nature of our wrongs.

Why do we need to pray for our repentance and forgiveness? After all, the psalmist tells us that God already knows:

Before a word is on my tongue you, Lord, know it completely.

PSALM 139:4

Prayers of repentance/forgiveness, then, are not for God's benefit. There is nothing we can confess of which He does not already know. Instead, prayers of repentance/forgiveness are for the sanctification of our own hearts from past deeds. One of the struggles that men and women have in addiction is not being *totally* honest about their past and how they are struggling today. Remember, God already knows … so be honest! The two most important aspects of prayers of repentance/

forgiveness are that they are offered honestly and with an open heart. To support this, breathe deeply and fully as you pray.

 Take a few minutes to pray. Allow this to be an outpouring of your heart to God, confessing past sins, asking contritely for forgiveness, and offering to God your disposition to change your behavior.

 After finishing your prayer, reflect and journal on your experience. Focus on whether you feel an unburdening or are still holding on to your regrets.

Prayers of deliverance. Prayers of deliverance are about asking God to deliver you from the bondage of addiction. At the core is an acknowledgment—you need God in your recovery program.

Often, we have seen people pray for deliverance while clinging to some aspect of their old behavior. This does not work. Their prayers are only earnest if they are accompanied by a willingness to let go completely, to surrender their addiction to God.

Prayers of deliverance are an important part of recovery. At the same time, we want to emphasize that these prayers are not a substitute for the other spiritual and psychological work of recovery. All too often, we have seen earnest Christians engage in prayers of deliverance and then do nothing else—arguing that since God was in control, this was all they needed to do. While we certainly believe that God is in control, we have seen time and again that these men and women failed in their recovery and, having put all their eggs in one basket, were either angry at God for failing to deliver them or ashamed that their prayers must not have been righteous since they were unanswered. A more viable approach, from our perspective, is to integrate prayers of deliverance into the other tasks of recovery. Accordingly, when praying for deliverance, take an additional step and focus on the small things you can do each day to reach certain goals. Commitment is saying, "Today I will do my part."

 Take a few minutes to pray, focusing solely on asking God to deliver you from your addiction and the shortcomings that undermine your recovery.

 After praying, reflect and then journal on your experience.

Jesus prayer. The Jesus prayer is a short one-line prayer:

Lord Jesus Christ, Son of God, have mercy on me, a sinner.

The prayer can easily be adapted to focus on your addiction:

Lord Jesus Christ, Son of God, have mercy on me, a sex addict.

You can say the Jesus prayer silently at any point in your day. If you find yourself drifting off into fantasy or euphoric recall (recall of past sexual experiences with an accompanying feeling of euphoria that can trigger additional acting out), the prayer can help ground you in the reality of the moment. As an ongoing practice, use the Jesus prayer continually to cultivate a quiet mind and an open heart.

 Repeat the Jesus prayer for five to ten minutes. Experiment by saying the prayer both silently and aloud. Set a timer to help you focus on the prayer without concern for time. When your mind drifts from the prayer (and it assuredly will), gently bring yourself back to the repetition of the Jesus prayer. Remember that you are asking for mercy, so be gentle and noncritical with yourself when your prayer time is imperfect. In no way does God want perfect prayers, only earnest ones.

After finishing your prayer, reflect and journal on this experience.

Prayers of submission. Prayers of submission are literally words of surrender to God's will. The best example is the prayer of Jesus in the Garden of Gethsemane:

"Father, if you are willing, take this cup from me; yet not my will, but yours be done."
LUKE 22:42

Luke tells us that Jesus then prayed some more because he was in anguish (Luke 22:44), another example that Jesus offers us. Luke 22:42 is an interesting passage. Jesus first offers a petitionary prayer ("take this cup from me") but then offers a prayer of submission ("yet not my will, but yours be done").

We all struggle with ego and willfulness. Quite simply, it is at the core of the human condition. This is the very reason that hitting "rock bottom" is such a grace-filled experience. For most of you, when you hit rock bottom, your ego was broken and your willfulness defeated. In your anguish, you may have realized that the hole in which you found yourself was too deep to possibly claw your way out of.

In that moment, there is nothing to do but surrender. Rather than climb out, you fall through. Fortunately, by grace, you fall into the arms of a loving God. Just as Jesus prayed in the garden, prayers of submission are prayers to lay down your own will and accept the will of the Father. This is the spiritual antidote to ego and willfulness.

 Spend a few minutes offering prayers of submission. You might begin the prayer with the words "not my will, but yours be done," following the example of Jesus. From there, go on to confess to God how you have been willful and how you struggle with willfulness, and then pray for God's will to be done in your life.

After finishing your prayer, reflect and then journal on this experience.

Eleventh Step Prayer. This prayer emphasizes the spiritual stance that is necessary for recovery. It refers to Step Eleven of the Twelve Steps (see Appendix A for a complete listing of the Twelve Steps).

> *Sought through prayer and meditation to improve our conscious contact*
> *with God* as we understood Him, *praying only for knowledge of His*
> *will for us and the power to carry that out.*

Prayers of submission and Eleventh Step prayers are cogent reminders that God is the ultimate orchestrator of life. While prayers of petition and intercession are valuable prayers, the potential pitfall of such prayers is that they are ego-driven (that is, they are about what you want for yourself and others). How can we rectify ego-driven prayers to a God who is

- omniscient (knows everything there is to know)
- omnipotent (capable of doing anything)
- omnibenevolent (perfectly good)
- impassable (unaffected by outside sources)
- immutable (unchanging)

To help make sense of this, think of a young child walking down the cookie aisle at the grocery store with his mother. He tells his mother he wants a particular type of cookie and, when she says no, he throws a tantrum, collapsing on the floor and screaming. All too often, this is how we approach God with our prayers.

Part of putting away childish things (I Corinthians 13:11) is recognizing that

- We do not always get our way.
- It is possible (perhaps even likely) that we do not know what is best for us.

In effect, then, any prayer that asks for knowledge of God's will for us and the power to carry that out is an Eleventh Step prayer. This is an extension of prayers of submission. You are praying here not only for God's will to be done in your life (submission), but also that you would come to know God's will (discernment) and have the courage to act on this will (action), even when it is in opposition to your own will. In the book *Twelve Steps and Twelve Traditions*, the Prayer of Saint Francis of Assisi is affectionately called the Eleventh Step Prayer, as it provides a spiritual stance for a life of recovery:

> *Lord, make me an instrument of thy peace.*
> *That where there is hatred,*
> *I may bring love.*
> *That where there is wrong,*
> *I may bring the spirit of forgiveness.*
> *That where there is discord,*
> *I may bring harmony.*
> *That where there is error,*
> *I may bring truth.*
> *That where there is doubt,*
> *I may bring faith.*
> *That where there is despair,*
> *I may bring hope.*
> *That where there are shadows,*
> *I may bring light.*
> *That where there is sadness,*
> *I may bring joy.*
> *Lord, grant that I may seek rather to comfort,*
> *than to be comforted.*
> *To understand,*
> *than to be understood.*
> *To love,*
> *than to be loved.*
> *For it is by self-forgetting that one finds.*
> *It is by forgiving that one is forgiven.*

Take a few minutes to slowly and meditatively read the Prayer of Saint Francis of Assisi. Reflect on the following questions.

- What parts of this prayer are you already living out in your life and have committed to continuing?
- What parts of this prayer are more difficult for you to manifest in your daily life?

Commit to revisiting the prayer of Saint Francis periodically and asking for God's help to become a living example of this prayer.

 Now, spend a few minutes asking for knowledge of God's will for you and the courage to carry this out. You might begin the prayer with the words "God, give me knowledge of Your will for my life and the courage to carry this out." From there, speak openly with God about how you have struggled to discern God's will from your own, how you have struggled to hear the "still small voice" (I Kings 19:12, KJV) amidst the storm of your life. Pray earnestly for knowledge of God's will and the courage to carry this out. And be patient. God reveals his plan over time and teaches us patience.

 After finishing your Eleventh Step prayer, reflect and journal on this experience.

Breath prayer. One way you can begin to "pray without ceasing" (I Thessalonians 5:17) is to develop what is called a "breath prayer." Your breath prayer brings you into communion with God. It is a way of coming to God that brings peace. The very words of Jesus support this idea:

Come to me, all you who are weary and burdened, and I will give you rest.
MATTHEW 11:28

To develop a breath prayer, choose a phrase between six and twelve syllables that has specific meaning to your recovery journey. The following are some examples:

1. Lord Jesus Christ, Son of God, have mercy on me. (A shortened version of the Jesus prayer)
2. I belong to you, O Lord.
3. Lord, I give myself to you.

4. Not my will but yours be done. (Prayer of submission)
5. May all I do praise the Lord.
6. Jesus, my light and my love.
7. Holy Spirit, breathe in me.
8. Speak Lord, your servant is listening.

Alternatively, write a breath prayer based on your favorite scripture passages. Another option is to spend a few moments in silence where you envision Jesus standing before you, asking you what you need from him. Then combine the responses with your favorite name for God (such as Father, Heavenly Father, Jesus, or Lord) to create a breath prayer. Examples include

1. Lord Jesus, give me peace.
2. Father God, give me courage.

Commit to remaining in God's presence as you begin saying your prayer. Ponder the meaning of what you are praying. Pray slowly, inhaling deeply on the first part of the passage and exhaling slowly and fully on the last part of the phrase. Pray and breathe *slowly*, that you might "be still and know that I am God" (Psalm 46:10a).

You may commit to spending a few minutes each day in breath prayer or you may draw upon it when needed, such as when you are being triggered sexually or "lost" in fantasy or euphoric recall. At these times, using your breath prayer will reconnect you to God and calm the emotions and physiological sensations that you are experiencing. Similarly, when you experience anger, resentment, or fear, the breath prayer can restore your restful peace in God. In such instances, uttering the breath prayer should not have a time limit.

 Now it is time to actually write down the six to twelve syllables that will serve as your breath prayer. You can change your breath prayer at any time. Complete the following tasks:

- Write your breath prayer.
- Journal situations and circumstances in which you expect your breath prayer will be helpful to your recovery. Include both external events and internal processes, such as fantasy.

 Now, spend a few minutes silently speaking your breath prayer. Set a timer so you can focus solely on the prayer. Lose yourself in the beauty and meaning of your chosen phrase. When your mind wanders (and it will), simply return to the prayer without being critical of yourself.

 After finishing your breath prayer, reflect and journal on this experience.

Listening Prayers

Although God can speak to us at any point, certain forms of prayer cultivate our ability to listen. Discerning the will of God for our lives is central to recovery. These approaches cultivate this listening heart. The following is a chart with a few examples of listening prayers.

Type of Listening Prayers	Description
Centering	A contemplative practice that will open you to God's will and actions
Daily Examination of Consciousness	A time of prayer to make you more aware of God's presence in your life

Centering prayer. Centering prayer opens you to God's will and actions. It has been used for centuries as a Christian spiritual practice but is taught only infrequently in modern churches, many of which have lost the contemplative traditions.

Centering prayer is deceptively simple. You select a sacred word as a symbol of your submission to God and then silently repeat this word for a few minutes. What makes this deceptively simple is that the mind tends to wander. You may be amazed at how quickly you get distracted, yet you may be able to learn something from noticing where your mind wanders off to. In short, then, centering prayer is simple… but not easy!

What you do when your mind wanders is a very important part of this practice. When you get distracted from your centering prayer, return yourself *gently* to the sacred word, without self-judgment or self-criticism. To begin a practice of centering prayer:

1. Choose a sacred word (such as *Jesus, Abba, Father, Mother, Peace,* or *Love*) as a symbol of your opening to God's presence in your life.
2. Sit comfortably in a chair, arms and legs uncrossed and feet on the floor.
3. Begin to gently say your sacred word silently, bringing your focus more fully to God.
4. When you become distracted, gently return to the sacred word.

5. At the conclusion of your centering prayer time, let go of the word and sit in silence for a few minutes.

6. You may choose to close out this time of prayer with a familiar prayer, such as the Lord's Prayer.

People who practice centering prayer as a primary practice typically do this twice a day (morning and night) for about twenty minutes. For those new to centering prayer, begin with a more modest practice of about ten minutes and then increase over time.

 Now it's your turn. Select a sacred word by closing your eyes and asking God to help you discern the best word for your centering prayer. Once you are clear about your word, write it down.

 Spend ten minutes in centering prayer. Use a timer so you can focus on your sacred word. When you conclude your prayer, rest in silence for a few minutes and then recite the Lord's Prayer, either silently or aloud.

 After finishing your time of prayer, take a few minutes to reflect and journal on this experience.

Daily examination of consciousness. Scripture tells us that God knows you better than you know yourself.

You have searched me, Lord, and you know me.
PSALM 139:1

From this, it follows that as God knows us, we can enter into a conversation with God to more fully understand ourselves and our God-given place in this world. Such a time of prayer has been called by many names but we will call it a daily examination of consciousness. This practice makes you more aware of God's presence in your life and helps you reflect on the events, experiences, and emotions of each day. Because it is a reflection of the day that has just passed, this practice is commonly used at night. The following is one simple approach to the daily examination of consciousness. Feel free to adapt.

Ten Steps in the Examination of Consciousness

1. If you use a daily calendar to track your activities, look at it to recall what happened today and what is scheduled for tomorrow.

2. Create an opening ritual (for example, light a candle or say a short prayer acknowledging God's presence).

3. Contemplate for a few moments in God's loving presence.

4. Reflect upon your day. Start with what you are thankful for. Here are some questions you might ask:

   a. What was the moment today for which I am most grateful?

   b. When was I happiest today?

   c. When did I feel the most alive today?

   d. Where today was I most cooperating with God's will for my life?

5. Now reflect on the more difficult moments of your day without seeking solutions or denying emotions that might emerge. Here are some questions you might ask:

   a. What was the moment today for which I am least grateful?

   b. When was I most unhappy today?

   c. When did I feel life draining out of me today?

   d. Where today was I resisting God's work in my life?

6. Turn your awareness now to unfinished business. What do you need to confess to God? What do you need to confess to another person? Is there anyone to whom you need to apologize or make amends? Commit to make these confessions, apologies, and amends as soon as possible.

7. Turn your attention to tomorrow. As you consider this day, what feelings emerge? Turn these feelings into prayers for comfort, courage, guidance, or whatever else will support you in the day to come.

8. Offer thanks to God for what you have experienced through this time of prayer.

9. Close out your prayer with the Lord's Prayer.

10. Journal your experiences from this prayer, including any actions that are needed, such as an apology or amends to someone you may have harmed this day.

 After finishing your prayer, reflect and journal on this experience.

Meditation

For some Christians, the term "meditation" has a strong negative connotation connected to other religious traditions. As we said before, your personal spiritual practices must fit with your belief system. If the very idea of meditation suggests something negative for you, skip this section and move on to the next spiritual practice (Study) on page 52.

There is a very thin line between prayer and meditation. For example, many consider breath prayer and centering prayer to be a form of meditation.

The Eleventh Step calls us into a stance of both prayer and meditation: *Sought through prayer and meditation to improve our conscious contact with God* as we understood Him, *praying only for knowledge of His will for us and the power to carry that out.*

The distinction we make here between what constitutes prayer versus meditation is based on our understanding. We encourage you not to get bogged down in these semantics, but rather to work in collaboration with the Holy Spirit to develop your spiritual discipline. The following chart includes some different examples of meditation.

Meditation Types	Description
Palms Down, Palms Up	A meditation that uses palm placement to indicate postures of surrendering and openness to God
Concentration on Breathing	A meditation that uses your breath as a vehicle for surrendering and accepting
Meditation on Scriptures	Interacting with God using scriptures as a meditation
Watchful Meditation	More of a "way of being" than a specific practice

In his classic work *Celebrating the Disciplines*, Richard Foster speaks of Christian meditation:

> *It is a sad commentary of the spiritual state of modern Christianity that meditation is a word so foreign to its ears. Meditation has always stood as a classical and central part of Christian devotion, a crucial preparation for and adjunct to the work of prayer.*[2]

Similarly, scripture supports the practice of meditation:

> *May my meditation be pleasing to him, as I rejoice in the Lord.*
> PSALM 104:34

Foster distinguished between Christian meditation and those of other traditions.[2] Christians do not engage in meditation simply to empty the mind. Instead, the process of Christian meditation works to empty the mind so that it can be filled with godly thoughts. Meditation clears the path to God. Interestingly, in the New International Version (NIV) of the Bible, the word "meditate" is used eighteen times while "memorize" is not used at all. While memorizing scripture is a useful and viable tool, creating a process of meditation deepens our connection with God.

Foster described two specific techniques for Christian meditation that will form the foundation for our approach to Christian meditation. They include *Palms Down, Palms Up* and *Concentration on Breathing*.

Palms Down, Palms Up

The first process—palms down, palms up—is a daily practice that takes between five and ten minutes. Begin by sitting with your feet flat on the floor and with a straight, but not rigid, back. Place your palms on your legs in a posture of surrendering your concerns to God. Then, start talking to God about what you are ready to release or surrender. You might say, "I release my anger toward my husband/wife" or "I surrender my need to manipulate others." Do this slowly and reflectively as it is ultimately an act of the heart.

After several minutes of doing this, turn your palms face-up on your legs as a symbol of your desire to receive from God. Now, start talking about what you are opening to receive or accept from God. You might say, "I open myself to fully experience your grace" or "I accept your forgiveness."

After doing this for several minutes, spend some time in complete silence. Be present in the silence without expecting any outcome.

Carefully go through this meditation. You may discover that while you are asking to surrender or receive some things, in reality you are not yet fully willing to surrender or accept them. Do not judge this, but rather pray for the growing willingness to surrender or accept, as appropriate to the awareness that God is growing within you.

 After completing the meditation, journal on your experience.

Concentration on Breathing

A second act of meditation described by Foster is to use your breath as a vehicle for surrendering and accepting. To do this, begin by sitting comfortably in a chair. Place your hands palms up or down depending on what feels most comfortable/

right for you in this moment. Inhale deeply, tilting your head back slowly as you do. Then, exhale slowly and fully, bringing your head forward as much as is comfortable, perhaps until your chin nearly rests on your chest. Repeat this several times, focusing solely on your breath and the slow movement of your head.

Then, with each inhale, pray silently for something that you wish to draw in, such as, "God, I breathe in your love and light." With each exhale, pray silently for something you wish to release, such as "God, I exhale my resentment about my recovery." Do not feel as if you have to pray words with each inhale and exhale. Rather, let the words come to you as they do, and speak them inwardly with the next appropriate breath. Do this slowly and watchfully. If you find yourself distracted, simply exhale with "I exhale my distractions" and "I inhale my focus on this time with you."

 After completing the meditation, journal on your experience.

Meditation on Scriptures ("Divine Reading")

Meditation on scriptures, or divine reading, involves interacting with scriptures in an alternative way. Rather than focusing on the critical understanding or interpretation of the text, as is usually done when studying scripture, this approach to reading scriptures is more heart-focused and contemplative. Also, it involves selecting a shorter passage than is the norm in Bible study. Follow these seven steps when using this process:

1. **Choose scripture.** Select between one and three verses of scripture—a favorite passage, a passage that calls to you for this reading, or a passage that you are guided to after a period of silent prayer.
2. **Be silent.** Enter into a short period of silence (at least three to four minutes). When your mind wanders, gently return a focus to your breath and the silence. The silence creates "space" for receiving God's Word.
3. **Read.** Now thoughtfully and slowly read the brief passage you selected. Experiment with reading the text aloud and silently. Reread the passage, emphasizing different words and phrases. Visualize what is occurring in the passage. Read through the passage several times in this way, reading for at least three to five minutes.
4. **Meditate on the Word.** Reflect on words or images that are most poignant for you in the reading.

5. **Speak.** Having meditated on the scripture, begin to speak to God, opening your heart to express the thoughts and feelings that emerged from your meditation. You may speak aloud or inwardly.

6. **Contemplate.** Having spoken to God, simply rest in His presence, surrendering to His care. In the silence that follows, God may speak to you, but this is not necessary and you should not try to force this to happen.

7. **Embodiment.** In the final step, reflect on how this meditation calls you to live differently in your daily life and commit to any call that you hear for change.

 Take some time to go through the seven steps now. Then, journal about your experience.

Watchful Meditation

Watchful meditation is less of a specific practice and more of a "way of being" both as you engage in other spiritual practices and as you go through your day-to-day activities. Scripture calls us to be watchful:

Be dressed ready for service and keep your lamps burning, like servants waiting for their master to return from a wedding banquet, so that when he comes and knocks they can immediately open the door for him.

LUKE 12:35–36

Devote yourselves to prayer, being watchful and thankful.

COLOSSIANS 4:2

What, then, does it mean to be watchful and thankful? During your active addiction, your addictive sexual behavior likely served, at least to some extent, to help you avoid, deny, or suppress experiences that were unpleasant. Perhaps it was feelings of anxiety or depression, a sense of shame over past sexual acting out, or something else. Regardless, research tells us that your addictive behavior helped you avoid unpleasant aspects of your experience.

It seems important, then, that your spiritual practices support you in accepting the parts of your experiences and emotions that you previously avoided through addictive sexual behavior.

Perhaps this is part of what Jesus meant when he said,

Watch and pray so that you will not fall into temptation.
The spirit is willing, but the flesh is weak.
MATTHEW 26:41

Of what, then, should you be watchful? For one thing, avoid being hyper-vigilant about your addiction, as this often causes increased anxiety, which may be a trigger for you. Instead, be watchful and remember that, even though you are in recovery, you remain an addict with the potential for relapse. It is from this watchful stance that you can best maintain your program of recovery.

As a recovering person, remaining watchful reminds you to rely on God:

Turn to me and be gracious to me, for I am lonely and afflicted.
PSALM 25:16

Further, a watchful spirit keeps us mindful of the gift of grace that is freely given:

For I have always been mindful of your unfailing love and
have lived in reliance on your faithfulness.
PSALM 26:3

 Make a list of behaviors that are not, in and of themselves, sexually acting out but do comprise high-risk behaviors that may trigger you to relapse into your old addictive behaviors. Here are some examples:

- looking at websites that are not pornographic but might nonetheless include images that are sexually triggering
- sexualizing others by staring at them and focusing on only certain body parts
- cruising areas where you once sexually acted out
- leaving "hook-up" apps on your phone or tablet even though you do not intend to use them
- looking at hook-up apps just to see who is there, telling yourself that you will not make contact
- looking at personal ads, promising yourself that you are not going to act on this but are "just looking out of curiosity"
- harboring resentments toward others, such as being angry at a partner for being sexually unavailable to you recently

• channel surfing on the television, looking for something to turn you on

It is unlikely that any of these behaviors alone would be considered a relapse. Now carefully review the list and try to discover why these behaviors could trigger relapsing behaviors.

 Answer the following questions in your journal:

- What are your own "slippery slope" behaviors, things that you know you need to watch? Create a list.
- What are you willing to commit to do when you watchfully notice any of the "slippery slope" behaviors? Brainstorm a list of possible healthy actions.

Study

The spiritual practice of study is popular. We recommend some form of small group Bible study, as the dialogue around scriptures often provokes new insights and perspectives. At the same time, solitary Bible study is a fruitful practice.

Here are a few recommendations to enrich your time of study:

1. Begin and end your time of study with prayer.
2. Select passages to study with intent.
3. Avoid the trap of studying too large of a passage in one sitting; remember that sometimes less is more and a focused study on just a few verses may have more meaning than a superficial reading of a longer passage.

 If you are looking for a starting place, the parables of Jesus are rich sources. For an initial study, select one of the following parables of Jesus:

- Parable of the Pharisee and the Tax Collector (Luke 18:10–14)
- Parable of the Rich Fool (Luke 12:13–21)
- Parable of the Two Houses (Matthew 7:24–27)
- Parable of the Good Shepherd (Luke 15:3–7)
- Parable of the Unmerciful Servant (Matthew 18:23–35)
- Parable of the Hidden Treasure (Matthew 13:44)
- Parable of the Five Foolish Maidens (Matthew 25:1–13)
- Parable of the Good Samaritan (Luke 10:25–37)

- Parable of the Sower and the Seed (Matthew 13:1–23)
- Parable of the Barren Fig Tree (Luke 13:6–9)

 Pray for guidance as you study the parable. Then, read it slowly, as if for the first time. Discover the Truths that Jesus is revealing through his story-telling. Reread the passage several times, searching for any deeper meaning. Consider that the parables are timeless. Ask yourself how this parable speaks to you at this moment.

 Now, write about your experience and what you've learned by studying the parable.

Simplicity

Our life is frittered away by detail. Simplify, simplify.
HENRY DAVID THOREAU

When you were actively in your addiction, your addictive behavior most likely created a certain chaos in your life, and possibly in the lives of those around you. Missed responsibilities, under-performance, lack of sleep, hyperfocus on your addiction, secrets, lies, and shame all led to a chaotic and overly complicated life-style. Some of you may have unconsciously created this lifestyle, at least in part, to justify your sexual acting out ("I work so many hours and my life is so difficult, I deserve to unwind a little bit sometimes").

If you are working a program of recovery from sexual addiction but are continuing to live a chaotic lifestyle, this may ultimately undermine your recovery. The spiritual solution to chaos is simplicity. Whatever your current life circumstances, it is possible to simplify your life. Some of you may be facing legal consequences, changes in relationship status, changes in financial circumstances, and other significant changes while working on your recovery. It is probably a difficult period in your life, perhaps one of the most difficult you have ever faced.

As a spiritual practice, prayerfully consider how you can simplify your life. Consider all of the areas in which you commit your time, energy, and resources. Consider how your living space and work space is chaotic. How can you practice simplicity in all aspects of your life?

 To begin, write down at least three things that you are willing to do (or not do) *right now* to simplify your life. Develop this list prayerfully to ensure that these plans are aligned with God's will for your life.

This is only a starting point. As an ongoing spiritual practice, continue to look for ways in which you can simplify your life.

Confession

The confession of evil works is the first beginning of good works.
—SAINT AUGUSTINE

Confession is an important spiritual practice for all Christians, and in Catholicism it is considered a sacrament. Whether done in a confessional to a priest, in a meeting with a Twelve Step sponsor, in a therapy session with a therapist, in a group counseling session with other recovering addicts, or in a coffee shop with a trusted companion, confession is, as the Scottish proverb encourages, good for the soul.

Scripture provides a clear explanation of why we must make confession:

*Whoever conceals their sins does not prosper, but the one
who confesses and renounces them finds mercy.*
PROVERBS 28:13

All too often we fail to confess our sins to God and to others because of our deep shame. Yet Scripture clearly speaks to the depth of God's redemption when we confess:

Surely the arm of the Lord is not too short to save, nor his ear too dull to hear.
ISAIAH 59:1

This wisdom also was embedded in the Twelve Steps. Step Five calls us to a confession of our past misdeeds and sins:

*Admitted to God, to ourselves and to another human being
the exact nature of our wrongs.*

Step Ten calls us to make confession an ongoing part of our lives:

Continued to take personal inventory and when we were wrong promptly admitted it.

Why do we confess to God when He already knows all? Scripture tells us:

Before a word is on my tongue you, Lord, know it completely.

PSALM 139:4

Clearly, then, your confessions to God are not so that God will know. He already does. Instead, your open and honest confessions to God are an expression of your responsibility, your awareness, and your remorse for acts that have hurt others and, indeed, your own communion with God.

Your confessions to others also are vital. Unlike God, others do not know of your past behaviors. Why is it vital to confess these acts to another person? Largely, because shame fuels addictive sexual behavior. In all likelihood, when you were active in your addiction, you believed that if others knew what you were doing, they would judge you, condemn you, ask you to leave their group (church, work, etc.), or otherwise cast you out. If they knew the truth, you said, they could not possibly love and accept you. The act of a fearless and searching inventory followed by confession to God, yourself, and another person, then, is an act of faith that you are lovable, forgivable, and redeemable. There will always be people who will judge you, often in hurtful ways, whatever your past deeds. In the end, that is about their shortcomings, not yours.

To Whom Should You Confess?

Be very judicious to whom you confess your sins. A trusted companion such as a Twelve Step sponsor, a therapist, or a clergy member may be your best choice. We want to caution you, though, that sponsors, therapists, and clergy members are not automatically worthy of hearing your confessions. The person should be trustworthy and somewhat detached from the situation. This is why a spouse or family member may not be the best person to hear your confessions.

Practice a confession to God. Remember that God already knows all, which frees you to confess whatever most needs confession. It may be a secret from others, but not from God.

 Write down two or three things that you did in your addiction that you would like to confess.

 Next, to prepare for your time of confession with God, read Psalm 32:5–7 silently as a reminder of what God has already promised if you confess your transgressions to Him:

> *Then I acknowledged my sin to you*
> *and did not cover up my iniquity.*
> *I said, "I will confess*
> *my transgressions to the Lord."*
> *And you forgave*
> *the guilt of my sin.*
> *Therefore let all the faithful pray to you*
> *while you may be found;*
> *surely the rising of the mighty waters*
> *will not reach them.*
> *You are my hiding place;*
> *you will protect me from trouble*
> *and surround me with songs of deliverance.*

 Enter now into a time of prayer, confessing what you've written about in your journal. Think of your prayers of confession as a pouring out of your heart what you have done and who has been hurt, and asking God to deliver you from the "guilt of your sin" (Psalm 32:5). In the passage of Psalms above, the psalmist reports that he did not cover up his iniquity. This tells us that as we practice prayers of confession, we should be especially watchful that we are honest about our sins, how others have been hurt, and how we have been separated from God. Prayers of confession are not superficial, intellectual, and detached. Instead, they are honest, heartfelt, and often emotional.

After your prayers of confession, record your experience about this. Consider whether you should talk to trusted counsel about your prayers of confession.

Solitude

Loneliness is painful, solitude is peaceful.
PATRICK J. CARNES

When you were active in your addiction, you may have never experienced solitude. Instead, in unscheduled and alone times, you probably felt lonely and longed for connection. This may have, in part, fueled your addictive behaviors. In recovery, Jesus calls you to shift from loneliness to solitude.

In early recovery, though, you may find yourself creating a busy life that leaves little time to act out. During "down time" you may experience an increase in fantasies and struggle more to maintain your sobriety. Even so, it is important to strike a balance here. When people overschedule themselves as a protection against acting out, fearing that unscheduled time will lead them into temptation, they are not planning for the exhaustion that comes with a hectic pace of life, an exhaustion that actually makes them more vulnerable to acting out. If entitlement was an issue for you in your addiction ("I work really hard, so I deserve ... "), this can be problematic in recovery as well, as the old justifications are more likely to creep in when you are tired.

Know that overscheduled chaos and loneliness are not the only choices. Cultivating internal solitude will leave you more at peace. At its core, solitude is not about being by yourself; it is more a state of mind, heart, and soul. Cultivating inner solitude quiets the chaos within regardless of external circumstances. This will leave you unafraid of being alone, for you will know at a deeper level that you are never alone.

In Jesus' documented ministry, he provided a great example of this. He started his ministry with a time of solitude (Matthew 4:1–11), spent time in solitude before making important decisions (Luke 6:12-13), grieved losses in solitude (Matthew 14:13), and encouraged his disciples to similarly spend time in solitude (Mark 6:31). Perhaps the most important example of solitude was when Jesus retreated to pray in the Garden of Gethsemane as he prepared for his own death. Indeed, Jesus sought out solitary places and solitary times.

For you, this may be simply about carving out time each day to engage in recovery work. It is important to remember, though, that there is a connection between internal solitude and internal silence. Part of practicing solitude is quieting the mind and body as an antidote to the busyness epidemic in our society. There is, indeed, "a time to be silent and a time to speak" (Ecclesiastes 3:7b).

Foster lists several ways to practice solitude:[4]

- Take advantage of the "little solitudes" in your day; for example, while having your morning coffee, while stuck in traffic, walking

Are You Doing Twelve Step Work? If So, Read This

Step Five calls you to confess your wrongs to God, to yourself, and to at least one other person. Many people in recovery, having done Step Four, assume that all has already been admitted to God who surely watches over our Fourth Step work. This assumption could cost you the wonderful opportunity to cry out to God in prayer and, as the psalmist so eloquently promises, be protected from trouble and surrounded by songs of deliverance.

from one place to another. Often we miss these mini-retreats because we are not focused on the present moment and being still.

- Find or develop a specific place for solitude; for example, you might designate a small area in your home as a place where you and others can go for respite and quiet.

- Find a place outside your home to practice solitude, such as a church sanctuary or a nearby park.

- Practice using fewer words and speaking with intent. Francis of Assisi often is quoted as saying "Preach the gospel, and if necessary, use words."

- Set aside a day for silent retreat; arrange to spend the entire day in silence, without any use of electronics. (Note: before doing this, consult with others, such as your therapist or sponsor, to make sure you are sufficiently solid in your recovery.)

- Set an electronics curfew, a time each day at which all electronics will be turned off.

- About once every three months, set aside time to withdraw for three to four hours and *prayerfully* reorient your life goals, purpose, and how you spend your daily energy. Often, amidst their busyness, people do not take the time to make sure they are living purposefully.

- At a point when you are solid in your recovery, plan a two- or three-day retreat focused on spiritual practices and recovery work.

Take a day to practice solitude. First, commit to trying out Foster's "little solitudes." Then, set aside thirty minutes in that day simply to be in solitude. Turn off all electronic devices and other potential distractions. Explain to your family of your need for quiet time and, if needed, reassure them that your practice of solitude is different from any isolating behavior that was a part of your addiction. For this initial time of solitude, simply take time to reflect on the following:

1. Your experiences of the "little solitudes" in your day
2. The gifts of recovery
3. Any changes that you need to implement to support your recovery

 You might integrate brief prayer time into your period of solitude.

 After completing your day-long experience of focusing on solitude, write about your reflections and experience.

Forgiveness

Forgiveness is the final form of love.
REINHOLD NIEBUHR

A complete and detailed discussion of forgiveness is well beyond the scope of this chapter. We introduce it here as a spiritual practice but encourage additional study if this becomes an important spiritual practice for you.

Many people make "unforgiveness" a practice. They harbor resentments, expend great amounts of energy judging other people, and are generally angry most of the time. Ultimately, they rent out a lot of space in their head to grievances against others. This only fuels anger and additional resentments. Refusing to forgive others is like drinking poison and waiting for the source of your resentment to die. For people in recovery, in particular, resentments are a problem.

Further, as a Christian, you have a clear mandate to practice forgiveness. In teaching us how to pray, Jesus included words about forgiveness:

Forgive us our sins, for we also forgive everyone who sins against us.
LUKE 11:4A

One of the last documented utterances of Jesus, as he literally hung dying on the cross, was an act of forgiveness:

Jesus said, "Father, forgive them, for they do not know what they are doing.
LUKE 23:34

Clearly, then, we are directed to forgive others. Unfortunately, because of these mandates, some religious leaders reduce forgiveness to a single act of will. Directives from the pulpit can sound like a commercial for an athletic shoe: Just do it.

Yet forgiveness is far more complex than "Just do it." It is human nature to resist forgiveness. Acts of forgiveness

- call to mind painful memories or feelings, which we may prefer to avoid
- may leave us feeling vulnerable
- lead us to admit that we, too, are in need of forgiveness
- rob us of self-pity and self-indulgence ("Oh, poor me")

In short, we are all inclined to avoid forgiveness work, but the practice of forgiving others increases the serenity that supports recovery. The other problem with the "just do it" proposal is that it fails to recognize that forgiveness is not a single act. Forgiving someone who has aggrieved you in some way is a process. Making forgiveness a global practice, so that you are practicing forgiveness on an ongoing basis, is a process. When we consider forgiveness work, the adage "Ready, willing, and able" is important.

Forgiveness is *not* the same as forgetting. Forgiveness simply releases the negative emotion associated with memories of past grievances. The memory stays with you but the emotions linked to the memory are now different.

 Focus on one specific event connected to one person whom you hope to forgive. Write down the details of what happened and then answer the following questions:

- What emotions arise as you recount this event? Do not try to change the emotions at this point; just be aware of them. What do you feel and where do you feel it in your body?

- Are you ready to forgive this person? If not, what do you need to do to become ready?

- Are you willing to forgive this person? If not, what do you need to do to become willing?

- Do you believe that you are able to forgive this person? If not, what support do you need to be able to forgive?

Service

The best way to find yourself is to lose yourself in the service of others.
MAHATMA GANDHI

Many of the spiritual practices we've discussed so far help strengthen our inner experience and encounter of a living God. At the same time, service to others is another vital spiritual practice. Jesus explicitly said this was true for himself:

*For even the Son of Man did not come to be served, but to serve,
and to give his life as a ransom for many.*
MARK 10:45

Scripture also clearly tells us the spirit within which we should serve:

Shadows of the Cross: A Christian Companion to *Facing the Shadow*

I served the Lord with great humility and with tears.
ACTS 20:19A

Herein lies a caveat about the spiritual practice of service. What is the difference between the Mother Teresas of the world and the most codependent people in our midst? Codependency happens when people constantly put the needs of others before their own. As a result, they forget to take care of themselves. The difference between Mother Teresa and a codependent person is one of intent. Codependent service is self-serving and self-righteous, an act of serving others in an effort to somehow bolster the self. Mother Teresa, in contrast, was a servant of God, unselfishly giving of herself and expecting nothing in return. As you consider the spirituality of service, prayerfully consider intent. There is a reason that service is only introduced in the last of the Twelve Steps of Sexaholics Anonymous:

Having had a spiritual awakening as the result of these steps, we tried to carry this message to others and to practice these principles in all our affairs.

That is, you are called to serve others within the Twelve Step tradition only *after* doing work on yourself. By no means does this suggest that you have to "finish" your own work before serving others. Rather, the wisdom of the Twelve Steps and the words of Acts 20:19a stress that it is not just *what* we do in service to others; it is *how* we do it and *why* we do it that matter. Also, service to others cannot replace our own interior work as spiritual practice. In short, we can only contribute to the healing of others when we are continuing to work on our own healing. At the same time, serving others gets us out of our own ego-centered worldview and is an important component of recovery.

 Reflect and journal on your own views of service by answering the following questions:

- What do you know of your personal challenges regarding self-righteous service versus true (that is, selfless) service? Are there specific ego-driven challenges that you know you face?
- What acts of service are you willing to commit to at this point in your recovery?
- What are some possible hidden acts of service (things that will largely be unseen and unnoticed) that you could do?

Committing to Action

In the end, spiritual disciplines are not about having a pious heart; they are about action.

 Before reading more about and experimenting with specific spiritual disciplines, review the preliminary plan that you created in your journal. Then add the "what" to your plan by doing the following:

- Commit to a *specific* daily spiritual practice. Write the specifics of *what* you are committing to do each day as a spiritual practice.

- Does your plan include specific disciplines that you plan to practice daily? If not, describe some that you may consider using.

- Which parts of the plan need to be modified to fit the details of your spiritual practice plan? Make those modifications in your journal.

As you continue through this book, consider how your daily spiritual practice can support your ongoing journey of recovery.

Practice.

Practice.

Practice.

Chapter Three
Jesus and the Twelve Steps

The original Twelve Step program was developed for alcoholism, but now we have programs for many different addictions. Why are they so prominent? Because they work! There is a saying in Twelve Step communities that "It works if you work it." Twelve Step programs do not change you, but you can be changed through the Twelve Step process. As you begin this chapter, turn to Appendix C to view the Twelve Steps of Alcoholics Anonymous.

In their wisdom, the program founders recognized that recovery required a spiritual component. At the same time, they wanted to create a program that could be used by anyone, regardless of where they were in their faith journey. Toward that end, they developed a program that fully and centrally reflects the importance of God and having a relationship with God, but is also acceptable and workable by people who were not Christian.

Because Twelve Step programs do not explicitly reference Jesus, however, some Christians choose not to follow them. While your community may offer faith-based sex addiction recovery groups (such as Celebrate Recovery, Faithful and True, and Recovered through Christ), the most prominent groups—Sexaholics Anonymous (SA), Sexual Compulsive Anonymous (SCA), and Sex Addicts Anonymous (SAA)—are not overtly Christian, though Christians likely attend these groups.

The best group is the one that works for you at this point in time. If you attend a group such as SA or SAA, we encourage you to recognize that the Twelve Steps are *highly* compatible with the teachings of Jesus.

 Read Jeremiah 38:21–22:

> *If you refuse to surrender, this is what the Lord has revealed to me:*
> *'Your feet are sunk in the mud; your friends have deserted you.'*

Although the context for this passage involves physical war and battles, these words speak eloquently to the spiritual warfare involved in recovery and the place you find yourself at the beginning of the recovery process.

In your *addiction*, refusing to surrender, you were stuck and felt alone. In *recovery*, you surrender to God through Jesus Christ and to a program of recovery.

This is the point in your life where you cannot crawl out of the hole into which you have fallen, but must instead fall into the arms of a loving God. The blood of Christ covers you. You are no longer stuck and you are most assuredly not alone. This is where the healing begins.

Jesus' ministry and teachings were consistent with the Twelve Steps in numerous ways. People in early recovery sometimes erroneously think that if they work through each of the Twelve Steps, from beginning to end, then they will be "done." It is a bit more complicated than that. Each Step is complex in its own way. People who work a solid program of recovery continue to work (and rework) the Steps over time, making the Steps more a way of life than a onetime activity or event. This is similar to how your Christian journey is an ongoing process of walking daily with God, not just your moment of salvation.

As a Christian, you are called to follow the Christ.

 Read Luke 9:23:

Then he [Jesus] said to them all: "Whoever wants to be
my disciple must deny themselves and take up their cross daily and follow me."

The first phrase that Jesus says in this passage, *"Whoever wants to be my disciple,"* is very clear. Of course, as a Christian, you want to be a disciple, which translates to student, follower, or adherent. It is the "how" of this work that is more complex. What does it really mean to

- take up your cross?
- deny yourself?
- follow Jesus?

The Twelve Steps complement your Christian worldview well and provide a structure within which you can return to a healthy sexuality. It works if you work it. Now, let's look at how each of the Twelve Steps of Sex Addicts Anonymous relate to your Christian values.

Step One

We admitted we were powerless over addictive sexual behavior—that our lives had become unmanageable.

Interestingly, Step One is about *undoing* rather than *doing*. What is being undone is your sense of personal power, ego, and the illusion of control. Undoubtedly, in your addiction you went to great lengths to control and somehow manage your addiction.

I do not understand what I do. For what I want to do I do not do, but what I hate I do. . . .
For I have the desire to do what is good, but I cannot carry it out.
ROMANS 7:15, 18B

Like a shepherd's tent my house has been pulled down and taken from me. Like a weaver
I have rolled up my life, and he has cut me off from the loom; day and night you made an
end of me. I waited patiently till dawn, but like a lion he broke all my bones; day and night
you made an end of me. I cried like a swift or thrush, I moaned like a mourning dove. My
eyes grew weak as I looked to the heavens. I am being threatened. Lord, come to my aid!
ISAIAH 38:12–14

When he saw the crowds, he had compassion on them,
because they were harassed and helpless,
like sheep without a shepherd.
MATTHEW 9:36

During your active addiction, you set goals to manage your behavior but could not sustain them (Romans 7:15). In your frustration with your inability to manage your addiction, you "cried like a swift or thrush" and "moaned like a mourning dove" (Isaiah 38:14). You became like "sheep without a shepherd" (Matthew 9:36) as you lost your sense of God's will for your life.

Fortunately, however, in fully recognizing that you are powerless over addictive sexual behavior and that your life has become unmanageable, you begin the process of recovery. You finally cry out, "Lord, come to my aid" (Isaiah 38:14) and Jesus looks upon your brokenness with compassion (Matthew 9:36).

Step Two

Came to believe that a Power greater than ourselves could restore us to sanity.

After acknowledging that we need help in Step One, Step Two taps us into our deepest longing for God. The phrase "Came to believe" emphasizes the belief that God will restore us to sanity through a practice and a process, not an event.

Some balk at the reference to "sanity" in this Step. Although addiction is a brain disease and not "insanity" in the usual sense, another definition of insanity is to do the same thing repeatedly expecting different results. Sound familiar?

Indeed, we felt we had received the sentence of death. But this happened that we might not rely on ourselves but on God, who raises the dead.

2 CORINTHIANS 1:9

The eternal God is your refuge and underneath are the everlasting arms. He will drive out your enemies before you, saying, "Destroy them!"

DEUTERONOMY 33:27

For it is God who works in you to will and to act in order to fulfill His good purpose.
Philippians 2:13

Richard Rohr, a Christian clergyperson, states that to fully engage in Steps One and Two, you must open three inner spaces:

- your opinionated head
- your closed-down heart
- your defensive and defended body[1]

Rohr goes on to state that coming to believe in God will restore you to sanity allowing the light of God to shine in you and through you to others.

 Read Matthew 5:14 and John 8:12. *You* are the light of the world if you will follow His path.

 In your journal, write about what you envision Step Two looking like for you over time. Specifically, describe what it will look like in your life and your relationships when you are

- restored to sanity
- less opinionated
- openhearted
- open to your embodied/physical experience

Step Three

*Made a decision to turn our will and our lives over
to the care of God as we understood God.*

The cycle of acceptance and surrender to God comes full circle with Step Three. Working Steps One through Three leads you to a more surrendered place as you realize you have a problem and need help (Step One), come to believe that God is that help (Step Two), and make a decision to surrender to God (Step Three).

Step Three packs a lot of information into twenty short words. Let's "unpack" those words.

Made a decision—It begins with a conscious choice. By focusing on the initial decision to turn over your will and life to God, you are making a commitment, one you will fall short of at times, but one to which you remain faithful. Faithful does not mean you have to be perfect. In the collective and God-given wisdom of those who developed the Twelve Steps, they recognized that the ego will always fight to maintain the status quo. Turning your will and life over to God begins with a decision in Step Three and continues with a lifelong process of acceptance and surrender.

turn our will and lives—You turn both your will and your life over to God. What does this mean? Your "will" is your attempt to engineer control that, of course, squeezes God out of the equation. When you are willful, you have made yourself into God. Step Three calls you to surrender your selfish willfulness, to continue to long for the will of God to become clear for you, and to live each day and moment in concert with God's longing for you.

over to the care of God—Here you are accepting and surrendering to the will of a caring and loving God. As explored in chapter 2, it is possible that you were taught to fear a wrathful and judging God. Through his death on the cross, however, it is clear that Jesus paid the ultimate price and so liberated you into the arms of a loving God. Part of what makes acceptance and surrender possible is the deep knowing that God is a caring God.

as we understood God—This simply acknowledges that God cannot be fully understood or discussed. At any given time, we all understand God as best we can.

*Therefore, I urge you, brothers and sisters, in view of God's mercy, to offer your bodies as
a living sacrifice, holy and pleasing to God—this is your true and proper worship.*

ROMANS 12:1

Ask and it will be given to you; seek and you will find; knock and the door will be opened to you. For everyone who asks receives; the one who seeks finds; and to the one who knocks, the door will be opened.

Decades before Twelve Step programs existed, Judson W. Van DeVenter wrote the text for "I Surrender All." Steps One through Three are eloquently captured in the chorus of this Christian hymn:

> *I surrender all,*
> *I surrender all,*
> *All to Thee, my blessed Savior,*
> *I surrender all.*

The verses of this song provide valuable insight into the stance with which this acceptance and surrender occurs:

- Surrender *all.*
- Give yourself *freely* to God.
- Ever love and trust God.
- Live in His presence daily.
- Bow humbly before God.
- Forsake worldly pleasures.
- In submission, pray to be *taken* by God.
- Pray to feel the Holy Spirit.
- Pray that you will act such that God will truly know you are His.
- Pray to be filled with God's love and power.
- Pray for God's blessing.
- Praise God.

The hymn writer also wrote of the promises of such surrender:

> *Now, I feel the sacred flame,*
> *Oh, the joy of full salvation!*

The key to working Step Three is to remain committed to the decision you made to turn your will and your life over to God as you understand Him.

Step Four

Made a searching and fearless moral inventory of ourselves.

Jesus wants us to be humble and honest. He returns to this theme often in his teachings.

Let us examine our ways and test them,
and let us return to the Lord.
LAMENTATIONS 3:40

But if you harbor bitter envy and selfish ambition in your hearts, do not boast about it
or deny the truth.
JAMES 3:14

 Read the Parables of the Prodigal Son (Luke 15:11–32) and the Pharisee and the Tax Collector (Luke 18:9–14).

In each of these stories, someone does something wrong but makes it wholly right simply by being honest and forthright about what he has done. This is the essence of Step Four. Beyond parables, Jesus gives a directive to essentially do a Fourth Step—two thousand years before the Steps came to be! He taught

How can you say to your brother, "Let me take the speck out of your eye," when all the
time there is a plank in your own eye? You hypocrite, first take the plank out of your own
eye, and then you will see clearly to remove the speck from your brother's eye.
MATTHEW 7:4–5

This is a direct call from Jesus to examine yourself, to look at yourself in a "searching and fearless" way, so that you might be able to genuinely be compassionate and show the love of God to others.

Step Five

Admitted to God, to ourselves, and to another
human being the exact nature of our wrongs.

Having looked in the mirror in a "searching and fearless" way, confess all you learned in your Fourth Step to God, to yourself, and to another person. The spiritual act here is one of confession.

If we confess our sins, he is faithful and just and will forgive us our sins
and purify us from all unrighteousness.
I JOHN 1:9

Therefore confess your sins to each other and
pray for each other so that you may be healed.
JAMES 5:16A

When I kept silent, my bones wasted away through my groaning all day long.
For day and night your hand was heavy on me;
my strength was sapped as in the heat of summer.
Then I acknowledged my sin to you and did not cover up my iniquity.
I said, "I will confess my transgressions to the Lord."
And you forgave the guilt of my sin.
PSALM 32:3–5

"But go and learn what this means: 'I desire mercy, not sacrifice.'
For I have not come to call the righteous, but sinners."
MATTHEW 9:13

 Read Proverbs 28:13:

Whoever conceals their sins does not prosper,
but the one who confesses and renounces them finds mercy.

Read this Proverbs verse slowly multiple times, out loud if possible.

 As you study this verse prayerfully, what does it say about either your active addiction or your current recovery?

Again, it is crucial to confess our wrongs "to God, to ourselves, and to another human being." Many people who have done a Fourth Step assume they have already confessed to God. Though this may be so, it is nonetheless important to offer heartful (and often emotional!) prayers of confession as part of the Fifth Step to actively confess to God. Why?

To answer this question, first read Psalm 38:18:

I confess my iniquity; I am troubled by my sin.

 One purpose of confession is to liberate yourself from the burdens of your past. How do you remain burdened by your past addictive sexual behaviors?

 Read Psalm 32:5:

Then I acknowledged my sin to you and did not cover up my iniquity.
I said, "I will confess my transgressions to the Lord."
And you forgave the guilt of my sin.

Confession is necessary, then, for God's forgiveness.

 Read Isaiah 59:1–2:

Surely the arm of the Lord is not too short to save, nor his ear too dull to hear.
But your iniquities have separated you from your God;
your sins have hidden his face from you,
so that he will not hear.

Read this verse several times, slowly, emphasizing different words and phrases each time. Remember that the word "sin" translates as missing the mark, like an arrow, or leaving a path, in this instance the path of God's will for your life.

 Reflect first on how your "iniquities have separated you from your God." Then reflect on what it means to you to know that the arm of the Lord is long enough to save you and his ear is tuned to your confession.

Confession to yourself and others becomes a logical extension of your confession to God. True confession requires honesty. So, before you can truly confess to others, you must be honest with yourself. Christians sometimes balk at telling others about their transgressions, believing that confession to God is what matters most. Being honest with God *does* matter most, but it is not enough and this is supported in scripture.

Read James 5:16:

Therefore confess your sins to each other and pray for each other so that you may be healed. The prayer of a righteous person is powerful and effective.

Indeed, you are called scripturally to confess not only to God but also to others. Confession to trusted others may provide the single greatest antidote to shame. Many addicts believe that past deeds are unforgivable. Perhaps you struggle with whether God can and will forgive what you have done. You almost certainly fear that other people will reject you if they know your whole story. While it is true that not everyone can support you in your "whole story," that is about them and not you. There are trusted souls in the world, such as your sponsor or therapist, who can hear your Fifth Step and remain a faithful supporter of your healing journey. Working the Fifth Step is vital to knowing at your deepest level that you are *not* beyond redemption and that you are loved.

The Fifth Step specifies that you admit "the exact nature" of past actions. Yet many people speak only in very general terms of their wrongful behavior. This is a subtle attempt to minimize what they have done because of the shame they feel. When doing your Fourth and Fifth Steps, be "strong and courageous" (Joshua 1:9).

Step Six

Were entirely ready to have God remove all these defects of character.

The Sixth Step presents you as a Christian with a paradox. You work to see your defenses, resistances, blocks, and excuses—namely, defects of character—but all of this work is simply to fully acknowledge that God alone can remove these defects of character.

Humble yourselves before the Lord, and he will lift you up.
JAMES 4:10

Because of the Lord's great love we are not consumed,
for his compassions never fail.
LAMENTATIONS 3:22

Many balk at the phrase "defects of character," thinking that this implies that God "messed up" when creating you and now must correct these mistakes. Not true. Part of your character defects are doubtlessly placed there by God to teach humility (II Corinthians 12:7). Others, however, you have learned along the way, often through psychological wounding from others. Part of the paradox of recovery is that you are not responsible for how these "wounds" came to be, but you are responsible for what you do with them now, as an adult. If you do not transform/heal these wounds, you will wound others. At the same time, you do nothing but prepare yourself for God, the ultimate healer, to remove these character defects. You wait … and prepare. You take responsibility … and surrender.

Step Seven

Humbly asked God to remove our shortcomings.

Ask and it will be given to you; seek and you will find;
knock and the door will be opened to you.
MATTHEW 7:7

If we confess our sins, he is faithful and just and will forgive us our sins and
purify us from all unrighteousness.
I JOHN 1:9

In another bit of paradox, Jesus both tells you to ask in Matthew 7:7 and reminds you in Matthew 6:6–8 to

- pray privately
- keep it simple rather than trying to impress God with many words
- acknowledge that God already knows what you need before you ask

If God already knows what you need, why are you called to ask? You are called to ask because the act of asking

- reminds you that you are not in control
- practices humility and avoids entitlement

Why does Step Seven direct us to humbly ask that God remove our shortcomings rather than instruct us to do this work ourselves? God seems to know that if we are left to our own devices, we will fail.

 Read Matthew 13:27–30. Read the verse slowly and reflect on what this means for your Step Seven work as a Christian.

"The owner's servants came to him and said, 'Sir, didn't you sow good seed in your field? Where then did the weeds come from?'

"'An enemy did this,' he replied.

"The servants asked him, 'Do you want us to go and pull them up?'

"'No,' he answered, 'because while you are pulling the weeds, you may uproot the wheat with them. Let both grow together until the harvest. At that time I will tell the harvesters: First collect the weeds and tie them in bundles to be burned; then gather the wheat and bring it into my barn.'"

 Write down your reflections on Matthew 13:27–30 and what this means for you in recovery. It can be cunning and baffling to discern your own "wheat" and "weeds." Commit to surrendering this to God and take time to talk to a trusted soul, such as a therapist or sponsor, about this.

The good news is that you are assured God will respond when you are ready. Although the following story is about a man with leprosy and not addiction, notice how he approaches Jesus to be healed. He takes a Seventh Step approach two thousand years before the Twelve Steps were written!

Read Luke 5:12–13.

While Jesus was in one of the towns, a man came along who was covered with leprosy. When he saw Jesus, he fell with his face to the ground and begged him, "Lord, if you are willing, you can make me clean."

Jesus reached out his hand and touched the man. "I am willing," he said. "Be clean!" And immediately the leprosy left him.

Pay particular attention to how the man humbled himself and approached Jesus about his healing. Journal about how you can use this same approach in your recovery. Notice how Jesus responded. Journal about Jesus' response when the man asked for healing and what this means for your recovery journey.

Step Eight

Made a list of all persons we had harmed and became willing to make amends to them all.

Steps Four and Five primarily address shame where you open yourself to God's forgiveness and unconditional love of you as you are right now. Similarly,

Steps Eight and Nine address your guilt over past deeds. You ask yourself, "Who have I hurt and how did I hurt them?"

Do to others as you would have them do to you.
LUKE 6:31

Therefore, if you are offering your gift at the altar and there remember that your brother or sister has something against you, leave your gift there in front of the altar. First go and be reconciled to them; then come and offer your gift.
MATTHEW 5:23–24

There are two action components of Step Eight. First, you make a list of people you have harmed because of your addiction. For many, this is a radically new behavior. If you are like most of us, you are far more likely to keep a list, in your head if not on paper, of people who have harmed you! Some of you may have used this "grievance list" to justify your addictive sexual behavior. Creating a very different list, one of your grievances against others, serves two purposes. It provides a structure for you to fully acknowledge to yourself how your addictive sexual behavior has affected others. It also serves to counter the resentments that you have been holding toward others.

The second action component of Step Eight is to become willing to make amends to everyone on your list. The wise writers of the Twelve Steps recognized that Step Nine—actually making amends—would be one of the most difficult aspects of working the Twelve Steps, so they acknowledged that you might need time to prepare yourself to make amends. How do you do this? Through prayer, meditation, and consultation with trusted companions in your recovery journey.

Step Nine

Made direct amends to such people wherever possible, except when to do so would injure them or others.

At this point in working the Steps, with God's help you have laid a foundation that will give you courage to face those you have hurt. Scripture tells you that you must *"make full restitution for the wrong [you] have done"* (Numbers 5:7). For a recovering sex addict, there may be many indirect amends. You may not know how to contact some of the people you have wronged (such as anonymous sex partners). In other cases, you may know how to contact the person but it would be unwise to do so. These are cases when indirect amends can and should be made. The distinction between when to make direct amends and when to make an indirect amends is nuanced. Consult with trusted souls about when a direct amends could be harmful to yourself or the other person, and discuss how an amends can be made without actually contacting that individual.

Fools mock at making amends for sin, but goodwill is found among the upright.
PROVERBS 14:9

Give, and it will be given to you. A good measure, pressed down, shaken together and running over, will be poured into your lap.
For with the measure you use, it will be measured to you.
LUKE 6:38

Making amends is a difficult and painful process, but it also liberates you from the guilt of past behaviors so that you can live more fully in the relationship you have with Christ. Be strong and courageous (Joshua 1:9).

Step Ten

Continued to take personal inventory and when we were wrong promptly admitted it.

Have you ever cleaned out a messy closet and committed to keep it free of clutter, only to "discover" later that the few things put in that closet over time evolved into new clutter? At a spiritual and psychological level, this is what Step Ten is about. Having worked to "clean your closet" in Steps One through Nine, you remain watchful for additional "clutter" of unfinished business with others. This is similar to doing Steps Eight and Nine daily, recognizing where you may have hurt someone else and making amends as soon as reasonably possible.

So, if you think you are standing firm, be careful that you don't fall!
I CORINTHIANS 10:12

But who can discern their own errors? Forgive my hidden faults.
PSALM 19:12

The daily examination of consciousness, described as a spiritual practice in chapter 2, provides an excellent structure for Step Ten work.

Step Eleven

Sought through prayer and meditation to improve our conscious contact
with God as we understood God, praying only for knowledge of God's
will for us and the power to carry that out.

Scripture says repeatedly, as the following examples demonstrate, that you are a child of God and that you have the capacity to grow each day in your "Christ consciousness." This occurs through spiritual disciplines—namely, prayer and meditation—as outlined in Step Eleven.

Let the message of Christ dwell among you richly as you teach and admonish one another
with all wisdom through psalms, hymns, and songs from the Spirit,
singing to God with gratitude in your hearts.
COLOSSIANS 3:16

He says, "Be still, and know that I am God."
PSALM 46:10A

You were taught, with regard to your former way of life, to put off your old self, which is
being corrupted by its deceitful desires; to be made new in the attitude of your minds.
EPHESIANS 4:22–23

Through these he has given us his very great and precious promises, so that through them
you may participate in the divine nature, having escaped the corruption in the world
caused by evil desires.
II PETER 1:4

Dear friends, now we are children of God, and what we will be has not yet been made
known. But we know that when Christ appears, we shall be like him, for we shall see him
as he is.
I JOHN 3:2

But we have the mind of Christ.
I CORINTHIANS 2:16B

In chapter 2, you were introduced to a number of "tools," also known as spiritual disciplines or spiritual practices. These practices will support you in removing obstacles and help you grow to be more like Christ.

What Jesus did better than any human to walk the planet before or after him was to practice the Eleventh Step. We know that Jesus often went into quiet places to pray and meditate. He did this to improve his conscious connection with the Father. How he lived his life was a testament to discerning God's will and having the courage to act on this discernment (that is, "the power to carry that out"). The wisdom of Step Eleven reminds you as a Christian that your path is not to invoke God to help you meet your goals, but rather to allow God to place within you the awareness of what you truly desire.

 Read the following words of Jesus several times, slowly and out loud, if possible.

If you then, though you are evil, know how to give good gifts to your children, how much more will your Father in heaven give the Holy Spirit to those who ask Him!"

LUKE 11:13

 What is Jesus teaching you in Luke 11:13 about your Eleventh Step work?

 Read the following passage slowly multiple times.

But when you pray, go into your room, close the door and pray to your Father, who is unseen. Then your Father, who sees what is done in secret, will reward you.

MATTHEW 6:6

 Reflect on the Matthew scripture. As you do so, keep in mind that some translations specify an "inner room" or a "private room," yet most homes in Jesus' day only had one room. If Jesus was speaking metaphorically rather than literally, what might he have meant? What does this mean for your daily spiritual practice?

Step Twelve

Having had a spiritual awakening as the result of these steps, we tried to carry this message to other sex addicts and to practice these principles in our lives.

As a Christian, you are called to care for others. In fact, Paul calls you to have the same mind-set as Christ in loving and valuing others. Similarly, Twelve Step programs include a final Step of providing service to others who are struggling.

Brothers and sisters, if someone is caught in a sin, you who live by the Spirit should restore that person gently. But watch yourselves, or you also may be tempted.

GALATIANS 6:1

Do nothing out of selfish ambition or vain conceit. Rather, in humility value others above yourselves, not looking to your own interests but each of you to the interests of the others. In your relationships with one another, have the same mindset as Christ Jesus.

PHILIPPIANS 2:3–5

There are two critical aspects of Step Twelve. First, you are not to carry this message to others without practicing these principles in your own life. That is, you cannot ask others to "do what I say and not what I do." Your Christian growth and continued working of the Steps are necessary before you try to help others. Second, this is the *last* of the Twelve Steps, a clear message that you are to do your own psychological and spiritual work before helping others. Doing Twelve Step service is not about *you* at all, but about others who are struggling and need the experience, strength, and hope that you can offer. This does not mean that you cannot do Twelve Step work until you are working a "perfect" program of recovery, for this never occurs. Do your own recovery work and continue to do so when you are providing service to others who are struggling.

Grace and Effort

At this point in your reading, you may see that working the Steps has a clear corollary in being a Christian. While an individual effort is certainly involved, there also is a level of surrender and acceptance. Many men and women struggle with finding an optimal balance. Some work too hard at recovery, which ultimately becomes an expression of willfulness and self-pride. Others expect God to heal them without taking personal responsibility for their recovery.

A helpful analogy is to think of a bird with two wings, one named *effort* and one named *grace*. For the bird to fly straight and true, both wings must work together. If either wing works harder than the other, the flight will soon veer off course. So, too, does your path of recovery require a path of balancing effort and grace.

 Do you anticipate that one of your "wings" will over-function or underfunction? What has this looked like in your past, especially around your addictive sexual behavior? If this is a common theme for you, what will you do to consciously watch and guard against this in recovery? In other words, how will you "stay awake, and keep your eyes open" (Matthew 13:37b)?

One, Two, Three . . . Twelve

Some people in early recovery "stall" at Step Four. Often, they have worked Steps One through Three well and are beginning to assume leadership or service opportunities within their Twelve Step communities. These people are caringly said to be adopting a One, Two, Three … Twelve approach to the Steps in which they surrender (Steps One through Three) and serve (Step Twelve). As you might imagine, though, such an approach is rarely if ever successful because it omits vital Steps in the recovery process. Steps Four through Eleven are active Steps that require a great deal of effort and tend to stir up shame, guilt, and fear. The work is not easy, but it is necessary.

 Read Job 23:11 several times slowly, being mindful of what emerges as most important for you at this point in time.

My feet have closely followed his steps;
I have kept to his way without turning aside.

 Take time to pray for the readiness, willingness, and ability to closely follow His steps and keep to His way without turning aside.

Spiritual Disciplines

Although many of the spiritual disciplines from chapter 2 may be useful as you reflect on the Twelve Steps and the teachings of Jesus, a few might be particularly salient.

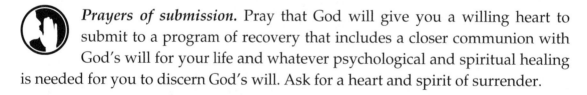 *Prayers of submission.* Pray that God will give you a willing heart to submit to a program of recovery that includes a closer communion with God's will for your life and whatever psychological and spiritual healing is needed for you to discern God's will. Ask for a heart and spirit of surrender.

 Prayers of thanksgiving. If you do not practice gratitude, you will practice resentment. Offer prayers of thanksgiving for what you have been given, including the gift of recovery, as a counter to any lingering resentments.

Eleventh Step Prayer. Say the following prayer:

> *Father God, as the deer pants for water, so do I thirst for you.*
> *My deepest desire is to know you more.*
> *From my connection to you, I long to live my life in accord with your plans for me.*
> *Give me an open heart and open mind to hear*
> *the wisdom of your still small voice as you speak to me.*
> *When I hear your voice, grant me courage, strength, and power*
> *to act with integrity as you would have me to act.*
> *It is in the name of your son Jesus that I pray.*
> *Amen*

Now, enter into a period of silent prayer, repeating lines of the prayer if needed. Breathe deeply and create space for God to speak to you.

Daily examination of consciousness. Review the directions for the daily examination in chapter 2. Consider whether this might be an important practice for you at this stage of your recovery. If so, engage in this practice now and commit to making it a daily practice.

Chapter Four
Who Am I in Christ?

Our addictions are our own worst enemies. They enslave us with chains that are of our own making and yet that, paradoxically, are virtually beyond our control.
GERALD MAY, ADDICTION AND GRACE

 This chapter parallels chapter 1 (What is Real?) in *Facing the Shadow.* Read and work through both simultaneously. Throughout the rest of this book, look for the icon indicating you should refer to *Facing the Shadow.*

Blessings to you as you continue on your journey of healing! This chapter focuses on how you have not been honest with yourself, others, and God. It is the very nature of addiction to deceive.

At the same time, we remind you that God's grace is sufficient. Period. It does not matter what you have done or where you have been. One of the most important tasks you have as a recovering person is to allow God's grace to heal your shame. To get started, let's distinguish between shame and guilt.

Guilt is a negative feeling over what you have done. *Shame* is a negative feeling about who you are. It is an important contrast. The voice of guilt says, "I have done bad things." The voice of shame says, "I am bad."

Guilt can be further broken down into two types, existential and neurotic. Existential guilt is a healthy guilt that tells us when we are living our lives without integrity and outside of the will of God. It is a course correction of sorts, a gentle pull within our soul to live our lives differently. Neurotic guilt, on the other hand, is a pervasive sense of never getting things right or quite good enough. Although this form of guilt also focuses on behavior (in contrast to shame, which focuses on the person), it exerts a negative influence in our Christian journey as we are consumed with feelings of inadequacy and an inability to ever be enough. Neurotic guilt leaves us in a chronic state of anxiety, lacking peace. It is simply not possible to be living in neurotic guilt and be in communion with God. What's more, there is a thin line between neurotic guilt and shame. If you live rigidly in neurotic guilt ("I can never do it right"), this inevitably leads to shame ("I am bad").

These distinctions are important to bear in mind as you begin to examine the ways in which you have been dishonest with yourself, friends and family, and God. As you shine the light of God into these previously hidden and dark parts of yourself, it is easy to feel a strong sense of shame ("I am such a bad person to have done those things") or a sense of neurotic guilt ("I never treat those around me well"). In the end, neither shame nor neurotic guilt will serve your recovery. As you do the exercises in this chapter, stop and talk to a trusted soul (for example, your therapist, sponsor, or pastor) if you find yourself in a place of neurotic guilt or shame. While a certain amount of existential guilt is useful, as it prompts you to make behavior changes in the present moment, neurotic guilt will leave you obsessing about the past or ruminating about the future.

Carl Jung, a psychologist of the early 1900s, taught that many of us are living someone else's life, with someone else's priorities, sabotaging our creativity and potential. Similarly, we are taught that "truth came through Jesus Christ" (John 1:17b). This chapter examines self-delusion and asks, "Who am I in Christ?" The intent is to begin deconstructing the core beliefs that have supported your addiction. You will learn to "let go" of past behaviors, critical inner voices, and feelings of bondage from familial, cultural, and organized religion doctrines.

Meditation

For the purpose of this chapter, read Luke 18:9–14; the Parable of the Pharisee and the Tax Collector. As you listen to Jesus' tale of the prideful Pharisee and the humble tax collector, notice that Christ is not interested in our list of good deeds. It is ridiculous for us to think we need to remind Him of our offerings. By speaking boastful words, we are deceiving ourselves into thinking we are better than, more important than, and more resourceful than the person with less means than ours. It is pride that gets in the way of how we should "see" and "be" like Christ.

Often, people in early recovery boast of their sobriety. Although sobriety is of the utmost importance to addicts and their families, it is the attributes of sobriety that need to be seen, but not often heard. What if instead of focusing on the things that create pride, we turned our interest on ways that God is showering grace and mercy on us?

In chapter 2, you worked exercises that guided you to a deeper understanding and recognition of God's Grace in your life. As a reminder, Grace can be defined as God's undeserved, unearned favor, goodness, kindness, and love toward us. Now, we turn our attention toward seeing the gift of Mercy. It shines through us every time we minister to people in emotional or spiritual pain; become willing to give ourselves fully to our spouses, friends, and family members in loving devotion; and rally with our friends who are hurt by rejection. We also can know God's mercy on us as we experience the newfound feelings of peace, calmness, and the sanity that follows us throughout the recovery journey.

Consider the following modern-day parable.

Blessed Are the Humble: A Modern Parable

Micah ran up the dusty path shouting, "Your dad is home!" Looking out the kitchen window, Jeannie watched as her husband, Dek, made his way toward the small wooden cabin they called home. Almost daily for the last ten years, she had stood in this place witnessing her husband's return from work. This time, her eyes saddened, as she noticed his gait was becoming slower, more tired.

"Quickly, Micah" she said to their only child. "Go get your dad some water. You know how hot and tired he is after working the ranch." Micah ran to the well and drew up the cool water, then handed it to his father.

"Thank you, son," said Dek as he playfully ruffled Micah's hair. "That's mighty kind of you to bring your old man some water." Taking the cup of water, Dek lifted it up to say thank you to the heavens before he drank. "You know, son, we might be poor according to the townspeople, but here on our own soil, we are rich. Remember that each time you give thanks to God for what he has given us."

During supper, Dek's family listened as he talked about his day. "I hear there is this fella coming from New York. Rumor has it that he wants to build a new town here. Says he's coming to build a school, better stores, and the like. And I hear that he is looking for folks to move in. Free land to those who ask for it."

"Dad, can we get some new land?" asked Micah.

Jeannie leaned over, patted her son's hand, and said, "Micah, it is time you understand. Things like that are for the rich people, you know, like Jake McCloud your dad works for. Mr. Jake gives so much to our town of McCloud, even owns McCloud bank that holds the deed to our house. Remember last year at the big party he threw for the town and how he told us all about the great things he has done for us. We should be grateful for his generosity. I am sure it is people like him that will receive the new land."

Looking thoughtfully, Dek said, "Maybe your mom is right, Micah. We don't deserve pieces of land, but I would at least like to speak to this fella about some work. We could certainly use a few dollars to fix the leaks in the roof, maybe get a couple more cows. I'll give it a shot, anyway. They say he'll be here next week."

"Now, son, go get ready for bed. And don't forget your prayers."

Micah smiled, "Alright, dad, good night. Good night, mom."

As foretold, Ben Smith arrived in town the following week. News spread quickly that he was interviewing people who were interested in moving into his new community. As Dek stood outside the doors listening to folks plead their case, he recognized his boss, Jake McCloud. Although Jake's voice is normally loud, today it was booming as he told Ben about all the great things he did for the townsfolk, details of the money he spent to build the town of McCloud, even built the church—McCloud's Place of Worship. Thirty minutes later, Jake's tales begin to cease and Dek continued to wait patiently for his turn.

Normally a mild and peaceful man, Dek grew uneasy as he waited in line, and he began to think about himself. Suddenly, he became anxious and sad, thinking and muttering to himself, "What right did I have asking for work? I have no education, no money to give, and sometimes I drink too much, even say a cuss word now and then."

"I am not going in there," he told himself. "After all, I'm nothing but a poor man who is a sinner. I have no right to ask for this man's kindness." Then he prayed, "Lord, thank you for giving me the thoughts of my sinful ways. You have given me so much, and I don't deserve any of it. Please have mercy on me and my family. Help me to remember your instructions to hide your words in my heart that I might not sin against thee. Placing his hat upon his head, he turned to head home.

"Dek!" cried out a voice. "Come here." Slowly Dek turned and looked up at the stranger in town. "Mr. Smith is asking you to come talk with him." Confused, Dek walked into the room where Ben Smith sat behind a wooden desk.

"Are you Dek Lamar?" asked Ben. "Yes sir, I am," answered Dek. "Then I am asking you to bring your family into the new town I am constructing. You can have the first pick of the land." Ben then pointed to a piece of paper that showed plots of land for Dek to choose from.

Dek replied, "I don't understand. I think you have the wrong person. My boss, Mr. Jake, who was just in here, he should get the pick of the land. You see, he has done great things for our town. I heard him tell you all about it just a few minutes ago. Me, I am just a poor man who doesn't always act right according to the Good Book. Sir, I can hardly look you in the eye right now."

Ben gave Dek a gentle touch on the shoulder and said, "Yes. I have met this man, Jake. I listened as he boasted of the many good things he has done. But, you are the man I am looking for. You see, as he was talking, I was watching you standing outside my door. I heard your muttering and saw your anguish as you searched your soul. I watched as you made repentance for sins and I watched you start to walk away feeling humbled and maybe defeated. You, sir, are the kind of person who will live in my town."

"Now, go home and gather your wife and son, for today you will receive greatness deserving of your humility. Understand this, men who boast about greatness will be made humble, but men who offer up their own humility will be made great."

Dek's eyes glistened with tears as he began to soak in all that Ben was saying. "Sir," he said, "before I go home to tell my family of your kindness, may I ask you a question?" "Go ahead, whatever your questions are, I will answer truthfully," said Ben. "What is the name of this new town you are building?" Smiling, Ben replied, "The town's name is Mercy and you, my friend, will live on the street I call Grace."

Justifying Addictive Behavior

Reflection on Scripture

 Reflect on the following scripture in your journal.

There is a way that appears to be right, but in the end it leads to death.
PROVERBS 14:12

- This proverb characterizes addictive sexual behavior. When you were actively in your addiction, you likely used many creative ways to convince yourself that your addictive behavior was "right." Journal about how you were dishonest with yourself and others to make your addictive sexual behavior "a way that appears to be right."

- This proverb also tells us that in the end, this justified way "leads to death." Although you are fortunate enough to have entered recovery and still be alive, consider what deaths you have nonetheless experienced. Journal about what you have lost (that is, what has "died" in your life) because of your addictive behavior. Also, write about how you might have physically died had you not started a healing journey of recovery.

The following scripture offers words of hope.

So if anyone is in Christ, there is a new creation: everything old has passed away; see, everything has become new!
II CORINTHIANS 5:17

Here, Paul shares with the church at Corinth words that are encouraging to this day. If you are "in Christ," you are being transformed. The bondage of addiction passes away and the new (in this case, a sexually healthy you) begins to emerge. Unfortunately, some Christians believe that to be in Christ simply means to believe in Jesus. But being in Christ is more than a set of passive beliefs. It is establishing a disciplined daily spiritual practice that draws you into closer communion with God.

There are many beliefs that can keep you from being in Christ. These include the ways in which you deluded yourself and others to justify your addictive behaviors. One of the problems in early recovery is that you may unconsciously hang on to some of these delusions. As Twelve Step communities like to say, "The results were nil until we let go completely." This means letting go not only of the addictive behaviors that plagued your past, but also of the thoughts that supported these behaviors. This is what it means to let go of childish things (I Corinthians 13:11) and to be in Christ.

We turn our attention now to some common things addicts say to themselves to support their addictive behavior and to mislead themselves, others, and God. You may or may not relate to all of these forms of deceit.

 Before you begin, say a brief prayer asking God to help you be "searching and fearless" in your reflections, fully honest with Him and yourself.

"I cannot really trust God."

For many, the struggle to fully rely on God is very real and tangible. Addictive sexual behavior often is, at least in part, an attempt to cope with difficult circumstances, experiences, and/or emotions. Not being able to fully trust God results in fear. If we refuse to trust God with our life, we will almost certainly be plagued with fear. Fear takes many forms, including

- fear of inadequacy
- fear of being left or abandoned
- fear of being unlovable
- fear of saying/doing the wrong thing
- fear that previous actions are unforgivable
- fear of how others perceive you
- fear that the current struggles will never improve
- fear that recovery will always be difficult
- fear that you cannot remain in recovery from your addiction

The results of fear are predictable. At an emotional and psychological level, though, fear always results in anger (and its more gentle counterparts, irritability and frustration), insecurity, paranoia, and pain. This separates you from a communion with God.

 How have you failed to trust God? Which of the fears listed above can you relate to most?

It is difficult to fully trust God. It takes practice supported by the spiritual disciplines you developed in chapter 2. Your particular fears depend on your experiences. To address your fears, you must counter them with something else. Consider the scriptural foundation for this.

In this world we are like Jesus. There is no fear in love. But perfect love drives out fear, because fear has to do with punishment. The one who fears is not made perfect in love.
I JOHN 4:17B–18

For the Spirit God gave us does not make us timid, but gives us power, love and self-discipline.
II TIMOTHY 1:7

The antidote to fear, then, is not courage … but love. The NIV version of the Bible mentions fear 336 times, so it is clear that God understands fear as part of our human experience. The Bible not only references fear as part of the human condition but also provides guidance on addressing our fear. The following are some examples of fear and soothing scriptural responses.

Fear of abandonment:

We are hard pressed on every side, but not crushed; perplexed, but not in despair; persecuted, but not abandoned; struck down, but not destroyed.
II CORINTHIANS 4:8–9

Fear of being unlovable:

For God so loved the world [meaning not the planet, per se, but all of the people, including you] that he gave his one and only Son, that whoever believes in him shall not perish but have eternal life.
JOHN 3:16

Fear of saying/doing the wrong thing:

Love is patient, love is kind. It does not envy, it does not boast, it is not proud. It does not dishonor others, it is not self-seeking, it is not easily angered, it keeps no record of wrongs. Love does not delight in evil but rejoices in the truth.

I CORINTHIANS 13:4–6

Fear that previous actions are unforgivable:

For his anger lasts only a moment, but his favor lasts a lifetime; weeping may stay for the night, but rejoicing comes in the morning.

PSALM 30:5

And hope does not put us to shame, because God's love has been poured out into our hearts through the Holy Spirit, who has been given to us.

ROMANS 5:5

Fear that recovery will always be difficult:

But if we hope for what we do not see, we wait for it with patience.

ROMANS 8:25

Yes, my soul, find rest in God; my hope comes from Him.

PSALM 62:5

Fear that you cannot remain in recovery from your addiction:

But those who hope in the Lord will renew their strength. They will soar on wings like eagles; they will run and not grow weary, they will walk and not be faint.

ISAIAH 40:31

If any of these fears is particularly strong for you, take time to breathe and meditate on the scripture to counter that fear and ask God to help you open to the depth and breadth of His love for you.

Note that while the word "fear" occurs 336 times in the NIV Bible, the word "hope" is used 180 times. The full experience of the love of God does not happen quickly, but slowly, through practice, study, and spiritual disciplines. Sensitive therapists and sponsors also can help you work through your fears and open more fully to the love of God. Paul, in his letter to the church at Ephesus, captures the vision of hope that you may have in Jesus:

I pray that the eyes of your heart may be enlightened in order that you may know the hope
to which he has called you, the riches of his glorious inheritance in his holy people.

EPHESIANS 1:18

Slow down and reflect and contemplate the verse above. Using practices discussed in chapter 2, you might

- engage in a contemplative reading of this verse
- say a breath prayer: (inhale) I pray (exhale) that the eyes of my heart be enlightened
- say a breath prayer: (inhale) I know (exhale) the hope to which God has called me

In whatever way is right for you, reflect on this part of the verse, "the hope to which he has called you" and how it applies to your recovery.

"I am God."

Although you probably never spoke these exact words during your active addiction, the reality is that if you felt unable to fully trust God, you probably tried to act like God yourself. We act like God when we pretend to not need God or the help of others. Also, when people are actively in their addiction, they often try to control and manipulate others to serve their self-interests, acting as if they know what is best for everyone.

> In the movie *Rudy*, the story of an undersized athlete who wants to play football at Notre Dame, there is a poignant scene in which Rudy meets with a priest. Father Cavanaugh tells Rudy: "Son, in thirty-five years of religious study, I have only come up with two hard incontrovertible facts: there is a God, and I'm not Him."

Scriptures speak to this issue very clearly. In Paul's second letter to the church at Corinth, he wrote:

For God, who said, "Let light shine out of darkness," made his light shine in
our hearts to give us the light of the knowledge of God's glory displayed in the
face of Christ. But we have this treasure in jars of clay to show that this

*all-surpassing power is from God and not from us. We are hard pressed on
every side, but not crushed; perplexed, but not in despair.*

II CORINTHIANS 4:6–8

There is much in this passage that is important for your recovery. When God said, "Let light shine out of darkness," He was saying to you, "Let recovery shine out of addiction." Paul goes on to tell us that the light is not us, not of us, and not from us, but rather was placed in our hearts by God. Something so powerful, so magnificent, certainly should be protected in a vault or a strong secure place, but instead, Paul tells us, it is stored in a fragile and easily broken container, one that is certainly flawed and chipped. You are that jar of clay! The chips, irregularities, and flaws in that vessel represent all of your shortcomings, mistakes, poor choices, and character defects— in short, all that makes you human. Yet, however flawed the fragile jar of clay may be, it contains something priceless, the light that God has placed inside your heart.

Just a few verses later, Paul offers encouragement for what the light can bring to us:

*Therefore we do not lose heart. Though outwardly we are wasting away, yet inwardly we
are being renewed day by day. For our light and momentary troubles are achieving for us
an eternal glory that far outweighs them all. So we fix our eyes not on what is seen, but on
what is unseen. For what is seen is temporary, but what is unseen is eternal.*

II CORINTHIANS: 4:16–18

 Reflect on the following questions in your journal:

- In your addiction, how did you pretend not to need God's help?
- In your addiction, how did you pretend not to need the help of other people?
- In your addiction, in what ways did you manipulate and try to control those around you for your own gain, essentially "playing God" with them?
- During your active addiction, in what ways did you hide the light that God placed in your heart?

"I deserve it."

To continue your addictive sexual behavior, you may have clung to the lie that you deserved to engage in that behavior. Often, this is referred to as *entitlement*. God does, indeed, entitle us in our human form to the pleasure derived from a healthy sexuality. This is very different, though, from addictive sexual behavior.

Shadows of the Cross: A Christian Companion to *Facing the Shadow*

In our work as therapists, we often hear the following statements of entitlement to which we offer these responses:

"I work really hard. I deserve to have some fun."

We agree that all people need breaks from hard work. What is needed, though, is fun that nurtures your soul and connects you to healthy people in healthy ways. Addictive sexual behavior does not nurture your soul and is disconnecting rather than connecting.

"My spouse just isn't as sexual as I am."

Many couples do struggle with sexual compatibility and varying levels of desire. It is particularly common for the partner of a sex addict to withdraw from his or her partner sexually, often as an attempt to avoid the fear of being inadequate sexually/unable to meet the partner's sexual needs. So in some instances the partner's sexual withdrawal (what some call sexual anorexia) is, at least in part, a reaction to the partner's sex addiction. Whatever the cause of the sexual difficulties in the relationship, the answer is not pornography, one-night stands, or other attempts to make a connection with another. Rather, the solution lies in genuinely working on the relationship, perhaps with the support of a therapist who specializes in treating couples.

"God made me a highly sexual person and I need outlets for that."

Like all humans, you are a sexual being and this is a gift from God. He did not create you, however, for addictive sexual behavior. That is a function of your emotional and psychological woundedness, and it has separated you from God.

"I do a lot of good for other people. Looking at pornography doesn't hurt anyone and it makes me relax. It's just me doing something for me."

This statement contains a number of flaws. First, you are using your good deeds to justify acting out. We are called by God to do good to others with no expectation of return. This is stated clearly in Luke 6:35:

> *But love your enemies, do good to them, and lend to them without*
> *expecting to get anything back. Then your reward will be great,*
> *and you will be children of the Most High, because*
> *he is kind to the ungrateful and wicked.*

Additionally, viewing pornography does, in fact, cause a great deal of harm to others, as it supports prostitution and human trafficking.

There are many variations on these statements of entitlement. In what ways did you justify your addictive sexual behavior as something to which you were entitled?

"I am different/special."

In *The Wizard of Oz*, there is a poignant scene where Dorothy and her friends have finally entered the wizard's castle and are standing in fear and awe before him. As Dorothy's dog, Toto, pulls back the curtain to reveal a very ordinary man at the controls, the "wizard" speaks words that every sex addict has uttered in some form: "Pay no attention to that [person] behind the curtain."

That is, we are so uncomfortable with our "ordinariness" that we strive to make ourselves special somehow. As an addict, you also use this illusion of being special or different from others to justify your addictive sexual behavior.

C. S. Lewis wrote, "As long as you are proud, you cannot know God." His statement is firmly grounded in scripture. Consider the following passages:

Pride goes before destruction, a haughty spirit before a fall.
PROVERBS 16:18

So then, no more boasting about human leaders! All things are yours.
I CORINTHIANS 3:21

Do nothing out of selfish ambition or vain conceit.
Rather, in humility value others above yourselves.
PHILIPPIANS 2:3

To the extent that you have manipulated or controlled family members to promote your self-interest, the Bible also has a clear mandate for families:

Submit to one another out of reverence for Christ.
EPHESIANS 5:21

There are two sides to the "I am special" mentality. On the one hand, this mentality is used to justify and rationalize addictive sexual behavior. On the other hand, people often struggle to present themselves as special or worthy because of the deep shame they feel over their hidden addictive sexual behavior. This is a near constant battle to be "good enough." By feeling "superior" in some respect, you may have been trying to balance how inferior you felt in your addictive cycle.

Respond to the following questions:

- In what ways have you presented yourself as special in some way to either (a) justify or rationalize your addictive sexual behavior or (b) reduce your shame over your addictive sexual behavior?

- If you manipulated family members during your addiction in any way, what will it look like now for you to submit to them out of reverence for Christ, as directed in Ephesians 5:21?

"Being 'found out' would be terrible."

If you are like most sex addicts, you went to great lengths to hide your addictive sexual behavior. Concealed in your mire of shame, you may have acted out only when you knew you would not be "caught." Doors were locked, lies were told, and computer and phone settings were manipulated. We have heard many stories revealing the great lengths to which people went to hide their addictive sexual behavior. Quite simply, you thought that the most terrible thing possible would be for anyone else to learn of your behaviors.

Some of you may have entered recovery precisely because what you feared most has happened. Someone did find out. A web cache, a stray email that was not deleted, a public sighting while you were engaged in addictive behavior, an arrest, a lost job, a pregnancy, a sexually transmitted disease, or other occurrences often lead to "discovery" by another person. Others of you found recovery when you could no longer hide in the shame and so disclosed your addiction to someone else. However recovery began for you in a moment your worst nightmare came true.

Or did it?

Whether you are in the "recovery by discovery" group or the "recovery by disclosure" group, the shame of being known in this way was no doubt painful and the minutes, hours, and days that followed were some of the most difficult in your life. In no way do we wish to minimize how painful that process is.

At the same time, for many men and women, this represents the "worst moment" or, as it is commonly called, their "rock bottom." As anyone in recovery will tell you, though, hitting rock bottom is the most grace filled moment of their lives, one in which the web of secrecy, deceit, and lies came crashing down in an instant. The resulting shame, fear, and pain is immense. Yet it is precisely amid this anguished experience—your worst moment—when recovery begins. This is the instant where the veil of deceit is lifted.

Consider the Samaritan woman at the well (John 4:3–42). Part of what was so upsetting for her was that she had been "found out." Jesus told her things about herself of which she felt shame and which she thought were unknown. While it must have been very difficult for her to hear this Jewish man naming her sins, this is the very moment where her healing began. So it is for you.

If there were somehow a gathering of everyone in the world experiencing their rock-bottom moment, Christ would undoubtedly be in their midst. Jesus commonly sought out people at their most painful time. Without a doubt, in your own experience of discovery or disclosure, even as you struggled with overwhelming emotions, the Holy Spirit was with you, rejoicing in what you will eventually see as the most grace-filled moment of your life—the moment you began your healing journey of recovery.

After your initial shock at being "found out," you may have been surprised to experience relief. The hard work, years or decades for some of you, of hiding in the dark takes a devastating toll. Whatever consequences you may yet face, you may nonetheless feel some relief that you no longer have to spend so much energy maintaining the deceit and lies and that you can begin to be healed from addictive sexual behaviors.

 Take a few moments now to offer a prayer of gratitude to God. Here is an example:

Prayer of Gratitude

Holy Father, I have amends to make to you, to those in my life, and to myself. In this moment, though, I offer my heart to you with thanks that I can lay down the lies and deceit that have been such a large part of my life for so long. Now I stand, not in the darkness of my lies, deceit, and addictive sexual behavior, but in the shadow of the cross. Amid the difficulties that I know lie ahead, help me to always know you are with me. I love you and thank you for loving me just as I am in this moment.
Amen

While the gratitude prayer like the one provided may be useful to you, never forget that Paul reminded us to pray continually (I Thessalonians 5:17). In this instance, you may simply wish to close your eyes, take a deep breath, and heartfully say "thank you" to God.

For those of you who are married, who have a partner, or are in a committed dating relationship, there is an important caveat here. You may feel relief at loosening the old burden of deceit, lies, and behaviors over which you feel deep shame while admitting you have a problem with addictive sexual behavior. This is not "news" to you. However, your partner is likely facing new and often traumatizing information. Because of this, partners often heal and recover at a slower pace than the addicts themselves.

In early recovery, addicts often express frustration that their partner "can't let go of the past" and feel grateful that they are now in recovery. Your objective at this point, though, is to understand and accept that your partner's healing journey may be happening on a different time frame than yours, perhaps a radically different time frame. Respecting and honoring your partner's healing process is part of making amends to him or her. It may help to recall the words of Paul in I Corinthians 13:4, which remind you how to respond to your partner during this time:

Love is patient.

Love is kind.

Some relationships survive sex addiction. Others do not. Either way, love is patient and kind. Paul did not say that love is patient and kind if you stay together or if your spouse forgives you. Regardless of your circumstances:

Love is patient.

Love is kind.

 Respond to the following questions:

- Now that your addiction is no longer a secret, either from others or from yourself, what blessings have you experienced? Acknowledge the difficulty of early recovery, but focus primarily on the blessings that have come with bringing what was in the dark to light.

- How you will manifest, with God's help, Paul's statements that love is patient and kind? This might be patience and kindness that you show to another, such as your partner, or it may be patience and kindness that you show to yourself as you move through recovery.

"No one is being hurt."

 At some point in your addiction, you likely told yourself this lie to reduce the shame you felt about your behavior. However, as you have learned in recovery, addictive sexual behavior is hurtful. See *Facing the Shadow*, chapter 1, on the consequences of your behavior.

Journal your responses to the following:

- How have you and one other person been hurt by your addictive sexual behavior? Who was hurt and how were they hurt?

- How have you "gone off the path" that God wants you to follow? Where have you strayed and where would God have led you differently if you stayed on the path?

With patience and persistence, through prayer, meditation, and trusted counsel, you can discern the path that God would have you follow. This is promised in scripture:

You make known to me the path of life; you will fill me with joy in your presence, with eternal pleasures at your right hand.

PSALM 16:11

"I can handle it."

At some point, most addicts recognize that they have a problem but hang on to the addictive behavior by convincing themselves that they can manage their "little problem" without help. You may have made promises not to engage in certain behaviors or to "manage" these behaviors by cutting back on them somehow. While personal contracts like these often do work for short periods, in time the addict returns to previous levels of the behavior. Here are some examples:

- Jorge was looking at pornography on his computer and masturbating for about three hours each night. He was losing sleep, which affected his work performance. He made a commitment to only watch pornography for thirty to forty-five minutes each night. He stuck to this for four nights, but then gradually began to increase the amount of time until he returned to his original level of about three hours each night. He went through this cycle many times before he finally sought help for his addiction upon hitting "rock bottom" by getting fired from his job for poor performance.

- Sally's acting out behavior involved going out to clubs, drinking excessively, and finding a sexual partner to take home. She always felt miserable the next morning, both physically and emotionally. She got stuck in a cycle where the only way to alleviate the shame was to repeat the cycle, which brought temporary relief but ultimately created more shame. At the peak of her addiction, Sally was engaging in this behavior every night. Her life was out of control, as many of the men would drop by her home later looking for sex. To combat this, she moved and vowed never to have another one-night stand. Shortly after her move, she decided to go out to a club, telling herself she would just have one drink and not meet anyone. When she awoke the next morning with a hangover and a stranger in her bed, the cycle had begun again.

- Tom was a married businessman who traveled frequently. When he traveled, he would go out in public and expose himself. At one point he was arrested for indecent exposure but had the charge reduced by claiming that he was urinating and thought he was in a secluded place. This is the same story he told his wife and she believed him. Terrified by the experience, Tom vowed to never engage in exhibitionism again. He continued work-related travel and had no problems for several months. Then, after a difficult day of business meetings in a town far from home, Tom decided to go for a walk "just to manage my stress." He exposed himself to a passerby, was arrested, and because it was his second offense, earned the lifetime label of a sex offender. He lost his job and his wife left him.

- Jake collected a stash of pornographic movies, which he kept well "hidden" on his password-protected computer. He would store about ten to fifteen movies and watch them for hours each night. Periodically, he would get discouraged at how much time he was wasting watching pornography and would delete his movies, vowing never to do that again. Within a few weeks, though, he would decide, "Well, I'll just download one movie and watch it every now and then." Soon, his pattern of amassing a collection of porn and spending increasing amounts of time watching it would resume.

 How did you try to manage your addictive sexual behavior? Include how your efforts worked and how they failed.

"God will deliver me from my addiction … so I don't need to do anything."

Carl presented himself in a sex addiction treatment group as a devout Christian. Although he had substantive legal problems as a result of his sexual behavior, he refused to call himself an addict, saying, "That sounds so permanent. I know that God will deliver me from this bondage." He only came to the group because he was mandated by the court to do so. As the group began working on various tasks, Carl failed to do his work, shared only minimally, and refused to attend support group meetings. Soon after, he was arrested in a sting operation in which he thought he was going to see a fifteen-year-old girl with whom he had flirted online.

We certainly believe in miracles and deliverance. The problem here, though, is that in these instances God is not being used as a source of strength, but rather as a defense mechanism to minimize the problem. Remember that the healthiest relationship with God to support your recovery is one of collaboration in which you surrender certain aspects of your recovery to God, accept personal responsibility for your behaviors, and work to discern what is within your control and what is not. This is the essence of the Serenity Prayer. When you try to take too much control (self-directing) or too little control (deferring) as Carl did, you miss the mark and increase the likelihood of relapse.

Remember the Serenity Prayer:

> *God, grant me the serenity to accept the things I cannot change,*
> *The courage to change the things I can,*
> *And the wisdom to know the difference.*

Take a few moments to reflect on the importance of these words. They provide guidance on how not to attempt to over-control or under-manage your addictive behavior.

 To begin, write each of the following prompts at the top of a page in your journal:

- God, grant me the serenity to accept . . .
- God, grant me the courage to change . . .
- God, grant me wisdom.

Then, on the first two pages (serenity and courage), list specific ways that you need to grow to accept and change, respectively. On the final page, journal about how you will collaborate with God to grow in wisdom and discernment.

Respond to the following:

- How do you plan to walk this recovery journey collaboratively with God, seeking the wisdom to discern between things that cannot be changed and those that can?
- Do you tend to say "God will deliver me" in a way that frees you from taking personal responsibility for your behavior and your recovery? How will you watch for this and instead work collaboratively with God?

"Reality is unbearable."

 Complete The Problem List in chapter 1 of *Facing the Shadow* (exercise 1.1).

In the past, you likely were in situations where you genuinely did not want to act out sexually after making a commitment to change, only to act out again in a time of stress or hardship. In these moments, you are using sexual behavior as an "escape," an avoidant coping strategy to deal with difficult circumstances. Here, we want to first and foremost validate your struggle. Life is, indeed, at times difficult for everyone.

> *But he said to me, "My grace is sufficient for you.*
> II CORINTHIANS 12:9A

For many sex addicts, stress triggers the physiological sensations that lead to acting out. Here are some preventive measures:

- Manage stress.
- Get enough sleep.
- Eat healthy.
- Enjoy aerobic activity consistent with your age and ability.
- Create healthy fun in your life.

We outlined the spiritual disciplines early on for a reason. Besides supporting your healing and spiritual growth, spiritual disciplines can help manage stress. When you are feeling triggered, you can use these practices to calm your mind and body.

 Review the spiritual practices discussed in chapter 2. Which are most effective at calming you? Write down the practices that calm you when your mind and/or body are triggered sexually.

"I can do just a little of my old behavior and be okay."

 This is similar to "I can handle it." What is different is that "I can do just a little … " is a trap you fall into after starting recovery, whereas "I can handle it" is pre-recovery behavior. If you have already been doing this, make sure that you include the "I can do just a little … " behaviors in The Secret List in chapter 1 of *Facing the Shadow* (exercise 1.2).

Consider the following examples:

- A man whose addictive sexual behavior involved a series of one-night stands decides it would be acceptable to go to a singles bar where he acted out.

- A woman who previously engaged in exhibitionism (flashing) decides it is okay to wear a very short skirt and low-cut top to a mall just to see what reactions she would get from others.

- A man who compulsively watched pornography as his primary addictive behavior decides it is okay to watch an R-rated movie that includes nudity and love scenes.

- A man in early recovery from sexual addiction whose primary behavior was voyeurism (peeping) decides to take his dog for long walks at night. He justifies this by saying that although he may be able to see into the windows of houses from the street, he is not going up to the houses and actively trying to look in windows as he once did.

Depending on your values, some of these behaviors, such as going to a club or watching an R-rated movie, may be inherently unacceptable on moral grounds. The key element of these scenarios, though, is that each person is trying to engage in a more socially acceptable form of their addictive behavior.

Scripture provides guidance here:

"No one can serve two masters. Either you will hate the one and love the other, or you will be devoted to the one and despise the other."

LUKE 16:13A

Although this particular passage refers to the "master" of money, it also applies to the master of addictive sexual behavior. An important distinction for you to make here is that it is not sex and/or your sexuality that is to be hated, as healthy sexuality is a godly gift. Instead, what is to be hated is your addictive sexual behavior, which at times has been your master, precluding you from serving God.

"It's not my fault."

 Complete the List of Excuses in chapter 1 of *Facing the Shadow* (exercise 1.3).

Some sex addicts manage the shame that accompanies their addiction by blaming others, focusing on injustices done to them or needs that were not met.

The research is clear here. Most sex addicts come from families that have dysfunction, including addictions. Many sex addicts are survivors of emotional, physical, or sexual abuse.

Commonly, sex addicts grow up in disengaged families where they do not learn how to connect with others in healthy ways. Being neglected as a child and internalizing the "I don't matter" message is a common precursor to sex addiction.

Others may be partnered with someone who has their own psychological struggles, such as an eating disorder, depression, anxiety, or their own addiction. At times, because of their own psychological struggles, such partners may be physically, emotionally, or sexually unavailable.

Blaming others for your addiction, though, is not the way of recovery. Many of you may have relationship issues that you will have to work through as part of your long-term recovery. For now, in this early phase of recovery, simply recognize that while not all of your developmental needs were met in childhood and perhaps not all of your emotional needs are met in your current relationship, you alone are responsible for your sexual behavior.

 When have you made excuses or blamed others to avoid responsibility for your addiction or your recovery?

Religious and Spiritual Consequences

 Complete the Consequences Inventory (exercise 1.4) in chapter 1 of *Facing the Shadow* to better understand the breadth of consequences you have experienced in multiple domains of your life related to your addiction.

 Then, in your journal, explore more deeply the following religious and spiritual consequences you have faced as a result of your addiction.

Religious consequences. Write about the consequences you have faced in your religious community. This might include being asked to leave, being bypassed for service opportunities, being judged by someone who knows of your addiction, or experiencing shame for having sexual fantasies or for sexualizing another person while in a church service.

Feelings of spiritual emptiness. Do you remember the "God-shaped hole" discussed in chapter 1? For many, addictive sexual behavior is an attempt to fill that void, which may be experienced as loneliness, sadness, shame, anxiety, fear, anger, or simply feeling unsettled in some indescribable way. Paradoxically, while addictive sexual behavior may bring short-term relief, over the long-term it intensifies the feeling of spiritual emptiness, often leading to escalation in the addictive behavior. In other words, it takes more acting out to mask the pain of the spiritual emptiness. Describe your own experience of spiritual emptiness and how your addiction affected this emptiness.

Feeling disconnected from yourself and the world. Addictive behavior often feels "out of this world" because, in a way, it is. That is, addictive behavior allows us to disconnect from reality. God is the Ultimate Reality, though, so when we disconnect from reality, we are also disconnecting from our true experience, from genuine connection with other people, and, ultimately, from God. Reflect on how your addiction left you feeling disconnected from yourself, others, and God.

Feeling abandoned by God. If your sense of disconnection from God grows, you may mistakenly assume that you have been abandoned, particularly if you had experiences of abandonment or neglect in your childhood. Describe any experiences where you felt abandoned by God.

Questioning God's existence. If you cannot find or feel God's presence, you may begin to question whether He exists. For some, this occurs during active addiction. For others, it occurs more in the aftermath of discovery or disclosure as you experience other consequences. Describe any experiences where you questioned God's existence.

Anger at God. Anger often emerges from fears and insecurities. If you have felt abandoned by God or question God's existence, such fears and insecurities are present. Often, you may not recognize these feelings because they may manifest as anger. Some will tell you it is not acceptable to be angry with God. We believe in a Big God, though, who understands and can handle your anger. Describe your experiences of being angry with God. Reflect on times you have been angry with God. Is it possible that your anger represented some other more vulnerable emotion such as sadness, fear, or shame? Even if you do not know what might have been going on underneath your anger, take a few moments to write about experiencing sadness, fear, and shame.

Loss of faith. Because of your addiction, you may have experienced a loss of faith in which you disconnected from your religious community, discontinued religious practices such as Bible study, or simply quit having faith in either God or your religious community. Write about any ways that your faith has lessened.

Other religious or spiritual consequences. Everyone has a unique experience of addiction and early recovery. Describe any other religious or spiritual consequences you have experienced.

The Highest Self

Take a few moments to meditate on the central scripture for this book:

*"For I know the plans I have for you," declares the Lord, "plans to prosper you
and not to harm you, plans to give you hope and a future."*
JEREMIAH 29:11

There are several key elements in this scripture. First, God has always had a plan for you. This is reiterated several places in scripture, perhaps most notably in the Psalms.

*Your eyes saw my unformed body; all the days ordained for me
were written in your book before one of them came to be.*
PSALM 139:16

Second, God has "plans to prosper you." Note that the active stance here, the "doing," is on God's part, not ours. Scripture does not tell us to go out and work hard so that our lives will be virtuous. Instead, Jeremiah seems to be saying that our "work" here is actually passive; that is, accepting the plan that God already has for us. As the authors of this book, we do not presume to know what that plan is. In large part, though, the purpose of this book is about helping you discern God's purpose for your life. To that end, we are reminded of the words of theologian Meister Eckhart who wrote, "God is not found in the soul by adding anything, but by a process of subtraction."

It seems clear, then, that part of accessing, encountering, and experiencing God in your own soul is "subtracting" addictive sexual behaviors and the underlying delusional thinking that support such behavior. In your addiction, you may have felt like you had the whole world. Addictive sexual behavior often feels powerful. Yet scripture reminds us of what we need to "subtract" here:

*What good will it be for someone to gain the whole world, yet forfeit their soul? Or what
can anyone give in exchange for their soul?*
MATTHEW 16:26

Recovery is about finding (or remembering) your calling from God and living your life in accord with the plan that has been made for you. This is part of God's promise to us:

*To be made new in the attitude of your minds; and to put on the new self, created to be
like God in true righteousness and holiness. Therefore each of you must put off falsehood*

and speak truthfully to your neighbor, for we are all members of one body.

EPHESIANS 4:23–25

There are promises in this passage:

- You will be "made new in the attitude of your minds"; if you are relatively new to recovery, you may be struggling with sexual fantasies and euphoric recall of previous sexual experiences. In short, your hijacked brain does not like the behavioral changes you have made. This will be discussed more in chapter 5. For now, know that if you continue on your path of recovery, these moments will become less frequent and less intense as you are "made new in the attitude of your minds."

- As your attitude changes, you will experience a "new self, created to be like God in true righteousness and holiness." If you have not yet healed the shame of your addictive behavior, it may be difficult for you to fully accept this promise. For now, simply recognize that Paul is clearly telling Ephesus that, with God's help, transformation is available.

Note, however, that Paul also gives two directives of how to step in to this "new attitude" and "new self":

- Put off falsehood.
- Speak truthfully to your neighbor.

At first glance, this might seem like one directive to be honest with other people. A different reading of this passage, however, is that there are two directives, first to be honest with yourself by consciously watching for the types of delusions discussed earlier in this chapter and second, to speak truthfully to your neighbor. This does not mean that you should tell everyone about your addiction. In early recovery, it means being fully honest with those who are supporting your recovery, such as a therapist, a therapy group, and members of your Twelve Step community. For many of you, this involves taking off the "mask" that you usually wear, the dishonest façade that you likely have shown others for many years to protect yourself from the shame of your addiction.

The Mask You Wear

 The following exercises will help you examine where you are right now and create a vision for the future God has promised you in recovery.

Shadows of the Cross: A Christian Companion to *Facing the Shadow*

1. Examine the mask you wear. This includes any aspect of the false self that evolved as part of your addiction, including
    *   delusional thoughts to which you held in the past and may, to some extent, continue to cling that allowed you to stay in your addictive cycle
    *   the persona of how you present yourself to the world, regardless of the truth
2. In your journal, draw a mask that you would wear to hide your face. Draw words, symbols, or images on the mask to represent the type of mask you wear. For example, a mask that always shows a happy face.
3. You put on the mask to hide parts of yourself from others (and yourself). These parts make you uncomfortable and, perhaps, ashamed. Now draw a blank face that would go under the mask. Draw words, symbols, or images that represent what the mask hides. As you do this, remember that the goal is honesty but not to increase your shame. If you find yourself experiencing shame as you do this activity, stop and finish it later while consulting with a trusted soul, such as a therapist or sponsor, who can help you look at yourself honestly without collapsing into your shame.
4. Begin to create a vision of yourself in long-term recovery, a self that does not need the mask because your attitude is new and you have a new self in Christ. Now draw another blank face that would go under the mask, and fill in words, symbols, or images that envision your new self in Christ. Begin by focusing on the thinking aspects. How will your new self in Christ think differently?

    Psalm 19:14 tell us:

    May these words of my mouth and this meditation of my heart
    be pleasing in your sight, Lord, my Rock and my Redeemer.

5. Now draw a picture of a heart in your journal. Using words, images, and symbols, visualize the meditation of your heart as a new creation in Christ.

    In the same way, faith by itself, if it is not accompanied by action, is dead.
    But someone will say, "You have faith; I have deeds." Show me your faith
    without deeds, and I will show you my faith by my deeds.
    JAMES 2:17–18

6. As the attitude of your mind and the meditations of your heart begin to change, so too will your deeds and actions. Now draw a picture of a hand in your journal. Use words, symbols, and images to represent these changes. NOTE: Look for the opportunity to share any or all of these drawings with a trusted soul such as a therapist, therapy group, or sponsor.

Cultivating Humility

When addicted, it's easy to feel entitled and arrogant. Addictive behavior is, in a sense, the ultimate form of selfishness. You may have become so focused on your addictive sexual behavior that you did not care about how your actions were affecting those around you. Cultivating the spiritual gift of humility will serve your recovery.

Humility gives us a framework for serving God amid our struggles of early recovery:

I served the Lord with great humility and with tears and in the midst of severe testing.
ACTS 20:19

Humility gives us a framework for our relationships with other people:

Do nothing out of selfish ambition or vain conceit.
Rather, in humility value others above yourselves.
PHILIPPIANS 2:3

Humility gives us a framework for discerning God's will in our lives. Remember the last line of the short version of the Serenity Prayer?

God grant me the serenity to accept the things I cannot change,
The courage to change the things I can,
And the wisdom to know the difference.

If part of what we are praying for here is wisdom, how then can we cultivate wisdom? Proverbs 11:2 tells us that when pride comes, then comes disgrace, but with humility comes wisdom.

How, exactly, do we cultivate humility to grow more wise? Rami Shapiro adapted Saint Benedict's twelve attitudes to cultivate humility, and we have modified Shapiro's adaptation to specifically focus on sex addiction.[1]

Shadows of the Cross: A Christian Companion to *Facing the Shadow*

1. As you go through each moment of recovery, be conscious of God's presence in all things. Every moment is an encounter with God and, as such, deserves our attention. Be aware of your tendency to "zone out."

2. Put God's will before your own. Your will, as part of the human condition, is to control situations and people in self-serving ways. When you cannot do this, you avoid God's will by denying your powerlessness over your addictive sexual behavior. God's will, on the other hand, is to liberate you from the bondage of sex addiction. Abiding by God's will, then, is to become a partner in this liberating process.

3. Seek counsel only from trusted souls. Many do not yet understand addictive sexual behavior. Further, many are uncomfortable with their own sexuality. Because of their ignorance of your struggle or their own sexual issues, they will not be able to support you in the process of becoming liberated from your sex addiction. Instead, they may shame you or reinforce your willfulness in recovery rather than your powerlessness.

4. When faced with difficulties, such as triggers, fantasies or euphoric recall, or injustice from others, be patient and still in responding. Slow your mind and body down so you can respond from a place of watchful calm. (Read Luke 12:35 and Colossians 4:2).

5. Recognize when sinful thoughts arise in your mind and heart. For a recovering sex addict, these often take the form of sexual fantasies, euphoric recall of previous experiences, blaming others for your addiction, harsh judgment of others, or resentments toward others or your situation. Such sinful thoughts are best released by confessing them to a trusted soul, such as a clergyperson, therapist, sponsor, or therapy group.

6. Be content with your life circumstances in this present moment. Avoid seeing all things as reward or punishment. Instead, see every experience as a chance to deepen your humility and the liberation it brings.

7. Prize and value others. Consider yourself lower than others, not so "the first can be last" (Matthew 20:16) but simply to act in humility rather than selfish ambition or vain conceit (Philippians 2:3).

8. Do nothing that serves only you. Make all of your deeds a benefit to the community. This does not include those acts that serve your community by supporting your healing journey. Here, remember the example of Jesus who frequently took care of himself spiritually so that he

could be of service to others. Jesus often withdrew to lonely places and prayed (Luke 5:16).

9. Discipline your speech and build your capacity to be in silence.

10. Avoid silliness, mockery, and playing the fool. In particular, be watchful of the use of

    - hostile humor; that is, humor at someone else's expense
    - sexual humor

11. Speak gently, honestly, and forthrightly to others and avoid the fog of deceptive speech.

12. Keep your heart humble and your appearance simple, seeing each moment as an opportunity to release the fear that triggers addictive behavior and the need to control situations, circumstances, other people, and your own addiction.

 Take a few moments to reflect on the twelve attitudes to cultivate humility and answer the following questions:

- Which of these are you already doing?
- Which of these will be most challenging for you?
- What are some strategies you can use to be watchful of these challenges? Be sure to include both internal (such as prayer) and external (such as confession and accountability to another person) strategies.

God Has an Answer

At this point in your journey, you have looked at many beliefs, justifications, and rationalizations that defended your addictive sexual behavior. You may be feeling discouraged that you clung to your addictive behavior for so long. For encouragement, then, we offer the following readings.[2] Take the time to read each of the suggested passages and to meditate on those that speak to your specific struggles.

YOU SAY	GOD SAYS	BIBLE VERSES
It's impossible	All things are possible	(Luke 18:27)
I'm too tired	I will give you rest	(Matthew 11:28–30)
Nobody really loves me	I love you	(John 3:16 and John 3:34)

Shadows of the Cross: A Christian Companion to *Facing the Shadow*

YOU SAY	GOD SAYS	BIBLE VERSES
I can't go on	My grace is sufficient	(II Corinthians 12:9 and Psalm 91:15)
I can't figure things out	I will direct your steps	(Proverbs 3:5–6)
I can't do it	You can do all things	(Philippians 4:13)
I'm not able	I am able	(II Corinthians 9:8)
It's not worth it	It will be worth it	(Romans 8:28)
I can't forgive myself	I forgive you	(I John 1:9 and Romans 8:1)
I can't manage	will supply all your needs	(Philippians 4:19)
I'm afraid	I have not given you a spirit of fear	(II Timothy 1:7)
I'm always worried and frustrated	Cast all your cares on me	(I Peter 5:7)
I don't have enough faith	I've given everyone a measure of faith	(Romans 12:3)
I'm not smart enough	I give you wisdom	(I Corinthians 1:30)
I feel all alone	I will never leave you or forsake you	(Hebrews 13:5)

Beyond Recovery? Not at All

There is another passage (Romans 11:11–24) in which the Apostle Paul is speaking of trees and branches. Although he is referring to the Gentiles and Israelites, we can learn much by reading it as a passage of recovery.

First, read verse 17:

If some of the branches have been broken off, and you, though a wild olive shoot, have been grafted in among the others and now share in the nourishing sap from the olive root
This passage is easily paraphrased for you as a recovering addict:

If you have been broken and separated from God and you, though an addict, have been reconnected to the Source of All Life, you now share in the nourishment that comes only from God.

We close this section by reminding you of the promise offered by Paul:
Again I ask: Did they stumble so as to fall beyond recovery? Not at all!
ROMANS 11:11A

Christian men and women often struggle with accepting the forgiveness of God because they have not yet forgiven themselves. For now, it's enough to reflect on the scripture above that plainly tells you that you have not stumbled beyond recovery.

Are you willing to accept this as truth? Write about what has helped you accept this or what keeps you from accepting this. Discuss your answers with trusted counsel as your willingness to accept this biblical truth will be central to both your sexual and spiritual recovery.

Spiritual Disciplines

Review and reflect on the spiritual disciplines in chapter 2. There is no "right" or "wrong" spiritual discipline, only those that are effective for you in drawing you closer to God and helping you grow in sobriety, recovery, and your walk with God.

In the next chapter, which parallels chapter 2 of *Facing the Shadow*, you will gain a broader understanding of your addiction within the framework of your Christian faith.

Shadows of the Cross: A Christian Companion to *Facing the Shadow*

Chapter Five
What Is an Addiction?

I do not understand what I do. For what I want to do I do not do, but what I hate I do. And if I do what I do not want to do, I agree that the law is good.

ROMANS 7:15–16

 This chapter parallels chapter 2 (What Is an Addiction?) in *Facing the Shadow.* The two chapters should be read and worked through together.

Paul's struggle described in Romans 7:15–16 certainly sounds like some type of addiction. By definition, your addictive sexual behavior was

- confusing ("I do not understand what I do")
- shaming ("I hate what I do")
- counter to your Christian values and beliefs ("I agree that the law is good")

Unfortunately, religion sometimes pathologizes healthy sexual behavior. For that reason, we want to highlight what separates addictive sexual behavior from healthy sexuality. In your sexual addiction, you

- engaged in behaviors inconsistent with your values and beliefs
- were unable to stop the behaviors despite adverse consequences
- were preoccupied with sex, evidenced by frequent fantasies, euphoric recall, or planning for your next acting out episode
- used strategies to justify, rationalize, deny, or minimize your behavior
- became unable to delay immediate gratification of acting out in spite of being aware of the long-term negative effects of your addiction
- experienced tolerance as indicated by increased frequency, intensity, or risk of sexual behavior
- experienced withdrawal when making attempts not to act out

In *Facing the Shadow*, Carnes characterizes addiction as ultimately an intimacy disorder. As an addict, you likely struggled to form intimate relationships with yourself, others, and God. One aspect of recovery, then, involves more fully understanding and healing distortions in your perspective on relationships.

Various theories and models of addiction characterize it as primarily physiological, psychological, or spiritual. The reality is that it is all three.

As Carnes noted in *Facing the Shadow*, there is a clear and growing awareness of the neurobiology of sex addiction. Your sexual acting out literally changed your brain chemistry and brain functioning. If you have endured the painful experience of early sobriety, you know how badly the brain wants the "hit" of a sexual experience. You can think of your addicted brain as a hijacked jet. It is traveling at great speeds, but you are no longer at the controls. Instead, the addict has pushed you aside and is now piloting the jet. In all likelihood, you tried to grab the controls back, perhaps many times. You told yourself, "This is the last time I am going to do this" or "I am only going to do this twice this week," only to fail.

Besides being physiological, sex addiction has a strong psychological component. Many sex addicts experience either hyper-arousal (too much emotion), which they medicate with sexual acting out, or they experience hypo-arousal (emotional suppression) and struggle to live in integrity with their emotional experiences. Emotions are part of your addiction and recovery. The primary focus of this chapter will be understanding sex addiction with a focus on the spiritual aspects of addiction.

The Parable of the Rich Fool

The applause rolled like thunder throughout the convention center as Princess Antoinette took center stage accepting the annual Global Humanitarian Action Award. The award was given to her for her tireless efforts promoting Saving Steps around the World, a charitable organization instrumental in providing shoes to children in third world countries. Selfishly, representing this foundation was the perfect mask she wore to cover her secret addiction.

Princess Antoinette was a shoe collector. Over the years, her shoe collecting had turned into an obsession. The shoe collection was a problem passed down through generations. Her own mother, the Queen, was a shoe collector, as was her grandmother. Each woman in the Princess's life had passed down an unnatural relationship with shopping, particularly for shoes, as a way to celebrate special events or self-medicate when feeling low.

Over the years, the Princess's preoccupation with shoes began affecting her daily activities. She planned her days around shopping for shoes, fantasized about wearing the shoes, and routinely put her shoe-related activities before time for self-care activities such as exercise, spending quality time in intimate relationships, or carefully managing her personal staff. In time, her shoe collection grew so large that she needed to hire someone for the sole purpose of caring for her shoes, making sure they stayed cleaned, polished, and organized.

She began to justify her shoe-filled closets to herself, by believing shoes represented happiness and a sense of confidence—especially shoes with high heels and sequined designs. As an only child, she had found joy in shoe shopping replaced her feelings of loneliness, sadness, or moments where she felt unloved. Now as an adult, when she found herself crying and depressed, she could find instant gratification through her addiction to shopping. Over time, her addiction became her idea of a spiritual connection to feelings of satisfaction and sense of worth.

Princess Antoinette spent her lifetime representing the Saving Steps around the World and believing she was doing good work for a worthy cause. But at the time of her death, it was her secret addiction to collecting shoes that became the shock heard around the world. The people were saddened by the thought of their beloved princess spending so much money on her shoes. They were especially saddened to realized that during the times where funding for the foundation was low and little money was available to buy shoes for the children, Princess Antoinette was building more closets for her enormous collection of shoes. In the end, she was remembered for her unhealthy relationship with shopping, not the philanthropic actions to which she had hoped would be her legacy.

Let's consider this modern-day parable and how it can be translated into our own lives today. As people in recovery, we will become sober in the behavior that got us into trouble, but we may unconsciously reinvent our addiction cycle into areas that are more socially acceptable, such as exercise, shopping, and eating.

A bumper sticker reads, "Nowhere but in America ... do we have a fine expensive automobile—that sits in the driveway because the garage is full of junk." These words give cause to think about the reality of our nation. Researchers have found that children begin collecting things somewhere between the age of two and six years old. Sounds odd, but reflect back on the toy "rages" that have run rampant through the United States in the past two decades. Remember the Beanie Babies fad, trolls, dolls, and many other objects that have currently little to no value, yet as adults we have a hard time letting go of these childhood possessions. Why do we feel it is important to collect things, store things away in dusty attics, and spend money on storage buildings to hold stuff we no longer enjoy?

Typically, people with a lot of stuff are known as collectors. There isn't anything wrong with collecting stuff, as long as it is within rationality. But when the hobby of collecting turns into a compulsion or obsessive behavior, the behavior becomes out of control affecting our mental and physical health.

Jesus addresses the addiction traits of escalation, selfishness, and isolation in His Parable of the Rich Fool (Luke 12:13–21). He tells the story of a rich man who stored his "things" in warehouses. Each time the man filled a warehouse, he would build another, collect more "stuff," and fill it completely. Again, he would build another warehouse. When people came to him and asked to borrow something, he would answer no because he felt the need to hold on to his things.

Any addiction, not just sexual addiction, can be an illness—a very serious disease. In fact, problems such as chemical dependency, food, gambling, gaming, and sex are related. They all involve negative belief systems and the impaired thinking of the addict.

So what does the Bible say to us about addictive behaviors? In Luke 12:13–21, Jesus used the Parable of the Rich Fool to help us see how our actions can become selfish, greedy, and purposeless. Even though the parable is about hoarding possessions of wealth, this same attitude appears when addicts do things excessively and go further with their actions than first intended. Jesus said, "Life does not consist in an abundance of possessions" (Luke 12:15).

 Respond to the following:

- How does a person's quality of life differ from the quantity of his or her possessions?

- What was the source of the rich man's abundance (v. 16)?

- The farmer assumes that because he is rich, he will have many years to enjoy his wealth. He exemplifies the attitude "Take life easy, eat, drink and be merry" (v. 19). Do you believe this?

- Why does God call the rich man a fool (v. 20)?

- If Jesus were telling this story today, the rich man might have added an extra room, filled his basement, or rented a storage unit to house extra possessions. Consider this fact: Did you know that there are now more than 30,000 self-storage facilities in America offering a billion square feet for people to store their stuff? One common attribute of any addiction is fear of economic insecurity, of not having "enough." Can you relate to having so many things that you don't have space for them all?

- What is the potential eternal cost of hoarding money or valuable possessions during your lifetime?

 Read James 5:1–3. The essential characteristic of a covetous man is that he lays up treasure for himself. His aim is to please himself and gratify his greed. Does this sound familiar as you begin to identify your own addictive behaviors?

Addiction as Spiritual Bondage

Besides thinking of your brain as a hijacked jet during your active addiction, you may find it helpful, as a Christian, to think of your sex addiction as being spiritually enslaved and held in bondage. The compulsive nature of your sexual behavior kept you ensnared in these bonds. As a person in recovery, though, you are being released from this bondage. Scripture is clear on this point:

It is for freedom that Christ has set us free. Stand firm, then, and do not let yourselves be burdened again by a yoke of slavery.
GALATIANS 5:1

That the creation itself will be liberated from its bondage to decay and brought into freedom and glory of the children of God.
ROMANS 8:21

It is all well and good to speak of addiction as bondage and of recovery as liberation from bondage. While this is accurate, it does not fully capture the struggle of becoming liberated from your bondage. The process is difficult and, at times, painful.

We know that the whole creation has been groaning as in the pains of childbirth right up to the present time.
ROMANS 8:22

At a deep spiritual level, analogies of slavery/freedom and new birth are appropriate for recovery. Think of the process of recovery as a route to a new life. Jesus said, "No one can see the kingdom of God unless they are born again" (John 3:3), which many believe means that we need a salvation experience, a moment of being "born again." While not diminishing the "road to Damascus" salvation experience, we can think of our spiritual journey, including the journey of recovery, as a series of deaths and births. In this framework, "death" refers to those parts of you that grow weak and die or that are surrendered to God. Death involves loss, so we refer here to things that are "lost" in your recovery. Birth involves new life. As a person in early recovery, you likely are "groaning as in the pains of childbirth."

It is through this process of repeated death and birth that we are created anew as promised in scripture:

Therefore, if anyone is in Christ, the new creation has come:
The old has gone, the new is here.
II CORINTHIANS 5:17

He saved us, not because of righteous things we had done, but because of His mercy. He saved us through the washing of rebirth and renewal by the Holy Spirit, whom He poured out on us generously through Jesus Christ our Savior, so that, having been justified by His grace, we might become heirs having the hope of eternal life.
TITUS 3:5–7

 Reflect on these images of death and birth and the "washing of rebirth" as an analogy of your own recovery process. Remember that what you are recovering is your freedom from the bondage of sex addiction.

As you are becoming a new creation in Christ, consider first the process of death, not your physical death, but the many "mini-deaths" that are occurring as part of your recovery. What is dying so that you might grow in Christ?

It may seem odd, but it is important to grieve the loss of your addictive sexual behavior. You are, of course, grateful for the changes you are making and can now see that your addictive behavior was unhealthy on many levels, yet this behavior was a central part of your life, perhaps for many years. Though an unhealthy coping strategy, your addictive sexual behavior nonetheless helped you to cope. Accordingly, it is possible to fully recognize how damaging your addictive behaviors were and still need to grieve the loss of that behavior.

 Journal your thoughts about the following:

- It seems paradoxical that you might need to grieve something that so badly needed to "die." At this point in your recovery, how have you grieved or not grieved this loss?
- Consider now the birth part of this cycle. What are the "pains of birth" that you are experiencing? Reflect here on the most difficult aspects of recovery for you.
- Finally, take a few moments to reflect on what is being "born again" inside of you as a result of your recovery journey.

Sex Addiction in the Church

In the past, an alcoholic who disclosed his disease to his pastor or his church likely would have been judged harshly and perhaps asked to leave the church. Although that could still happen today, it is much more likely that the congregation would pray for the alcoholic and the pastor would look outside the church for treatment options. In short, the alcoholic would be loved and supported in his faith community.

In some churches, a sex addict would have the same experience. In many other churches, however, the reaction would be more like what the alcoholic experienced fifty years ago. Indeed, there is a "double whammy" for the sex addict as many churches do not fully understand addiction *and* they have a difficult relationship with sexuality. Because of this, we recommend being cautious about disclosing your addiction within your faith community. It is not for us to say you should or should not. We have seen many instances where disclosure to a pastor resulted in a healing experience that supported recovery. In other cases, however, the pastor clearly did not understand sex addiction and judged the parishioner harshly, in some instances asking the person to leave the church. Inevitably, this rejection and abandonment by the church is harmful. While we support honesty as an important part of your recovery, we encourage discretion as to whom you share.

Although there are a number of groups that are addressing sexual addiction in the church, many churches seem blind to this problem. In all likelihood, the number of people who struggle with sex addiction in your church is far higher than you would think. Researchers have speculated that as many as 50 percent of people in churches struggle with sexual integrity.[1] The reality is that researchers do not have accurate data about this because of underreporting. What is clear, though, is that sexual integrity is a major issue in the church.

In one sense, then, you are not alone. At the same time, because you may not be able to disclose your addiction within your faith community, you may feel very isolated. If there is an addiction recovery program in your church, you may benefit from becoming involved in that smaller community. If not, you may need to find a community such as Sexaholics Anonymous or Sex Addicts Anonymous where you can be fully honest with your disclosures. This will not replace the sustenance you receive through your church life, but rather provide some support that the church might not yet be ready to offer.

Early recovery is about coping and community. It is unfortunate that most local churches, in our experience, are not yet ready to fully support the recovering sex addict. Even so, it is vital that you find a supportive community. Remember that you cannot do recovery alone!

Write about your experiences with disclosure in the church. If you have disclosed to clergy or to other members of your church, what were your experiences? If you have chosen not to disclose, write about your experiences related to non-disclosure. Do you wish you could disclose? Have you experienced frustration or sadness over this?

Shame: Fuel for Addiction

Review the visual depiction of the addictive system as presented in chapter 2 of *Facing the Shadow*, including the cognitive, behavioral, and emotional components of this cycle. At the core of this cycle is shame. Shame reinforces the belief system and impaired thinking that supports the unmanageability of the addictive behavior. As your addiction progressed and you became increasingly preoccupied with sex and your behaviors became more compulsive and ritualistic, the resulting despair may have heightened your shame.

Shame is the internal voice that says, "I am a bad person." This differs from the internal voice of guilt, which says "I have done bad things." At some point in your own addictive system, you likely crossed the line from feeling guilt about your behaviors to feeling shame about who you are. Even as you progress in recovery, you may still feel that sense of shame for past deeds. There is hope in recovery and we remind you:

Hope does not put us to shame, because God's love has been poured out into our hearts through the Holy Spirit, who has been given to us.

ROMANS 5:5

Remember, also, that Christ dwells in your heart. Paul wrote to the church of Ephesus a hope that people would grow to know the depth of Christ's love for them. Growing in your knowledge of Christ's love for you, just as you are in this moment, may be the single greatest antidote for your shame:

So that Christ may dwell in your hearts through faith. And I pray that you, being rooted and established in love, may have power, together with all the Lord's holy people, to grasp how wide and long and high and deep is the love of Christ, and to know this love that surpasses knowledge—that you may be filled to the measure of all the fullness of God.

EPHESIANS 3:17–19

Use your journal for the following activities:

- Draw a picture (without words) of your addiction-related shame.

- Now draw an image that represents your full knowledge and acceptance of "how wide and long and high and deep is the love of Christ" and what this does to your shame.

- Now review the images you have drawn. Write about your thoughts and reactions to this experience. Consider showing and discussing these pictures to another trusted soul, such as a therapist or sponsor.

- Review your second drawing again and then answer the question, "What concrete steps are you ready, willing, and able to take to begin realizing the fullness of Christ's love for you and releasing the shame that binds you to the past?

Working with shame is tricky especially when reflecting on our past. Part of what is cunning, baffling, and powerful about shame is that we can experience meta-shame; that is, we can feel shame over the fact that we feel shame. Because of this, it may be important for you to talk with trusted souls, such as a therapist or sponsor, about your struggles with shame. Consider this hope-filled reminder:

No, in all these things we are more than conquerors through him who loved us.
For I am convinced that neither death nor life, neither angels nor demons,
neither the present nor the future, nor any powers, neither height nor depth,
nor anything else in all creation, will be able to separate us from the
love of God that is in Christ Jesus our Lord.

ROMANS 8:37–39

Through Jesus, who loves you just as you are, you are more than a conqueror. Nothing, absolutely nothing, can separate you from the love of God through Jesus.

Acting Out and Acting In: Shame, Religion, and Sexual Anorexia

Virtually every time that the word "sex" is used in the New Testament, it is accompanied by language of problematic sexuality:

- *sexual sin*
- *sexual immorality*
- *sexual impurity*

If you grew up attending church, you may have gotten messages that sex is sinful, bad, or wrong. Yet, scripture tells us that you are "fearfully and wonderfully made" (Psalm 139:14), which includes your sexuality. What is problematic, then, is not that you are a sexual creature, as this was divined by God, but that you have compulsively and addictively engaged sin, immorality, and impurity.

For many Christians, the struggle is to *embrace* a healthy sexuality. If you grew up with childhood messages that sex is sinful, you likely struggled in late childhood and adolescence to deal with your developing sexuality. Psychotherapist Carl Jung spoke of a process whereby you deny parts of yourself by moving them out of your conscious awareness and into what he termed *the shadow*. For Jung, the shadow included disliked parts of the self. You then psychologically "hide" these parts so that you do not see them in yourself. Jung suggested that the more you ignore this part of the self, the stronger it grows and the more you have to work to keep it out of your awareness. Taken to an extreme, this helps explain your addictive behavior and the defense mechanisms, such as denial, minimization, rationalization, and justification, that support addictive sexual behavior.

For many people, the attempt to deny sexual urges and impulses creates a self-shadow split. Often, Christians try to subjugate the sexual self by denying it, thinking erroneously that if they are good Christians, they will have no sexual desires or impulses. From this, they tend to go to one of two extremes. Some over-focus on repressing their sexuality, viewing any sexual thought or impulse as deeply sinful and shameful. Others simply deny their sexuality, relegating it to shadow. There is the potential for a vicious cycle here. A hyperfocus on what you have done in the past may heighten your shame and increase the likelihood of spinning back into your addictive cycle. To deny your past, though, is to miss the opportunity to work through and heal those parts of you that underlie your addiction and undermine your recovery.

 Read through the extensive self-reflective process on sexual anorexia, or an aversion to sex found in chapter 2 of *Facing the Shadow*.

As part of your recovery, you may need to abstain from any sexual behavior for a period of time. This is intended to support your recovery by allowing your brain to return to healthy functioning where you are not preoccupied with sex and sexuality. This abstinence from sex is not sexual anorexia. Sexual anorexia is an aversion to sex. In your addiction, you may have gone through periods where you committed yourself to being nonsexual to try to control your addictive behavior. This aversion to your sexuality may increase your vulnerability to relapse. Just as an anorexic has a hate-based relationship with food, during sexual anorexia, you are more than just avoiding sex. You are demonizing sex and sexuality as something that must be fully subjugated or controlled.

In chapter 2 of *Facing the Shadow*, Carnes walks you through a series of reflections on sexual anorexia. For our purposes here, we will focus on internalized messages, shame, and the shadow.

 Respond to the following:

- First, reflect on your earliest memories of sex and sexuality. What did you experience?

- What were you told as a child or adolescent about sexuality? How did these early messages affect you?

- If you grew up attending church, what messages did you receive as an adolescent about sex and sexuality?

- What were your first experiences as a sexual being?

- After your early sexual experiences, how did you feel? Proud? Ashamed? Fearful? Explain.

- How does Jung's idea of the shadow fit your experience with sexual addiction? Did you try to hide your sexual behavior while presenting yourself very differently in public? In other words, how did you compartmentalize and create two lives, one public and one private?

- Jung suggested that when you relegate a part of yourself to the shadow, you become more likely to project that on to someone else. When you project, you turn what you experience as a personal deficit or weakness in yourself into a moral deficiency in someone else. Commonly, projections are harsh moral judgments made of others about parts of ourselves that we dislike. If you relegated your sexuality to the shadow, you may have been hypercritical and judgmental of others for their sexual behaviors. List examples where you did this.

- Projections serve as a buffer, insulating you from looking at these parts of yourself and creating a deepening gap between self and full reality. This creates an illusion. Reflect on how you used projections, perhaps in concert with denial, minimization, justification, and rationalization, to maintain the illusion that you were not sexually addicted.

- Amid your addiction, did you ever engage in periods of sexual anorexia as an attempt to control your addiction? If so, describe these experiences.

As an example of sexual anorexia, consider the case of Beth. She is a forty-five-year-old woman who partied heavily and engaged in a number of "one-night stands" while in college. A strong Christian, Beth experienced a great deal of shame about her premarital sex. In college, she vacillated between periods of devout religiosity and asexuality and periods of heavy partying and sexual promiscuity. She hit her worst moment when she woke up in bed with a strange man and a bad hangover, looked at the clock, and realized she had missed a church service in which she was to sing a solo. Rather than work through this shame with a sensitive clergyperson or therapist, however, Beth decided that the only solution was to deny her sexuality. This went to such an extreme level that Beth made an unconscious decision not to be in a relationship that involved any type of intimacy, even emotional intimacy. Whenever men showed interest in her, she would look closely to see their faults and why they were not good for her. She was still a single woman when she entered therapy. She would go for months with no sexual or physically intimate behavior at all but then go on a binge for several days, picking up men in bars or masturbating compulsively. After a few days of this, she would return to her sexual anorexia and relationship avoidance. She went to therapy after one of these sexual binges, suicidal over her inability to stop this cycle and the great loneliness and despair she felt. Over time, Beth began to realize that she had internalized some negative messages about sexuality from her childhood (from both her parents and her church) that left her thinking that anything sexual was "dirty" and "bad." These messages became more fully embedded in Beth after her sexual experimentation in college and led to a cycle of sexual anorexia and compulsive sexual binging.

Part of Beth's work in therapy was to unpack her negative view of sexuality and her avoidance of emotionally intimate relationships. In essence, she had to bring her sexuality out from the shadow and into the light, accepting that her sexuality was a gift from God and that, with this perspective, she could seek God's guidance to define what healthy intimacy (both emotional and physical) meant for her.

Experiencing Freedom from Bondage

Earlier in this chapter, you reflected on two passages of scripture on bondage:

It is for freedom that Christ has set us free. Stand firm, then, and do not let yourselves be burdened again by a yoke of slavery.

GALATIANS 5:1

That the creation itself will be liberated from its bondage to decay and brought into freedom and glory of the children of God.

ROMANS 8:21

Sexual addiction kept you bound up, unable to experience the "freedom and glory of the children of God." For this activity, you will create two contrasting images in your journal.

- Use crayons, markers, pens, or pencils to create an image that represents the "yoke of slavery" you experienced when you were actively in your sex addiction. Be sure to include a visual representation of where Jesus and/or God were during this time of your life.

- Now, draw a contrasting image that captures the "freedom and glory of the children of God" that you have begun to experience in recovery. Again, be sure to include a visual representation of where Jesus and/or God are now in your life.

Known of God

The two drawings you created likely provide a stark visual contrast between the "yoke of slavery" and liberation. As you look at those drawings, the importance of recovery may be very clear. At the same time, we know that recovery is an experience of "progress not perfection."

During these times, remember that God knows not only the parts of you that you freely show to the world but also those parts with which you are deeply ashamed. God loves you. Period. This is why grace is so amazing. Although you may struggle at times to maintain sobriety and to accept the depth of God's grace and forgiveness, God is always there. As you continue in your recovery journey, look back from time to time at the drawing you made of your "yoke of slavery" and reflect on the words of Paul:

> *But now that you know God—or rather are known by God—how is it that*
> *you are turning back to those weak and miserable forces?*
> *Do you wish to be enslaved by them all over again?*
> GALATIANS 4:9

Take comfort in the absolute knowing that even as you imperfectly recover from your addiction, God is ever-present with you:

> *For he has been mindful*
> *of the humble state of his servant.*
> *From now on all generations will call me blessed.*
> *Luke 1:48*

Yes, even in this moment, God is mindful of the humble state of you, His servant.

Spiritual Disciplines

Continue to practice your spiritual disciplines. While the disciplines you use should ultimately evolve out of conversations with God, there are some specific practices that may particularly support your healing work at this point in recovery. The following disciplines are offered here not as substitutes for your daily practice but to enhance what you already do as you focus on this chapter's content.

Prayer of Continued Deliverance

In John 8:12, Jesus spoke to the people saying, "I am the light of the world. Whoever follows me will never walk in darkness, but will have the light of life." Part of this chapter has focused on how you may have relegated your sexuality to darkness, in the shadows of your unconscious. Part of recovery, then, is shining light into those dark places, bringing them forward and revealing them to yourself and others, as appropriate.

 Pray for your continued deliverance, focusing specifically on

- actively following Jesus so that you will not "walk in darkness, but will have the light of life"
- praying that you will accept the "light of the world" into the dark places inside of you
- continued guidance in your recovery journey

Prayers of Thanksgiving

As you have worked through this chapter, you likely have grown in your awareness of the blessing called recovery.

 Take some time to *pour out your heart* to God, focused on your gratitude for the many spiritual gifts in recovery. Remember that, more than eloquent words, God longs to hear a heartfelt "thank you."

Meditation on Scripture

 Read and meditate on the following passage:

"My soul glorifies the Lord and my spirit rejoices in God my Savior,
for he has been mindful of the humble state of his servant."
Luke 1:46b–48a

 Do the following:

- Start by entering into a period of silence.

- Now read the passage above thoughtfully and slowly, multiple times, both silently and aloud. On each reading, emphasize different words and phrases in the passage.

- Remember that this is the beginning of Mary's outpouring to God about being chosen as the mother of Jesus. Visualize her speaking these words aloud to God.

- Now, reflect on words or phrases that are most poignant for you.

- Based on what is on your heart and in your mind, speak to God either silently or aloud, opening your heart to express your thoughts and feelings.

- Rest in the silent presence of God.

- Reflect and journal about how this meditation calls you to live differently in your daily life and commit to accepting any call that you hear for change.

Chapter Six

What is a First Step?

 This chapter parallels chapter 4 (What is a First Step?) in *Facing the Shadow* and should be read and worked through together with this chapter. Review the First Step content thoroughly in *Facing the Shadow*.

This chapter will help you continue to reflect on shame and denial, which keep you from fully acknowledging your powerlessness over your addiction *and* reaching out for help and support. In an effort to begin to *fully* accept your addiction as a problem, you will explore, write, and confess your own story. Throughout the process you will discover your need for mercy, grace, and forgiveness.

Shame and denial, the barriers to a First Step, are critical both in addiction and in recovery. Scripture provides clear descriptions of the mind and heart ensnared in addiction:

> *The mind governed by the flesh is hostile to God; it does not submit to God's law,*
> *nor can it do so.*
> ROMANS 8:7

> *How long will you people turn my glory into shame?*
> *How long will you love delusions and seek false gods?*
> PSALM 4:2

Addictive sexual behavior involves delusional thoughts such as "No one is being hurt by this" and becomes, at some point, a false god that is wholly incapable of filling even the smallest portion of the God-shaped hole. From a spiritual standpoint, Step One of the Twelve Steps is an act of surrender. In your active addiction, you may have consciously or unconsciously bargained, rationalized, justified, minimized, and denied to maintain your addictive sexual behavior. Because all of these behaviors do not involve the spiritual act of surrender, they are best considered half measures. The Big Book of Alcoholics Anonymous is clear on this issue, "Half measures availed us nothing. We stood at the turning point. We asked his protection and care with *complete* abandon." (italics added)

Step One, then, is an act of surrender, the recognition that you *cannot* handle your addiction by yourself. You need

- the mercy and healing afforded by Jesus Christ
- other people to hold you accountable and to support you and encourage you in recovery
- a program of recovery that will provide sufficient structure, contact, and coping skills/resources for you to maintain your sobriety

A First Step is the opposite of struggling and straining one more time to change your addictive sexual behavior. Most people have many "false starts" at recovery in which they try to claw their way out of the hole of addiction that they have once again fallen into. True recovery is no longer "white knuckling" to hang on. Instead, it is a letting go. It is only when you let go that you can fully fall into the arms of a loving God. As the Big Book of AA states, "Some of us tried to hold on to our old ideas, but the results were nil until we let go absolutely...."

For many of you, the idea to "let go absolutely" might seem counterintuitive. For now, we ask simply that you trust that this might be true. Scripture makes great promise of what will happen to you if, in your brokenness, you bow before God:

The Lord upholds all who fall and lifts up all who are bowed down.
PSALM 145:14

Undoubtedly, you have stumbled and fallen in your addiction. Now, through surrendering in a First Step, you will be upheld and lifted up by God.

Modern-Day Parable—The Tale of Two Gardens

The empty bags that once contained Grandpa's treasured vegetable seeds lay crumpled on the floor of Ted's bedroom. The perfectly round seeds sailed across the room as Ted thumped them from the desk. Ding—another one hit the window and bounced sideways into the wall and rolled onto the floor. Smiling, Ted positioned his thumb and finger, carefully aimed and … thump … another seed hit the window.

While visiting his grandparents last Christmas, both Ted and his brother Tim were given bags of seeds as a special gift. A small note was attached to the bags, carefully explaining the proper planting for each type of seed: corn, okra, carrots, and squash.

Grandpa's note read, "These bags of seeds come from the vegetable garden my father grew for us when I was a little boy. Even though we had no money for food, we never went hungry because of the abundance of nutrition God provided us through our garden. Every year, I have planted our vegetable gardens for your Grandma and me, and then I harvest the seeds for the next year. I want to pass these along to you. Please follow the planting instructions carefully as you plant your own garden this spring."

Down the hall from Ted, his brother took out a wooden box from underneath his bed and carefully placed his bags of seed in the box. "I will start getting my garden spot ready tomorrow," thought Tim.

For the next several months, once a week, Tim pulled weeds, turned the soil, and prepared the area in the backyard for his spring garden. Ted would sit on the porch, laughing and making fun of his brother. "You are making way too big of a deal of this, Tim. All you really have to do is stick the seeds in the ground and watch them grow." And off Ted would go to play.

Spring came and planting season arrived as scheduled. Tim was ready. His plot was laid out, the dirt was healthy with fertilizer and weed preventers, and his rows were perfectly formed. Systematically, he placed seeds in the ground: one row each for the carrots, corn, okra, and squash. He watered his garden every two days and pulled the weeds every week. He felt good that he was following his Grandpa's instructions exactly as they had been written.

Ted's plan for his garden was different. "Now where are my seeds?" said Ted, suddenly remembering the earlier game he had made out of them. Once he had gathered the seeds from his bedroom floor, he began to push them into the hard ground. "No worries about watering the little guys; it will rain soon enough," he said and then ran off to play with his friends.

Weeks went by and Tim's garden grew and grew. The carrot's green leaves began to poke out of the ground, the corn and okra stalks grew tall and straight, and the yellow squash blossoms were numerous. Tim's garden supplied vegetables for his family for the summer.

Ted's garden did nothing.

The story of Ted's and Tim's gardens is a modern-day version of Jesus' Parable of the Wise and Foolish Builders (Matthew 7:24–27). Both stories speak to us about the importance of obeying. Whether we are building houses or planting gardens, there are instructional words to follow that provide guidance, wisdom, and purpose.

Recovery from addictive sexual behavior is much like the story of the brothers' gardens. In the end, we alone cannot make vegetables grow. This is the work of God. At the same time, we can prepare the soil, carefully attend to the planting, and weed and water as needed. Such is the active work of recovery.

 Read Matthew 7:24–27. As you read the Parable of the Two Houses, think about the story you just read of The Tale of Two Gardens. Both stories contrast two people—one who wisely acts on correct instructions and one who foolishly neglects or ignores vital information. The metaphors of the house and the garden are symbolic of decisions we make when living our Christian life, our actions and projects, and our addiction recovery. The application is clear. If these instructions are ignored or not carefully followed, growth will not happen.

It is important to determine exactly what would be destroyed and what consequences would occur if you do not follow your recovery program.

The consequences: Jesus said, "Therefore, everyone who hears these words of Mine and puts them into practice is like the wise man who built his house on the rock" (Matthew 7:24). Because addiction is a disease of the brain, learning to follow instructions is vital to improving the neuroplasticity, or changing, of the brain. In fact, your obedience to your recovery program makes the difference between survival and destruction, between sobriety and relapse.

The dangers: Often, recovering addicts live in a state of delusion, believing they are able to work their recovery program by using just some of the Twelve Steps and some of their therapist's suggestions or treatment plan requirements. In this way, the addict attempts to maintain control. That is, he or she has not surrendered to the reality of the addiction.

Are there some pieces of your recovery program where, like Ted, you are only pretending to do the work that is needed? If so, what are they? Make a list of consequences that can happen if you do not follow your recovery plan completely.

The hope: Revisit Jeremiah 29:11, reading slowly and prayerfully:

"For I know the plans I have for you," declares the Lord, "plans to prosper you and not to harm you, plans to give you hope and a future."

Imagine for a moment that God had a refrigerator. Visualize that it is your picture He would display on the front of it! God loves you. He desires great and wonderful things for you. No matter what you have done in the past, through Christ's mercy and His Grace, your future is bright and full of hope. No matter how lonely you may feel at times, you are never alone.

God also provides other healthy recovering people to support you. People who float in and out of your life for the purpose of making your daily life better are "God with skin on." Maybe you have someone in your life right now who fits this description, such as your sponsor, a member of your support group, a neighbor, or a co-worker.

 Reflect on the people in your life who are encouraging and supporting, who take time to listen, or who just give you a friendly smile. They could be someone you are close to or even the cashier or clerk at the grocery store or the teller at your bank. These people have been put in your life by God to give you hope. It is up to you to want a better future, one filled with communion with God, and then to do your part to make it happen.

Read II Corinthians 12:9–10:

> *But he said to me, "My grace is sufficient for you, for my power is made perfect*
> *in weakness." Therefore I will boast all the more gladly about my weaknesses,*
> *so that Christ's power may rest on me. That is why, for Christ's sake,*
> *I delight in weaknesses, in insults, in hardships, in persecutions, in difficulties.*
> *For when I am weak, then I am strong.*

Paul addresses the people of Corinth instructing them to become aware that Christ's grace is sufficient. He reminds them to remember that when they feel weak, he (Christ) is strong.

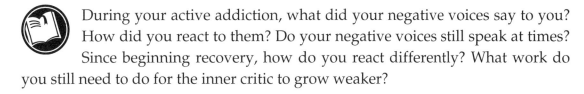 During your active addiction, what did your negative voices say to you? How did you react to them? Do your negative voices still speak at times? Since beginning recovery, how do you react differently? What work do you still need to do for the inner critic to grow weaker?

 Reflect on this verse:

> *I am worn out from groaning. All night long I flood my bed with weeping and drench my*
> *couch with tears. My eyes grow weak with sorrow; they fail because of all my foes.*
>
> PSALM 6:6–7

 How do you relate to these words? As you reflect on this scripture, what emotions do you feel?

Next read Deuteronomy 30:19–20:

This day I call the heavens and the earth as witnesses against you that
I have set before you life and death, blessings and curses. Now choose life,
so that you and your children may live and that you may love the Lord your God,
listen to his voice, and hold fast to him.
For the Lord is your life, and he will give you many years.

 First, reflect on the "death and curses" portion of the passage. List the events in your life that cause you the most pain along with the accompanying emotions.

Now focus on the "life and blessings" portion of the above passage. What does it mean for you to "choose life" at this point? List the greatest blessings in your life along with the accompanying emotions.

 Now consider Mark 4:35–40:

That day when evening came, he said to his disciples, "Let us go over to the other side."
Leaving the crowd behind, they took him along, just as he was, in the boat.
There were also other boats with him. A furious squall came up, and the waves
broke over the boat, so that it was nearly swamped. Jesus was in the stern,
sleeping on a cushion. The disciples woke him and said to him,
Teacher, don't you care if we drown?" He got up, rebuked the wind and
said to the waves,
"Quiet! Be still!"
Then the wind died down and it was completely calm.
He said to his disciples, "Why are you so afraid? Do you still have no faith?"

As a person in early recovery from sex addiction, you almost certainly face a storm that rages within you. Can you hear the words of Christ speaking to the storm within you?

Quiet! Be still!
Why are you so afraid? Do you still have no faith?

 Think about your faith in Christ. On a scale of 1 to 10, with 1 being "no faith" and 10 being "fully trusting in Christ," how do you measure your

Faith Scale today? If you choose a low number, how can you raise your faith level? If you choose a high number, what events have you overcome by placing more faith and trust in Christ?

Expect a Miracle

When a rabbi saw that the Jews were being mistreated, he went into the forest, lit a sacred fire, and said a special prayer asking God to protect his people. And God sent him a miracle.

Later, his disciple went into the same part of the forest and said, "Master of the Universe, I do not know how to light a sacred fire, but I do know the special prayer; please hear me!" And the miracle happened again.

A generation passed, and another rabbi, seeing how his people were being persecuted, went into the forest and said: "I do not know how to light a sacred fire, nor do I know the special prayer, but I still remember the place. Help us, O Lord!" And the Lord helped them.

Fifty years later, another rabbi, who was crippled, spoke to God, saying: "I do not know how to light the sacred fire, nor do I know the special prayer, and I can't even find the place in the forest. All I can do is tell this story and hope that God will hear me."

And again the miracle occurred.[1]

Strength is found in telling your story, especially the recovery pieces. The Twelve Steps are based on two things: spiritual practices and service to others. Go forth, then and tell your story to others. And expect a miracle in return.

Elements of a First Step

 Read the introduction to chapter 4 (What is a First Step?) in *Facing the Shadow*.

A First Step is essential to recovery as it begins to break down (1) the old excuses you once used to support addictive sexual behavior and (2) the belief that you can handle this on your own. In recovery, you need help. As a Christian, you may receive help in the form of a loving God along with the support of others, such as a therapist, sponsor, and Twelve Step group members.

The Four Pillars of Addiction

When you were actively in your addiction, it almost certainly stood on four pillars: denial, minimization, rationalization, and justification. Use the following definitions as you continue working through this chapter:

- **Denial** ("I'm fine, I don't have a problem")—you refused to acknowledge that you had a problem. It is the very defense mechanism that probably kept you from taking a First Step for so long. The shame of acknowledging your addiction seemed overwhelming, so you hold your addiction in the shadows to avoid bringing it to light.

- **Minimization** ("I'm not that bad")—you minimized the magnitude of your bondage to addictive sexual behavior.

- **Justification** ("All I want is a little relief")—you somehow justified your sexual acting out in a way that often was self-pitying and manipulative of others.

- **Rationalization** ("It's not my fault")—you somehow vindicated your addictive sexual behavior by explaining it in a logical manner to avoid the true reasons for the behavior; you may have used platitudes, such as "Everything will work out for the best," "Life goes on," or "Everything happens for a reason" in an attempt to find comfort from your psychological or physical pain.

In this chapter, we will look at each of the four pillars of addiction separately to unpack the defense mechanisms, or mental "tricks," that you used to maintain your addiction.

 Respond to the following questions:

- In what ways did you deny your addictive sexual behavior?
- How did you minimize your problems with addictive sexual behavior?
- How did you justify your addictive sexual behavior?
- How did you rationalize your addictive sexual behavior?

Religion and Sexuality History

 Complete your Sexual Addiction History (exercise 4.1) in chapter 4 of *Facing the Shadow*.

 Now write a history of your Christian journey. To help you get started, answer the following questions:

- What is your earliest memory of being in church?
- At what age do you believe you became a Christian?

- If you attended church as a child, what are the most important memories you hold from your childhood of participating in religious activities?

- If you attended church as an adolescent (approximately twelve to twenty years of age), what are the most important memories you hold of religious activities during this period of your life?

- Thinking of your church-related experiences as a child and adolescent, what were the lessons you learned, if any, about yourself as a sexual being?

- Throughout your life, have you had periods of questioning or crises of faith, in which you particularly struggled in your Christian journey? Describe these times.

- As an adult, what messages about sexuality have you received from religious communities?

- As an adult, what are the most critical *positive* experiences you have had within your religious community?

- As an adult, what are the most critical *negative* experiences you have had within your religious community?

- If you were religiously active throughout your addiction, how did you "manage" the double life you were living?

- How has starting recovery from your sexual addiction affected your religious life and your relationship with God?

- Anything else you would like to share?

Reflect on any connections between your history of sexual addiction and your spiritual history. Look for any themes and specific connections. The goal here is not to blame the religious community for your addiction and early perceptions of sex and sexuality, but rather to learn about you as both a religious and a sexual being.

To help you get started, consider the following:

- When did your sexual addiction begin?

- What was going on in your religious and spiritual life at that time?

- During periods of escalation and de-escalation of addictive sexual behaviors, what was happening spiritually for you?

Worst Religious or Spiritual Moments

 Complete the Ten Worst Moments activity (exercise 4.6) in *Facing the Shadow*.

 What are your ten worst moments related to your religious or spiritual life? Examples might include times of fantasy or euphoric recall during church services, opportunities for worship missed because of acting out, sexually acting out with someone from church, or sexually objectifying church members. Include feelings you had then and feelings you have now as you look back on these moments. If this process leaves you in a vulnerable place, talk to your trusted guides.

Sharing Your First Step

 Read about sharing your First Step in *Facing the Shadow*.

Scripture provides helpful guidance around doing a First Step. Many people avoid acknowledging that they are powerless over their addiction and that their lives had become unmanageable for one primary reason—shame. When you were actively in your addiction, it is unlikely that others openly talked to you about your addiction. The secrecy of sex addiction, both how you hid your addiction and how others hid it, may have left you feeling ashamed of your behavior and believing that no one, perhaps not even God, could accept you as you are.

Nothing New under the Sun

Hopefully, in the process of beginning recovery you have seen that there are many who struggle with addictive sexual behavior. Many other Christian brothers and sisters have struggled and continue to struggle with sex addiction. As scripture tells us, *"There is nothing new under the sun"* (Ecclesiastes 1:9b). Addictive sexual behavior has been a part of society long before we had the language and research to understand it. You are not alone because God remains steadfastly with you. There is, indeed, nothing new under the sun.

Heartful Confession

It is possible to do a First Step but remain detached from your own story, as if you were describing the behavior of another or a television show you recently watched. Yet this is the equivalent of Ted carelessly tossing seeds around his room. It does not support the work to come. This is your story and it is important to confess it heartfully. Scripture shows us that heartful confession will be healing to us and touch the hearts of those to whom we confess.

While Ezra was praying and confessing, weeping and throwing himself down before the house of God, a large crowd of Israelites—men, women and children— gathered around him. They too wept bitterly.

EZRA 10:1

Passion and Compassion

The crucifixion of Jesus is sometimes referred to as the passion of Christ because the word "passion" comes from the Latin *passio*, which means suffering. As a recovering sex addict, you may certainly note the irony that these words are connected in this way. In your addiction and, indeed, in early recovery, you have no doubt suffered. As part of your recovery, you have already documented many negative consequences of your addiction. You likely have struggled emotionally, relationally, and spiritually. In short, you have suffered.

In an odd way, the good news is that your trusted guides understand your suffering precisely because they have struggled themselves. When you tell your story to your sponsor or at a Twelve Step meeting, those who are hearing it deeply understand the struggle. Whether your therapist is in recovery or not, he or she likely is drawn to a helping profession because of personal suffering as well. Because all of these individuals have suffered, they better know how to "suffer with," the definition of compassion.

 Read Ephesians 3:17–19:

So that Christ may dwell in your hearts through faith. And I pray that you, being rooted and established in love, may have power, together with all the Lord's holy people, to grasp how wide and long and high and deep is the love of Christ, and to know this love that surpasses knowledge— that you may be filled to the measure of all the fullness of God.

The single greatest antidote to suffering (passion) is to have someone "suffer with" (compassion). This is, in part, the wisdom of sharing your First Step. While it may be obvious, it seems important to highlight that only those who are compassionate toward your suffering should be trusted with your First Step. If you participate in a religious community, such trusted souls likely exist in your community. However, watch out for those who are judgmental and, perhaps, wrathful.

We have seen church members shunned, publicly judged, and asked not to return to the congregation. It is beyond the scope of this book to address this broader problem. For you as a person in early recovery, though, it is critical to find a balance between sharing your First Step appropriately and protecting yourself from those who will harm you.

You might think of this as looking for those who can be an *anam cara* for you. In Irish, *anam* means soul and *cara* means friend. So, an anam cara is a soul friend, someone who can experience your essence as deeper than any behaviors you might confess or any story you might tell. Because of this, an anam cara is capable of accepting you just as you are. The Irish believe that whenever you are in the presence of an anam cara, you are home.

Thorn in the Flesh

 Read II Corinthians 12:7b–10:

> *Therefore, in order to keep me from becoming conceited, I was given a thorn in my flesh, a messenger of Satan, to torment me. Three times I pleaded with the Lord to take it away from me. But he said to me, "My grace is sufficient for you, for my power is made perfect in weakness." Therefore I will boast all the more gladly about my weaknesses, so that Christ's power may rest on me. That is why, for Christ's sake, I delight in weaknesses, in insults, in hardships, in persecutions, in difficulties. For when I am weak, then I am strong.*

As an addict, you likely have practiced control, sometimes even controlling things that matter little to you, just for the sense of control. This is the opposite of *powerlessness*. As such, powerlessness may feel like a foreign concept. You may even erroneously equate powerlessness with weakness. From a spiritual standpoint, though, the opposite is true. As Paul wrote, "When I am weak, then I am strong."

Shapiro explained it this way: "The more clearly you realize your lack of control, the more powerless you discover yourself to be. The more powerless you discover yourself to be, the more natural it is for you to be surrendered to God. The more surrendered to God you become, the less you struggle against the natural flow of life. The less you struggle against the natural flow of life, the freer you become. Radical powerlessness is radical freedom."[2]

 First, pray for guidance as you complete this activity. Then, reread II Corinthians 12:7b-10 several times, identifying words and phrases that mean something to you in particular. Journal about what the passage reveals to you about your addiction, recovery, and telling your story to others as a First Step to recovery.

While He Was Still a Long Way Off

 Read Luke 15:20, a verse from the story of the prodigal son.

> *So he got up and went to his father. But while he was still a long way off,*
> *his father saw him and was filled with compassion for him;*
> *he ran to his son, threw his arms around him and kissed him.*

Read the verse several times, keeping in mind that you are reflecting on the importance of a First Step. Focus on the part of the passage when the father is filled with compassion and runs to his son. This is the only place in the Bible where Jesus (or anyone else) characterizes God as running. He runs to you when you turn toward Him, even while you are still a long way from home.

 Write about what this passage means to you at this point in your recovery process.

Compassion and Self-Compassion

As you reflect on the importance of First Step work to the recovery process, consider the roles of self-compassion and compassion. Scripture is clear that Jesus had great compassion for others who were struggling:

> *When he saw the crowds, he had compassion on them, because they were harassed and*
> *helpless, like sheep without a shepherd.*
>
> MATTHEW 9:36

Perhaps from all of the challenges you have faced, you can relate to feeling "harassed and helpless" and in need of a compassionate Shepherd to help you find your way. Similarly, scripture is crystal clear on the importance of having compassion for others.

> *Even in darkness light dawns for the upright, for those who are*
> *gracious and compassionate and righteous.*
>
> PSALM 112:4

If you are around others in recovery, you may notice some who are not practicing compassion. Perhaps borne of their own fears, they are critical and judgmental of others. For example, partners may be criticized for not letting go of the past quickly enough. These types of criticism are the opposite of compassion and may quickly fester into resentments, which often sabotage recovery. Practicing compassion and Christ-centered love for others is the antidote for judgment and entitlement.

 Read Psalm 112:4:

> *Even in darkness light dawns for the upright,*
> *for those who are gracious and compassionate and righteous.*

 Consider your own recovery to this point. Are you harboring resentments toward others rather than practicing compassion? Write about your commitment to be compassionate toward those around you.

As a Christian, you may have been taught to "value others above (yourself)" (Philippians 2:3). While selflessness is indeed a Christian value, it does not mean that you should not value yourself. Interestingly, the words of Christ are poignant here. This is how Jesus replied when asked which of the commandments in the Law were greatest:

> *"Love the Lord your God with all your heart and with all your soul and with all your mind." This is the first and greatest commandment. And the second is like it: "Love your neighbor as yourself." All the Law and the Prophets hang on these two commandments.*
> MATTHEW 22:37–40

Most commonly, the passage in verse 39, "Love your neighbor as yourself," is taught as a lesson in compassion for others. If you are filled with self-loathing, self-contempt, and shame, however, and you are frequently hypercritical of yourself, surely Jesus would not want you to treat your neighbor the same way. To truly love others, you must love yourself, not in an ego-driven way but one that deeply knows and affirms that you are a child of God.

The reality is that many Christians are far more compassionate with others than they are with themselves, although Jesus clearly is encouraging us to be self-compassionate in Matthew 22:39. It is important, however, to distinguish between self-compassion and self-aggrandizing or self-promoting. In Matthew 22:39, Jesus is certainly not encouraging us to be egotistical or narcissistic. Neither is he calling

Shadows of the Cross: A Christian Companion to *Facing the Shadow*

us to minimize our faults and transgressions. That is not self-compassion. Jesus also is not calling us to make excuses for unhealthy behavior. That is not self-compassion but a subtle form of denial. Rather, Jesus calls us to be gentle and kind with ourselves, as we might be with others who matter dearly to us.

 Reread Matthew 22:37–40 several times slowly. Now focus on verse 39, where Jesus calls you to love your neighbor as yourself, but in so doing also subtly directs you to love yourself. How do you feel about that? Do you practice self-compassion? Write about your commitment to practice self-compassion daily.

Spiritual Disciplines

Prayers of Petition

In *Facing the Shadow*, Carnes provides a list of what full acceptance of a First Step looks like. Pray that God will help you

- make no excuses or explanations for your acting out behaviors
- understand and accept your powerlessness, partially by reflecting on previous unsuccessful efforts to stop your behaviors
- understand your unmanageability by looking honestly at consequences you have experienced
- understand your addiction fully
- take full responsibility for your actions, past and present
- experience your emotions appropriately in every situation
- experience grief, pain, sorrow, and remorse
- own the loneliness you feel
- commit to do whatever it takes to change

[adapted with permission by Gentle Path Press.]

 Reflect on your prayer of petition. As you pray for God's guidance to full acceptance, what will you need to focus on in the coming days?

Prayers of Intercession

 One way to move beyond the selfishness of addictive behavior is to pray earnestly for those who have been harmed by your addictive sexual behavior. Write down the first names of two or three people who have been harmed. Then look at the names one at a time and allow an image of that person to come to mind. Pray for each person and for God to use you in whatever manner He deems necessary to support the person in her or his healing. NOTE: Make sure your prayers are indeed prayers of intercession for the other person and not subtly prayers of petition for yourself.

Meditation on Scripture

It requires great courage to authentically do a First Step. The following meditation is a reminder that you do not face your First Step alone.

 Read Psalm 144:2a

> *He is my loving God and my fortress, my stronghold and my deliverer, my shield, in whom I take refuge.*

Read this passage several times, slowly, out loud if possible. Each time, emphasize a different word or phrase, allowing yourself to sink into a more contemplative state, noting how your body responds to these timeless words. Allow one word or short phrase from the passage to emerge as most important to you *right now*. Spend a few minutes repeating this word or phrase as a short prayer, breathing deeply with each recitation. Finally, sit in silence for several moments. When your mind wanders, return to your word or phrase as a focal point.

End with a short prayer of gratitude.

 Journal about your experiences with the above meditation.

Shadows of the Cross: A Christian Companion to *Facing the Shadow*

Chapter Seven
What Damage Has Been Done?

 This chapter parallels chapter 5 (What Damage Has Been Done?) in *Facing the Shadow* and the two should be completed concurrently.

This chapter focuses on helping you face the consequences of your addictive behavior by using recovery principles from a Christian perspective. The scriptural foundation for this chapter is Ecclesiastes 3:1–3, which focuses on the seasons of our life and how change is inevitable.

There is a time for everything,
and a season for every activity under the heavens:
a time to be born and a time to die,
a time to plant and a time to uproot,
a time to kill and a time to heal,
a time to tear down and a time to build.

Recovery from sexual addiction is, of course, about being sexually sober and sexually healthy. But it's about so much more. It's about "a time to heal" and "a time to build." To move forward, however, it is necessary to recognize that while the past cannot be changed, it must be acknowledged, owned, and worked through. In this chapter, we will help you look at the past, recognize damage you may have caused, and give instructions for making amends by carefully laying out an action plan. In Twelve Step groups, the first promise of recovery is "We are going to know a new freedom and a new happiness. We will not regret the past nor wish to shut the door on it." Like the passage in Ecclesiastes, this tells us that, in recovery, we are in a new season of life and that we must not shut the door on the past.

Modern-Day Parable: The Unmerciful CFO

It is 2:30 p.m. and the board meeting for Grace, Inc., is about to begin. The chief executive officer (CEO), Mr. Phillips, is becoming anxious because the complete set of financial reports is not in the board members' information binders. Frustrated, he calls the chief financial officer (CFO), Mike, into his office.

Mr. Phillips says, "Mike, can you explain to me why there is not a complete set of financial statements in this quarter's binder? We are about to start our quarterly board meeting and I have incomplete information to report."

Sighing, Mike replies, "I know this looks bad on my part. Last week I instructed my assistant to copy, print, and put the binders together. I never took the time to follow up with him before today. I am afraid it will not be done by the time of the board meeting."

"Mike, this incompetence you continue to show me is becoming a pattern. During your last review, not only did I document your failure to produce sufficient financial reports, but we also discussed the paid time off hours you owe our company. I understand that you have had family hardships and sickness this year, but Mike, the PTO you owe our company is equivalent to three month's pay. And, if we are considering your financial debt to the company, we need to include the loan you took against your 401K last year to purchase your new house."

Soon it became evident that Mike was struggling to keep his composure. "I am so sorry, sir. It is true that I have had to borrow time against my PTO and I understand that if you fire me, I would have a huge loan to pay back. I will put in overtime every day plus weekends to pay back what I owe the company. During this time, I will focus on analyzing the numbers and producing financial statements that are worthy of presenting to the board."

Having compassion for Mike, Mr. Phillips smiles and leans across his desk as he says, "Mike, because you are loyal to our company and a hard worker, I want to give you a second chance. Tomorrow I will call accounting and tell them to forgive the PTO time that is due plus pay you a bonus on your next check that will be enough to pay off your 401K loan."

Overwhelmed by the compassion that was being shown by Mr. Phillips, Mike thinks, "I have to tell my Sunday school members about this. It is so great to work for another Christian." He stands up and the men shake hands.

The next day, Mike walks down the hall and heads toward his assistant's cubicle. "Fred, I was called into Mr. Phillips's office yesterday. The full set of financial statements was not in the binder for yesterday's board meeting. It was your responsibility to see that the binders were completed probably. Do you understand how bad this looked for me and my department?"

Shadows of the Cross: A Christian Companion to *Facing the Shadow*

Fred replies that he feels bad about this, but explains how the multiple projects he was working on took more time than he had anticipated. He asks for forgiveness, promising to catch up on all of his projects. But Mike is furious and in no mood to listen to Fred's excuses and promises. "You owe me more than a promise. I will not tolerate employees whose incompetence makes me look bad. Clear out your desk—you are fired!"

When Mike returns to his office, Mr. Phillips is standing in the doorway. "Mike, may I see you in my office?" When Mike enters his boss's office, Mr. Phillips begins, "Please sit down, Mike. I heard what you told your assistant. Just yesterday, did I not confront you about your lack of responsibility and your debt to this company? Do you understand how bad I looked in front of our board members?" "Yes sir, I do," replies Mike.

Mr. Phillips continues, "I was willing to excuse your lack of management skills and even provide a bonus to help you cover your debts to the company. But the manner in which you just treated Fred is unacceptable. And for you to go so far as to fire him for the very same thing you have done helps me to see clearly that you do not possess the management skills we require for Grace, Inc. For this reason, it is you who will be let go and Fred will stay."

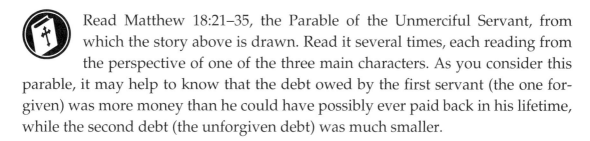 Read Matthew 18:21–35, the Parable of the Unmerciful Servant, from which the story above is drawn. Read it several times, each reading from the perspective of one of the three main characters. As you consider this parable, it may help to know that the debt owed by the first servant (the one forgiven) was more money than he could have possibly ever paid back in his lifetime, while the second debt (the unforgiven debt) was much smaller.

 Reflecting on the parable of the unmerciful servant, respond to the following:

From the king's perspective:

- Make a list of people you have forgiven and the specific acts that you forgave.
- What did these acts of forgiveness cost you?
- What did you gain from these acts of forgiveness?

From the first servant's perspective:

- Make a list of people who have forgiven you.
- Describe these experiences, focusing on both thoughts and emotions.

- Make a list of people you have not yet forgiven.
- Describe the emotions you experience when you think about those you have not yet forgiven.

From the second servant's perspective:

- Make a list of people who have not forgiven you.
- Describe these experiences, making sure that you *take responsibility for your acts rather than blaming those who have not forgiven you.*

Damage Control

 Complete the Damage Control Worksheets (exercises 5.3-5.10) in chapter 5 of *Facing the Shadow* which, in essence, becomes a strategic plan for addressing problems.

Because many people in early recovery are faced with immediate and rather severe consequences of their addiction, their initial problems list, which informs the damage control plan, is focused on these pressing problems. As a result, most people, even the best of Christians, do not initially think of their disconnection from God as one of their high-priority problems. Do you view your disconnection from God as one of your main problems?

At the outset of recovery, many people are dealing with distressing questions such as

- Where will I live?
- Will my marriage/relationship survive this?
- Should I/she keep the baby?
- How did I get this sexually tranmitted infection and what do I do now?
- What do I do now that I have lost my job?

Undoubtedly, you had your own pressing questions and problems. Now that you have been working a program of recovery for a while, it may be useful to consider your relationship with God as a "problem" that you are willing to work through.

 Using the Damage Control Worksheets (exercises 5.3-5.10) in *Facing the Shadow* as a guide for this activity, write down "Disconnection from God" as a current problem. As you think about ways to strengthen or re-establish this connection, respond to the following:

- **Best possible outcome.** What would be the best result of any actions you might take or plan you might devise?

- **Minimal acceptable outcome.** What is the minimal result that is acceptable?

- **Possible solutions.** Gather all the solutions that you and the people in your support system suggest. List each one, no matter how far-fetched it may seem.

- **Best solution.** From all possible solutions, combine and choose the ideas that you believe would work for you.

- **Action steps and target dates.** What concrete actions do you need to take? By what date will you take them?

- **Support needed.** What do you need in order to take these steps and who do you need to help you with this solution?

[reprinted with permission by Gentle Path Press.]

Minimizing Ongoing Damage

In addition to dealing with damage caused by your past behavior, avoid compounding this with additional and ongoing damage. In early recovery, you may continue to struggle with denial, repression, and deep regret for your past. As you begin to have difficult conversations with others as part of your recovery, be aware of the following potential hazards:

- **Denial.** Although you may no longer deny your addiction, watch for subtle ways you continue to use denial as an unhealthy coping strategy. For example, you may deny who was affected by your addictive sexual behavior or you may be in denial about the long-term commitment required for a life of recovery.

- **Emotional suppression.** You may have used addictive sexual behavior as a way to cope with difficult emotions, including fear, sadness, anger, and the shame of your addictive sexual behavior. In recovery, many men and women begin to experience strong emotions that may feel uncomfortable. This emotional release is a normal and healthy part of recovery. Energy spent suppressing emotions is better spent in recovery activities. Although there may be isolated instances where short-term emotional suppression is required (for example, to function on a particular day at work), it is generally unhealthy. Allow yourself to experience a full range of emotions and express these to healthy people in healthy ways.

- **Cognitive repression.** When you entered recovery, you may not have remembered many of your past sexual behaviors. You may begin recalling them now in bits and pieces. This is a benefit of doing a sexual history with a therapist or sponsor, as the process often will trigger additional memories. Compartmentalization and shame can cause you to repress memories. Many recovering addicts are surprised when new memories of their addictive behavior surface. This is a normal part of recovery. You are actually *recovering* parts of yourself that you had previously shut out, perhaps because of shame or fear. While you should not force the recovery of these memories, be open to the possibility that you may not initially remember everything you have done.

- **Inappropriate disclosure.** Now that you are no longer holding on to secrets, you may begin to feel the weight of your addiction lift and feel inclined to tell many others about your addiction. Before making a disclosure, review the list of suggestions in chapter 5 in the Damage by Disclosure section in *Facing the Shadow*. This is particularly applicable to disclosures within your church community. While it is important to stop keeping secrets and to create a support system of people with whom you can completely honest, remember that a shaming judgmental church member can do far more harm than good. You can always make disclosures to others later. Once they are made, however, they cannot be taken back.

 Respond and journal to the following:

- Are there any ways in which you may still be in denial? For example, are you minimizing damage done to yourself or others? Are you hanging on to hope for a "quick fix" from your addiction?

- What has your emotional life been like since you began recovery? Are you able to experience and express your emotions to healthy people in healthy ways? Are you aware of times that you "numb out" or otherwise avoid your emotional experience? Are you now more aware of emotional processes that may have triggered you to act out sexually?

- Have you had the experience in recovery of remembering some past behaviors that you had previously forgotten? What is it like for you to remember these experiences? Are you open to the possibility that there might be other memories that will be recovered over time?

There Is a Time for Everything

 Reread the passage (Ecclesiastes 3:1–3) with which this chapter opened.

 Reflect on this passage using the prompts below:

There is a time for everything, and a season for every activity under the heavens.

- Use words or phrases, or draw images to show how you would characterize your current "season" (that is, the recovery season).
- Use words or phrases, or draw images to show how you would characterize the season of life in which you were actively a sex addict.

... a time to be born and a time to die

First, consider your physical birth and death. When gravestones are engraved, the etchings typically include a date of birth and a date of death separated by a hyphen or dash. Of these elements, the dash is said to be the most important; that is, what you did with your life between birth and death. Here are some ways to reflect on "the dash":

- Write an obituary for yourself as if you had never started recovering from your sexual addiction. In other words, write about being an active sex addict for the rest of your life.
- Next, write an obituary for yourself as a person who maintains an active program of recovery and grows in sobriety and spirituality.
- Read over these two obituaries several times. What are the differences? This activity can be very emotional, so remember to reach out to your support system as needed.

Having reflected on your physical life, now turn your attention to your spiritual life. Not only is there a time to physically be born and physically die, but there also is scriptural precedent for spiritual birth and death.

 Read John 3:2–4. This is the story of a Pharisee named Nicodemus who came to Jesus in the secrecy of night as a member of the Jewish ruling council. We can assume that Nicodemus traveled in the shadow of night because meeting with Jesus would have been frowned upon by other members of the Jewish ruling council.

He came to Jesus at night and said, "Rabbi, we know that you are a teacher who has come from God. For no one could perform the signs you are doing if God were not with him."

Jesus replied, "Very truly I tell you, no one can see the kingdom of God unless they are born again.

"How can someone be born when they are old?" Nicodemus asked. "Surely they cannot enter a second time into their mother's womb to be born!"

Nicodemus longed to understand Jesus' teaching, but he clearly misunderstood Jesus to be talking about a literal physical rebirth, not a spiritual rebirth. This spiritual death and birth also is described in Romans 6:4:

We were therefore buried with him through baptism into death in order that,
just as Christ was raised from the dead through the glory of the Father,
we too may live a new life.

This passage plainly tells us that there is a spiritual death of the old so that "new life" may occur.

 Consider your own spiritual death and rebirth:

- What has had to die so that you can have new life?
- Have you grieved the loss of what had to die? Although it may seem strange, you need to grieve the loss of addictive sexual behavior.
- Using words and images, characterize your new life in recovery.
- Imagine a toddler taking his or her first steps, so unstable and uncertain. So, too, is the progress of spiritual rebirth. What do you need, both from yourself and others, to support your spiritual rebirth?

... a time to plant and a time to uproot,

"Plant" refers to anchoring specific behaviors that are vital to recovery. "Uproot" is the "digging up" and changing of behaviors that threaten your recovery.

 Respond to the following questions:

- What are the most important daily behaviors that support your recovery? What will it mean to "plant" these behaviors and water/nourish them daily?
- What are your behaviors that need to be uprooted so that they cannot live?

Shadows of the Cross: A Christian Companion to *Facing the Shadow*

... a time to kill and a time to heal,

Here, the author of Ecclesiastes (possibly Solomon in his old age, but this is debated by scholars) juxtaposes two interesting words, "kill" and "heal." This can be considered both between you and others (interpersonally) and within you (intrapersonally). At the interpersonal level, this is not a call to physically harm another person but a call to end (that is, kill) any relationships that do not support your recovery. In other relationships, you may need to make amends.

Similarly, in the intrapersonal realm, there is a time to kill and a time to heal. Here, it is important to distinguish "self" from "Self." We consider the Self (capitalized) to be the Self-in-God and God-in-Self. The True Self is not separate from God and does not see the Self as separate from others. The Self is in communion with God and lives close to God's will for her or him. No one is perfect and, accordingly, no one lives a life perfectly aligned with God's will for them. Those who are nurturing the Self, though, live closer to the ideal that God is in them and they are in God.

The self (not capitalized), in contrast, is not who you were created to be. It is a false self. The false self is ego-driven, selfish, and sees itself as separate from God and others. Often, this separateness is fueled, at least in part, by shame. This false self may be highly religious (that is, involved in religious activities), but it lives fairly constantly in sin (remember that sin is the translation of a Greek word that means missing the mark, such as an archer's arrow or straying from the path). Behaviors that support/feed the false self, then, become barriers to the True Self (Self-in-God and God-in-Self) and must be removed. How does this happen?

Certain aspects of the ego-driven self will die if not "fed." Other aspects of the self, however, are more entrenched. They must be "killed," an active process of avoiding behaviors that align with the ego-driven self.

Other aspects of the ego-driven self that keep you from a fuller communion with God must be surrendered. Unless you are different from virtually every other addict in recovery, though, the ego-driven self loves control and, accordingly, *hates* surrender. "Letting go" feels like a weakness, a death, to the ego-driven self. Because of that, you may find yourself clinging to some behaviors that are unhealthy. In Twelve Step language, these are called defects of character. Simply stated, the ego-driven self is strong and you will most likely need help in performing the necessary acts of surrender.

Step work can be very useful here. Steps Four through Eight focus on a "time to kill and a time to heal." In particular, Steps Six (*Were entirely ready to have God remove all these defects of character*) and Seven (*Humbly asked God to remove our shortcomings*) first acknowledge that we need God's help to do this work and, second, ask us to surrender. We can humbly ask God to remove shortcomings (Step Seven) but if we are not "entirely ready" to surrender these personal defects (Step Six),

God will honor our free will and allow us to continue to cling to these unhealthy aspects of self.

 Consider both the relational (interpersonal) and individual (intrapersonal) aspects of *a time to kill and a time to heal*. Answer the following questions:

- What relationships with others do you need to end in order to support your recovery?
- What relationships with others do you need to focus on healing?
- What are the three most prominent characteristics of your false self?
- Keeping in mind that the collaborative approach with God (in which you both take responsibility where you are able and surrender where necessary) is most effective, what action steps do you need to take? Note that prayer and meditation help reinforce the idea that you cannot do this work by yourself.

... a time to tear down and a time to build

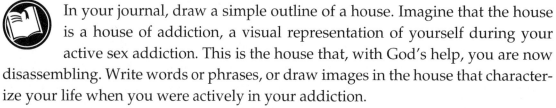 In your journal, draw a simple outline of a house. Imagine that the house is a house of addiction, a visual representation of yourself during your active sex addiction. This is the house that, with God's help, you are now disassembling. Write words or phrases, or draw images in the house that characterize your life when you were actively in your addiction.

Now draw another simple outline of a house in your journal. Visualize it as a house of recovery, a visual representation of yourself actively engaged in the recovery process. This is the house that, with God's help, you are building. Write words or phrases, or draw images in the house that characterize your life in recovery.

 Take time to compare the two house images you have just created. Carl Jung suggested that a house is a symbol for our soul that emerges from a deeper level of consciousness, such as when we have dreams. Thinking of the two houses as representations of your soul, one in addiction and one in recovery, reflect on the changes that are occurring at a soul level in recovery.

 Take time to open your heart to God in gratitude for changes that are occurring and pray for God to help you continue to build your house of recovery.

Healing the Spiritual-Sexual Split

In chapter 5 of *Facing the Shadow*, Carnes briefly discusses the split between one's spirituality and sexuality. To begin the healing of this split, Carnes encourages you to acknowledge "that sexuality is about meaning and spirituality is about meaning." According to author Mark Laaser, fantasies are another expression of the soul's deepest longing.[1]

What are some of your common sexual fantasies? Listing these fantasies can be triggering so it is a good idea to tell a trusted companion, such as a therapist, sponsor, support or therapy group about this work. The idea here is *not* to indulge the fantasy but to *reflect* on the types of fantasies you have and what this might say about your soul's deepest longing.

Respond to the following:

- Are you commonly seduced in your fantasies? Could this indicate a deeper longing to be wanted?
- Are you commonly dominant or submissive in your fantasies? Could this indicate a longing for control or a need to be taken care of?

Reflect on deeper longings that might manifest in sexual fantasy while being watchful of not being triggered. Remember that the focus is on the themes of the fantasies, not the fantasies themselves. Nonetheless, this work can be triggering so keep your support system informed and close by.

The problem with chronic sexual fantasies is that they are an unhealthy expression of the soul's longing. Having reflected on what your fantasies might tell you about your soul's deeper longings, take time to write down ways in which this longing can be met in spiritually and psychologically healthier ways.

Spiritual Disciplines

Continue the daily spiritual practice that you developed in chapter 2. Here are some additional practices that may help you with the content in this chapter:

Prayers of Petition

Pray for courage and strength to continue on this journey of healing and transformation.

Prayers of Repentance

As you reflect on the work in this chapter, you may feel remorse for your past behavior. Remember that remorse for past deeds is healthy as long as it does not spiral into a sense of shame about the self. Pray for mercy from our loving heavenly father and allow yourself to experience His unconditional mercy and grace.

Modified Jesus Prayer

Recite several times, aloud if possible, this modified Jesus prayer:

> *Lord Jesus Christ, Son of God, have mercy on me, a sex addict.*

Rather than just allowing this to be a rote prayer said without emotion, breathe deeply as you recite this prayer and allow yourself to feel God's love and mercy.

Contemplative Reading

 Read Ecclesiastes 3:1–3 again. Reflect on two distinct seasons of your life: life before recovery and life now that you are in recovery.

Chapter Eight

What is Sobriety?

 This chapter parallels chapter 6 (What is Sobriety?) in *Facing the Shadow*. The two chapters should be read and worked through concurrently.

As you may gather by this point, short-term recovery is largely about coping and community. The essential tasks discussed in *Facing the Shadow* are about building coping skills and strategies and highlighting the importance of a supportive community. *Shadow of the Cross* complements this by detailing spiritual coping strategies as well as emphasizing the importance of community. In the short term, coping strategies and healthy community are what will help you to stay sexually sober. This chapter explains how your spiritual path can support your sobriety.

The path of recovery and maintaining sobriety is, to a great extent, one of removing barriers to full communion with God. When you are in communion with God, your path is clear and your steps straight. As you continue on your healing journey, you can take comfort in knowing how your relationship with God is evolving:

You will call and I will answer you;
You will long for the creature your hands have made.
Surely then you will count my steps
but not keep track of my sin.
My offenses will be sealed in a bag;
you will cover over my sin.

JOB 14:15–17

As you begin this chapter, pause to reflect on this passage:

You will long for the creature your hands have made.

JOB 14:15B

Over and over again in this book, we have focused on helping you acknowledge your "God-shaped hole" and your deepest longing for communion with God. This passage reminds you, though, that God also longs for you!

 Read Philippians 4:8:

> *Brothers and sisters, whatever is true, whatever is noble, whatever is right, whatever is pure, whatever is lovely, whatever is admirable—if anything is excellent or praiseworthy—think about such things.*

 On the left side of your journal page, write down the key words from Philippians 4:8:

- excellent
- praiseworthy
- true
- noble
- right
- pure
- lovely
- admirable

Reflect on the qualities you already have that fit within each of these categories. Put a star by any entries that you wish to cultivate more fully.

A Modern-Day Parable: Pete and the High Street SA Group

> *Being strengthened with all power according to His glorious might so that you may have great endurance and patience.*

COLOSSIANS 1:11

At a local church, Pete sits in a circle of nine other men and says for the first time, "Hi, my name is Pete and I am a sex addict." "Hi, Pete," say the other men in a tone that is welcoming and calm. "I cannot believe I am in roomful of men all professing to be sex addicts. And at the Church of the Peaceful Dove!" Pete thought.

Many times during the meeting, Pete wanted to get up and run out. But he had promised his therapist he would attend a Sex Addicts Anonymous Twelve Step meeting every day for ninety days, along with finding a meaningful spiritual practice.

Bill, the group leader, made some announcements and then shared the meeting guidelines, after which everyone held up their hand pledging confidentiality to the group. At the end of the meeting, Bill read a section from a devotional book for sex addicts:

The best part of the day
Is the rest of the day,
For it is meant to be led from the heart.

But if for some reason
You find yourself teasing
With the *UnWelcomed Guest* from the past.

Do what you know
Run away from the foe
That reminds you of cravings that last.

"Foe? UnWelcomed Guest? What in the world is this man talking about?" wondered Pete. But, just then, Bill began to explain it. "Men, we must understand the meaning behind this poem. Think of the *UnWelcomed Guest* as your addict self. Even though we are in recovery and doing everything possible to stay in recovery, the addict self still lives within and from time to time, without warning, he will appear in the form of unhealthy thoughts, cravings, and a harsh inner critic voice. What are some tools you have learned that will prevent relapse from occurring?"

The other men responded:

"Call my sponsor."

"Call you people in my group."

"Call my therapist."

"These are all good choices," Bill continued. "Now, let's talk about the importance of self-care. What can you do for yourself that will condition your mind, body, and soul against the *UnWelcomed Guest* visit and his vicious attack on your recovery?"

Again the men took turns throwing out ideas and suggestions. "Go for a walk, run, or swim—anything to get out of the house." "Get plenty of sleep." "Hey, Cliff, how about laying off those Big Macs and shakes?" teased Miguel. Cliff tossed a pretend punch at him and everyone laughed. "Good work, guys. Let's close this session with the Serenity Prayer and go home," said Bill.

During the drive home, Pete replayed the conversation over in his head. "I can't believe that Bill expects me to call everyone I know whenever my urges begin. *And* start some kind of healthy living regime. You gotta be kidding me. Ain't gonna happen … this trying to stay sober is hard enough."

For the next days and weeks, Pete faithfully attended the SA meetings. By this time, he was enjoying the diversity of the men, attitudes, and conversation of each group. "What does it matter? My therapist says ninety meetings in ninety days, might as well have fun with it," he smirked.

The High Street Twelve Step Meeting quickly became Pete's favorite. The members were more relaxed than in some other groups and seemed to have more fun. Even though they were staying sober, they kept their old routines of staying up late, eating fast food, and going to movies, watching TV, or playing video games.

"I have decided to stay with this one group of guys," replied Pete when his sponsor, Ed, began quizzing him about the various SA meetings he was attending. "Tell me more about this group," said Ed, "Why this group?" "Oh, you know how staying sober is a tough deal. At least these guys don't try to cram all that healthy living stuff down my throat. That's the last thing I want to deal with." Pete said with a sly grin.

"Pete, listen to me. Your Addict Self *will* return. In fact, he lives inside you now just waiting for the moment when you are weak and vulnerable. Without the proper conditioning of your body, mind, and soul, he will attack in a vicious way and I am afraid he will win," warned Ed. "I am afraid you are in trouble, my friend."

Ed tried to discuss this a little bit further but Pete was not budging. After paying for the coffee and shaking hands, the two men parted ways.

That was three weeks ago …

Since then, Pete's life had cycled down in a spiral he was finding difficult to control. Just as he was warned about, the UnWelcomed Guest had returned. It was during an event when the High Street SA Meeting group members decided to go bowling at the local Let 'Er Rip bowling alley. What seemed to have started as an innocent evening of bowling, nachos, and sodas quickly turned into the night from hell—at least from the eyes of a sex addict new to recovery.

Ironically, members of the SA "church group" were also there. Pete waved and they waved back. "Hmmm … it is just men bowling with them. Geez, I am glad I am over here. At least my guys aren't afraid of letting women join us. Guess we are just a little stronger than they are."

These were words Pete would soon regret thinking.

The women were friendly, the food was tasty, and music and laughter filled the place. One thing led to another and soon the familiar flirting began and the hookup lines were uttered. Pete and his group were entertaining not only the women but the UnWelcomed Guest and, sadly, they didn't even know it.

 Reflect on the story of Pete. Everyone, yes everyone, in recovery from an addiction can relate to Pete. Does this story have a ring of familiarity to it? At this moment, how are you feeling about Pete? About yourself?

 Pete's story is a modern-day version of Jesus' Parable of the Wise and Foolish Maidens. Take time to prayerfully read Matthew 25:1–13.

After reading this passage, you may be wondering how Pete's story relates to the maidens with the oil lamps and oil.

Think metaphorically. Compare the oil lamps to your brain. If you think of your brain as an oil lamp, then what you put into your brain is the oil. Both the oil in the lamp and the neurochemicals in your brain provide forms of energy. In the lamp, oil creates the energy of light. In your brain, neurochemicals create the neuropathways of the brain. This is the path of recovery. What you get out of it depends on what you put into it.

The wise maidens who were successful in meeting the bridegroom had carried enough oil to make it through the night. The foolish maidens took only the lamp full of oil, but no more. Because their lamps ran out of oil (energy), these women stumbled in the dark.

Now consider Pete, who only worked his program to satisfy his therapist, but no more. Had he listened to his sponsor and "filled his lamp" with healthy living and a dedication to a daily spiritual practice, his choices and outcomes may have been different.

 Respond to the following:

- In what ways are you developing your recovery program today? Is it a program of convenience or a comprehensive recovery program?
- Consider your personal recovery program as it is today and write down your plan of action. For example: make a daily commitment to meditation, scriptures study, and journaling; exercise at least three days a week; and call your sponsor daily.
- Do you notice areas that have changed from the very first days of your recovery? If so, are they moving in a positive way? Are there areas you need to build and adhere to more diligently?

- Now, think about areas in your life that need more attention. Perhaps you need more exercise, spiritual practice, healthy eating, and proper sleep. What do you need to focus on *right now*?

> A successful recovery is one of endurance and resiliency with a dedication to stay the course no matter what. Consider this quote from Patrick Carnes: "We must know how to transform bad experiences into assets. We call this resilience."

The Parable of the Wise and Foolish Maidens is a story of endurance. By telling this parable, Jesus is empowering you to think of ways you can endure in the preparation of your body, mind, and soul so that you will be ready for what is to come.

 Similarly, the psalmist wrote of endurance in Psalm 119:

You're blessed when you stay on course, walking steadily on the road revealed by God.
You're blessed when you follow his directions, doing your best to find him.
That's right—you don't go off on your own; you walk straight along the road he set.
You, God, prescribed the right way to live; now you expect us to live it.
Oh, that my steps might be steady, keeping to the course you set;
Then I'd never have any regrets in comparing my life with your counsel.
I thank you for speaking straight from your heart;
I learn the pattern of your righteous ways.
I'm going to do what you tell me to do; don't ever walk off and leave me.
PSALM 119:1–8, THE MESSAGE

New Testament scripture also encourages endurance and perseverance:

Therefore, since we are surrounded by such a great cloud of witnesses,
let us throw off everything that hinders and the sin that so easily entangles.
And let us run with perseverance the race marked out for us,
fixing our eyes on Jesus, the pioneer and perfecter of faith.
For the joy set before him he endured the cross, scorning its shame,
and sat down at the right hand of the throne of God.
Consider him who endured such opposition from sinners,
so that you will not grow weary and lose heart.
Hebrews 12:1–3

The two Bible passages direct us to follow a path that has been marked. The psalmist encourages you to "walk straight along the road he set" and the author of Hebrews encourages you to "run with perseverance the race marked out for us." Both authors are telling you to persevere on God's path for your life. In your journal, reflect on these questions:

- What do you know about God's path for your life at this point in your recovery?

- What obstacles have you encountered because of your perseverance?

- How will you overcome those obstacles using recovery tools and spiritual practices?

Now, let's check back in with Pete. Unlike the foolish maidens who found a door slammed and locked, Pete's story takes a different turn. Pete relapsed. The shame he felt continued to feed the urges and cravings of sex addiction. "God, help me stop!" he screamed one morning after another night of looking at pornography on his computer. "Why am I doing the very thing I hate?" he cried. Hands in his face, Pete rocked back and forth, sobbing uncontrollably. Soon, he lay exhausted on his bed, shaken and numbed by the thoughts of what he was doing to himself.

Moments later, he heard a buzzing and turned his head slightly to see the light of his cell phone glowing on his bedside table. Picking up the phone, he saw *Ed—Sponsor* on the screen. "I can't answer his call. If he knew the shape I was in, he'd find out what a loser I am and that he is wasting his time with me." So, he set the phone on his chest and cried some more.

A few moments later, Pete heard the buzz indicating that Ed had left a voice-mail. Pete reluctantly decided to listen to Ed's message. The words he soon heard brought an unexpected feeling of comfort. Ed said, "Pete, it's me, Ed. I haven't heard from you for three weeks. Please let me know how you are and what I can do to help you." Then with great sincerity, he said, "Pete, it is quite possible that you have relapsed. If this is true, I beg you to contact me. I have been where you are now. Let me help you; let your group help. Please reach out today ... right now. Come on over, I am at home. I will be waiting for you. See you soon, hopefully today."

Silence filled Pete's bedroom. Feelings of courage grew and he began to get dressed. He knew he needed help. And suddenly, he wanted to talk to Ed about how to focus more fully on recovery. Slowly, Pete walked up the path to Ed's house. Though he was not sure that Ed would answer the door, Pete took the chance.

Knock, knock, knock. He heard footsteps coming closer to the door and suddenly there stood Ed, grinning ear to ear. Immediately, Ed wrapped his arms around

Pete and whispered, "Glad to see you, my friend. Come on in and let's talk."

 Matthew 25:11–13 tells of the outcome for the maidens who went to buy oil for their lamps. In the telling of this parable, Jesus closes with a phrase that is an important reminder for people in recovery.

Later the others also came. "Lord, Lord," they said, "open the door for us!"
But he replied, "Truly I tell you, I don't know you."
Therefore keep watch, because you do not know the day or the hour.

Both Pete's story and the Parable of the Maidens reveal that preparation is what distinguishes the wise from the foolish. As a recovering person, you will experience triggers and stresses that will cause your addict self to become louder. How you respond in those moments will depend on how prepared you are. You practice recovery daily for just those moments.

 Journal about the following:

- Jesus' statement in Matthew 15:13 that "you do not know the day or the hour" reminds us that triggers, urges, and cravings can occur unexpectedly in recovery. How do you "keep watch" daily so that you will be prepared when this occurs?

- They say "Practice does not make perfect. Perfect practice makes perfect." Although, as we have discussed, perfection is not the goal, this saying reminds us that sloppy practice makes for sloppy performance on game day. This is what Pete experienced at the bowling alley. Sloppy practice made for poor preparation when "game day" arrived. Thinking about your current program of recovery, what does it look like when you are practicing well? How do you know when you are practicing poorly?

- When unexpected triggers, impulses, and cravings occur (that is, when you face your "game day"), what specific things can you do to deal with these and maintain your sobriety?

 Read the opening section of chapter 6 in *Facing the Shadow* on how boundary failure happens in which Patrick Carnes discusses issues that often compound the problem of addiction. Some of these issues are likely to be more relevant for you than others. As you read this section, consider carefully what this means for you.

Thinking of your life as a Christian, write down each of the following issues in your journal, noting how prominent they figure into your life, steps you are taking to address them, and ongoing challenges you must face:

- achievement
- self-esteem
- accountability
- self-care
- conscience
- realism
- self-awareness
- relationships
- affect

Reflect on your commitment to make ongoing changes in these areas as needed. Then write down any awareness that emerges from this reflection.

 Thank God for changes that you have already made and pray for God to guide your steps for changes still in process.

 If you have not already done so, complete the Three-Circle Method (exercise 6.7) in *Facing the Shadow*.

After completing your three circles, look closely at your outer circle behaviors. These are behaviors that support your sobriety and recovery. What spiritual practices did you include in your outer circle? Consider whether you need to add spiritual practices or add more detail to make it clear. To ensure that there is integrity in your three-circle work, it is essential that you review this work with trusted souls, such as a sponsor, therapist, or therapy group.

Circle Behaviors

When you find yourself engaged in middle-circle behaviors, there is a tendency to look at the inner circle and either congratulate yourself for not engaging in any inner-circle behavior or hyperfocus on not engaging in any inner-circle behaviors. Neither of these responses are effective and useful. Congratulating yourself on not engaging in inner-circle behaviors excuses middle-circle behaviors, which is inherently problematic. Staring at the inner circle and hanging on with "white knuckles" to avoid acting out is not a long-term solution, either.

Instead, when you find yourself slipping into middle-circle behaviors, go to your three-circle chart and look at the outer circle. What recovery behaviors are needed? What spiritual practices will help?

By focusing on the outer circle during "slippery slope" times, your energy is moving in a positive direction. Inner-circle behaviors become "things of earth" as noted in the old hymn "Turn Your Eyes Upon Jesus" by Helen H. Lemmel:

Turn your eyes upon Jesus,
Look full in His wonderful face,
And the things of earth will grow strangely dim,
In the light of His glory and grace.

Three Facets of Spiritual Health

There is a poignant scripture passage in which Micah has asked God what he should do. Should he bring burnt offerings and should God be given gifts of rams or rivers of olive oil? Should one's first-born be offered for past sins? The answer is simple, although not easy.

 Read God's response to Micah's question in Micah 6:8:

He has shown you, O mortal, what is good.
And what does the Lord require of you?
To act justly and to love mercy
and to walk humbly with your God.

God seems to be saying that to obey is better than to offer sacrifices. What is required? Three things:

- Act justly.
- Love mercy.

- Walk humbly with God.

 Reflect on this response to Micah's question. Then consider what specifically it looks like for you, as a Christian who is in addiction recovery, to do the following:

- Act justly.
- Love mercy.
- Walk humbly with God.

Ask God to help you grow in humility, mercy, and just actions.

Serenity, Security, and Sobriety

Consider two people in recovery. One feels troubled, unsafe, and unprotected. He is tenuous in his recovery and has almost daily experiences of "white knuckling" to not fall into old patterns of acting out sexually. The second person feels a sense of calmness and safety as he goes through his day. He occasionally experiences triggers, cravings, and urges, but these are fleeting and usually not intense. It is, perhaps, a silly question, but which person is more likely to maintain sobriety? Which person would you rather be?

Cultivating serenity and security are important to maintaining your sobriety and growing both in your recovery and in your Christian faith. As a Christian, you are blessed to have a wellspring of teachings and disciplines that support serenity and security.

 First, scripture tells us that security and serenity are possible.

Peace I leave with you; my peace I give you. I do not give to you as the world gives.
Do not let your hearts be troubled and do not be afraid.
JOHN 14:27

Come to me, all you who are weary and burdened, and I will give you rest.
Take my yoke upon you and learn from me, for I am gentle and humble in heart,
and you will find rest for your souls. For my yoke is easy and my burden is light.
MATTHEW 11:28–30

And the peace of God, which transcends all understanding, will guard your hearts and your minds in Christ Jesus.

PHILIPPIANS 4:7

Biblical encouragement that Jesus has given you his peace and rest is important. It may be true, though, that you do not yet fully experience this "peace … which transcends all understanding." Unfortunately, sometimes people who have not yet experienced the promises of Jesus feel "less than," as if they are doing something wrong or, worse, that they *are* less than. That is, if you do not yet experience peace, you may be inclined to judge yourself negatively. Be not dismayed! Like all of the gifts of the Spirit, security and serenity must be cultivated, nurtured, and grown.

The good news is that you already have tools to cultivate security and serenity. The spiritual disciplines outlined in chapter 2 are practices that will help you draw closer to God through Christ Jesus. Security and serenity are by-products of such practices. Integrate some form of contemplative practice, such as breath prayer or contemplative reading, into your daily routine. Doing so will help you begin to feel more secure and serene. You will grow in your ability to rest in the spirit. And, over time, it will become possible to experience peace that passes all understanding.

This is what the psalmist meant when he wrote:

"Be still, and know that I am God."

PSALM 46:10A

Fruits of the Spirit

As you establish more time in recovery, you will experience spiritual growth as you live in greater accordance with God's will. That is, as you move closer to the path for which you were created, you become closer to God, for that is where He waits for you. From this, your experience of what Paul referred to as the fruit of the Spirit will deepen.

Read Galatians 5:22–23.

But the fruit of the Spirit is love, joy, peace, forbearance, kindness, goodness, faithfulness, gentleness and self-control. Against such things there is no law.

Paul chooses an interesting metaphor in this passage. For fruit to grow, a seed must first be planted. Then it must find the nutrients of fertile soil and have sufficient sunlight and water. Ideally, someone will trim and prune dead branches from the tree or vine.

What a beautiful metaphor for recovery! The seed of the fruit of the Spirit has been planted deeply within you. Your work is to nurture the seed, trim and prune what is no longer needed, and enjoy the fruit when it has fully ripened. It is your responsibility to bring alive what is already inside of you.

 Reflect on each of the following fruits of the Spirit. Rank each on a scale of 1 to 10 with 1 being "never experience" and 10 being "always experience." Then, for each fruit of the Spirit, write about how you can more fully cultivate and nurture that particular fruit:

- love
- joy
- peace
- forbearance/mercy
- kindness
- goodness
- faithfulness
- gentleness
- self-control

Select one of the fruits that seems particularly important for you at this time. Take ten minutes to engage in a breath prayer, asking God to increase this fruit in your life. Here are some examples of breath prayers:

- God, grant me better self-control.
- God, grant me a spirit of peace.
- God, give me a gentleness in my spirit.

Simplicity: The Antidote to Chaos

Complete the Personal Craziness Index (PCI) (exercises 6.8 and 6.9) in *Facing the Shadow*. If you have already completed the PCI, take time to review your results. Ongoing monitoring of PCI scores is a great way to be watchful of your lifestyle. For most recovering addicts, the movement toward the recovery zone is one of simplifying a life that has been overly chaotic. This is the power of the PCI, to help you identify areas of your life over which, with God's help, you need to be more watchful and intentional. Remember that simplicity is a spiritual practice. A chaotic life leaves little room for stillness of mind, body, and soul. We encounter God most fully in these still places.

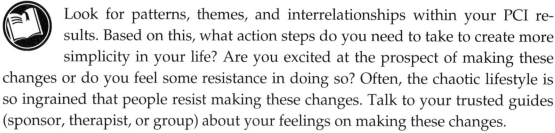 Look for patterns, themes, and interrelationships within your PCI results. Based on this, what action steps do you need to take to create more simplicity in your life? Are you excited at the prospect of making these changes or do you feel some resistance in doing so? Often, the chaotic lifestyle is so ingrained that people resist making these changes. Talk to your trusted guides (sponsor, therapist, or group) about your feelings on making these changes.

Simplify, simplify, simplify.

Spiritual Disciplines

Continue your daily spiritual practice plan. You may choose to add more spiritual practices into your daily plan to support your continued healing.

Prayers of Petition

1. Review the Relapse Scenario Worksheets (exercises 6.3 – 6.5) in chapter 6 of *Facing the Shadow* and pray for God to help you see the preconditions and challenges of the ego, and make good choices to avoid acting out.
2. Review your PCI scores and pray for continued progress in the seven areas you identified as being most important.

Affirmations

Affirmations are simply brief positive statements that help you to focus on what is good and holy. Identify one challenge you are still struggling with in your recovery journey. Now develop an affirmation that addresses this challenge and practice repeating it throughout the day. For example, if you are struggling to accept God's forgiveness, your affirmation might simply be

I am a child of God

Whatever your affirmation, get in the habit of saying it many times each day, either silently or aloud. When you say your affirmation, take a deep breath and allow yourself to really take in the Truth of the statement.

Meditation on Rock Bottom

Reflect on your own "rock bottom" experience by visualizing it. You may even feel some of the emotions from that experience just from remembering this time in your life. Do not hesitate to contact your guides (sponsor, therapist, or group) if you need support.

At the time, you probably felt as if this were the worst possible moment in your life. How do you think of this experience now? Are you at a place where you can begin, even if only slightly, to understand that "rock bottom," as difficult as it may have been, was the most grace-filled moment of your life? How did this experience allow you to begin recovering not only your sexual sobriety but also your walk with Jesus?

Chapter Nine

What Has Happened to Your Body?

 This chapter parallels chapter 7 (What Has Happened to Your Body?) in *Facing the Shadow*. The two chapters should be read and worked through concurrently.

Addiction hurts the body. Period. This chapter will examine how your body has been affected by your addiction and, more importantly, look at ways in which the damage can and will be healed over time with your faithfulness to recovery.

The Temple

 Read I Corinthians 6:19–20:

> *Do you not know that your bodies are temples of the Holy Spirit, who is in you,*
> *whom you have received from God? You are not your own;*
> *you were bought at a price.*
> *Therefore honor God with your bodies.*

In this passage, Paul writes of your body as a temple in which the Holy Spirit dwells as a gift given by God.

 Read the scripture several times slowly. Journal whatever comes to your mind and heart. Answer the following:

- Are you ready to receive the Truth that your body is a temple of the Holy Spirit?
- If not, what keeps you from knowing this as Truth?

- What does it mean to you that "You are not your own; you were bought at a price"?
- Being specific, what does it mean for you to honor God with your body?

Thieves in the Temple

Read Matthew 21:12–13:

Jesus entered the temple courts and drove out all who were buying and selling there. He overturned the tables of the money changers and the benches of those selling doves.
"It is written," he said to them, "My house will be called a house of prayer, but you are making it 'a den of robbers.'"

The passage speaks about the literal temple courts. For now reflect on the passage as if it was referring to your body as a temple of the Holy Spirit as referenced in I Corinthians 6:19–20. Read it slowly and prayerfully and then respond to the following:

- When you were actively in your addiction, in what ways was your body a "den of robbers"? (Consider your behaviors, thoughts, and emotions.)
- As a recovering person, in what ways is your body a "house of prayer"?
- Thinking of your addiction as those who did not belong in the temple, what are you doing to drive out the "money changers" and keep them out of the temple each day?

A Modern-Day Parable Based on Matthew 13:44

"Not again," Jeff said sadly as he hung up the phone. Once again, he needed to drive to the police station and pick up his son, Richard, who had been arrested for drunk driving. Jeff had been in recovery from alcoholism for the past ten years. His heart felt heavy as he watched his own son go down the same destructive path as he had so many years ago. Driving to the police station, he called his sponsor.

"Caleb, it's me … Richard is in trouble again. I don't know what to do. Am I a failure as his dad? Are his drinking troubles because of me?" Jeff cried.

"Richard is making his own decisions, my friend. It is easy for us to take on the responsibility of someone else, especially when they are our children. I hear how you are hurting tonight. My advice to you is to continue loving Richard, but this time, outline consequences he will suffer if he does not change. It is time that you set boundaries with him and for yourself."

"It's so hard. I was never good with disciplining my son. I thought that Martha would be the disciplinarian in the family. God, I miss her." And, with those words, Jeff began to sob uncontrollably. "Sorry, Caleb. I've got to pull over and get myself together before I see my son."

Martha had died when Richard was an infant. After her death, Jeff began drinking. It wasn't until he faced Child Protective Services and the possibility of losing Richard because of neglect that he went to AA and became sober.

The next day, Jeff was sitting in his AA meeting. He felt better talking to his group members about Richard's drinking. Al, the oldest member of the group, caught up to Jeff after the meeting. "Jeff, I had a similar experience with my youngest daughter. I sent her to treatment three times before she sobered up. I am proud to say she has been sober three years now. But the best thing she and I did to heal our relationship was to find something to do together. You know, like a hobby. Is there anything Richard likes to do that you think you could enjoy with him?"

Jeff said, "When he was little, we used to do wood craft projects. He seemed to like working with tools. I guess we could do something like this again."

This thought gave Jeff the confidence to go through with an idea he had been contemplating for some time. The next weekend, he made an offer to buy an old run-down house not far from his home. When Richard came home, Jeff took him to the house. Standing in front of the house, Jeff put his arm around his son and said, "She don't look like much, but with some hard work and long hours, I think we can make this old house look beautiful." Richard didn't seem interested but Jeff pressed deeper.

"Richard, you have two choices; you can begin attending AA meetings or go into treatment for your drinking. I am not going to watch you destroy yourself like I almost destroyed me and our family."

"Dad, I am not ready for treatment and AA meetings are for old folks like you. No one my age goes to meetings."

"Son, then as far as this house goes … I will work on this alone because it feels right to me, but I am asking you to help. Who knows, this could be a good thing for you, for us. What do you say—are you in?" Before Richard could answer, Jeff added, "Oh, and by the way … you *will* go to meetings and sober up or you will be finding a new place to live, understand?" Then Jeff smiled at his son.

Daily devotionals took on a new meaning to Jeff. While he used to study and meditate for himself, he now studied and meditated with Richard on his mind. Richard had started attending AA meetings and was working a Twelve Step program with his sponsor. He was now four months sober. Working on the house together had proved to be a blessing. Every night after dinner, they worked side by side. This project had turned into something much more than Jeff had expected or hoped for. Father and son had gained a feeling of closeness that they had never experienced before. They laughed, talked, and sometimes sang off-key to songs on the radio.

Jeff remembered reading about Jesus' Parable of the Hidden Treasure. Sometimes he felt that the hidden treasure of this house was finding his relationship with his son.

And time moves on …

One day as Jeff and Richard were scraping the interior walls of the old house, Richard yelled, "Dad, come here—look!"

They stood with wide eyes. Underneath the old wallpaper were hundreds of dollar bills tacked to the wall. Jeff remembered that back during the Depression, people would often hide their money in odd places. The owner of this house must have papered the walls with money, then covered it with actual wallpaper.

"Oh, God," Jeff said as he bowed his head that night. "Thank you for hidden treasures. Some can be physically seen and held, and some are found in the people you hold. In my case, you have given me back my son who is sober." Then he smiled, "And the money was a nice added blessing. Thank you, thank you, thank you."

 Read Matthew 13:44, the Parable of the Hidden Treasure:

The kingdom of heaven is like treasure hidden in a field. When a man found it, he hid it again, and then in his joy went and sold all he had and bought that field.

This parable is generally interpreted as highlighting the great value of the Kingdom of Heaven. It also highlights how what is hidden can be found and, if one is willing to sacrifice all, can be obtained.

Where is the Kingdom of Heaven? When this question was posed to Jesus, he provided an interesting answer.

 Read Luke 17:20–21:

Once, on being asked by the Pharisees when the kingdom of God would come, Jesus replied, "The coming of the kingdom of God is not something that can be observed, nor will people say, 'Here it is,' or 'There it is,' because the kingdom of God is in your midst."

According to a number of translations of this parable, Jesus says that the kingdom of God is *within you*.

As in the story of Jeff and Richard, the focus of this chapter is on healing what has been broken and claiming what is already there. Like money tacked to the wall, God is "in your midst" waiting for you to find Him.

 Read about addiction neuropathways in chapter 7 of *Facing the Shadow*. Complete (exercise 7.1) Your Sexual Addiction Matrix, (exercise 7.2) Your Sexual Health Matrix, and (exercise 7.3) Matrix Reflection Questions.

 Reflect on your responses to the *Facing the Shadow* exercises. What are the most important things that you learn from these exercises?

Write about whether or not you can relate to any of the following common reflections:

- My addictive sexual behaviors emerged as a way to avoid negative self-concepts.
- In my addiction, I confused sex and love and, in so doing, over-focused on sex as an expression of connection.
- My addictive sexual behaviors emerged as a way to avoid or overshadow undesirable emotional experiences.

Thoughts behind Addictive Processes

The addiction neuropathways and subsequent addictive behaviors emerge then, at least in part, as a function of your thoughts and feelings.

In act 2, scene 2 of *Hamlet*, Shakespeare writes, "For there is nothing either good or bad, but thinking makes it so. To me it is a prison."

No human avoids this self-made prison. Each of us experiences hurts and psychological wounds that make us who we are. Long before you became a sex addict, there were sown seeds of experience that would influence how you began to think about yourself, others, and your relationship to others.

John Bowlby, a noted psychologist, asserted that we develop internal schemas, which he called internal working models, based on our early experiences in relationships.[1] As a child, you had positive and negative experiences with early caregivers (parents, guardians, teachers, siblings, etc.) that shaped how you thought about yourself and other people. Based on this, you developed attachment strategies, or ways that you connect with other people, that are either secure or insecure.

People with a *secure* attachment tend to

- believe that it is safe to ask for help from others
- ask for support
- share with important others their personal struggles
- feel at peace in their relationships
- not become overly distressed when an attachment figure is temporarily unavailable

Bowlby suggested that people with insecure attachments could be further classified as having either an anxious attachment or an avoidant attachment.

People with an *anxious* attachment tend to

- worry about whether an attachment figure will be available to them
- feel anxiety, often to the point of panic, when they think the "other" is not available
- be driven by their anxiety/panic; they may over invest in primary relationships by compulsively reaching for the other (such as calling or texting their partner many times during the workday and feeling anxious if calls/texts are not answered quickly)
- fear abandonment

It is common for a person with an anxious attachment strategy to have a core fear of abandonment. Fueled by this fear, the person tries to cling to a romantic partner, often acting in ways that have a paradoxical effect of pushing the person away, particularly if the partner has a more avoidant attachment strategy.

Often, a person with an avoidant attachment strategy (either dismissive or fearful) has a core fear of inadequacy. Fueled by this fear, the person tries to avoid conversations, circumstances, and situations that have the potential to prove this fear is true. When it comes to avoidant attachment, attachment theorists now suggest we use one of two basic strategies, commonly labeled as dismissive-avoidant and fearful-avoidant. People who use the dismissive-avoidant strategy deny that they have any attachment-related needs while those who use the fearful-avoidant strategy are acutely aware of their attachment-related needs but fear that these needs cannot be met.

Accordingly, people with *dismissive-avoidant* attachment tend to

- believe they do not need any close relationships
- feel independent and self-sufficient

- view close relationships as unimportant
- get anxious when others try to get close to them
- seek less intimacy
- deny or suppress their feelings
- respond to perceived rejection by distancing from the source of rejection (such as a partner)

People with *fearful-avoidant* attachment tend to

- have a history of loss or abuse in childhood
- want close relationships but find it difficult to trust others
- worry about being hurt if they get too close to others
- have mixed feelings about close relationships
- believe they do not deserve responsiveness from partners
- mistrust the intentions of partners
- be uncomfortable expressing affection

Researchers have determined that attachment styles also can be understood in the context of how you tend to view yourself and how you tend to view others.

- *Secure attachment*—positive view of self and others
- *Anxious attachment*—negative view of self and positive view of others
- *Dismissive-avoidant attachment*—positive view of self and negative view of others
- *Fearful-avoidant attachment*—negative view of self and negative view of others

 Based on what you've learned about the various attachment strategies, respond to the following questions:

- What attachment strategies do you most often use?
- Would they best be characterized as secure or insecure? If insecure, are you more anxious or avoidant in your attachment strategies? If avoidant, are you more dismissive or fearful?

Often, we use attachment strategies to help us manage how we are feeling in a given situation. Strong emotions drive our behaviors or action tendencies. For example, an anxiously attached partner may try to always be "in touch" with the partner, expecting them to do everything together and have limited interests outside of the relationship. They may also "cling" to the partner by texting/calling with great frequency.

On the other hand, a more avoidant person may be aware that they need to be comforted in some way but be unwilling to ask a partner for this comfort.

Consider the following scenario as an example of how attachment strategies play out in relationships:

Danielle's mother died in a car crash when Danielle was four years old. The driver of the other car was legally drunk. Her father had always had drinking problems, but developed serious alcoholism and other drug addictions after her mother died. As a result, he was emotionally and psychologically unavailable to her. So, in essence, Danielle lost both parents at a very young age. She was basically raised by her maternal grandparents who were struggling with their own grief. As a result, Danielle developed separation anxiety and an anxious attachment style characterized by fear that her grandparents were going to die and she would be left alone.

Martin grew up in a family where both parents were hypercritical of everything he did. He received positive attention when he excelled at something and sharp criticism when anything was less than perfect. Often, he was negatively compared to an older sibling. As a result, he disengaged emotionally from his family. He experimented with drugs as a way to numb out, but generally became a loner and developed the belief that he didn't need other people to be happy. In short, he developed a dismissive-avoidant attachment strategy.

Danielle and Martin met in college and began to date. Initially, they were strongly drawn to one another for reasons that were not entirely clear to either of them. Soon, however, Danielle began to experience Martin as "aloof and unavailable," and Martin began to experience Danielle as "clingy and demanding." Danielle began to worry that she was going to lose Martin, and he began to fear that he could never be good enough for Danielle. Soon, the relationship became distressed. The more Martin seemed unavailable, the more Danielle tried to draw him closer. And the more Danielle tried to draw Martin closer, the more he pulled away. This cycle intensified and became increasingly intense on an emotional level until the two split up after only about four months of dating. Both were devastated by the breakup because they cared deeply for one another, but they were unable to work through their differences in attachment strategies. The couple had the potential to help each other heal old wounds but, instead, they ultimately hurt one another emotionally.

 Danielle and Martin's story is just one example of how attachment strategies can play out in relationships and create distress. At some point, addictive behaviors may be part of this cycle. Take time to reflect and journal about how your attachment strategies have affected your close relationships and what role they play in your addiction.

 Before moving forward, review the information on the arousal template in *Facing the Shadow* and complete (exercises 7.9 through 7.17), Your Arousal Template Worksheets.

People with secure attachments are comfortable with closeness but also feel safe when they are not in the immediate proximity of a partner. That is, they are not threatened by either closeness or distance as they trust the distance is temporary.

People with insecure attachments, however, are distressed either by closeness or a perceived loss of closeness.

It is not difficult to see how sex, sexuality, and your arousal template can easily become entangled in this process. In *Facing the Shadow*, Carnes invites you to look at the relationships between sex, romance, and relationships. In your addiction, you likely saw sex as the most important of these three and, perhaps, as the primary (or even sole) expression of romance or relationships.

Attachment strategies interact here in ways that are important. If you have an anxious attachment strategy, you may have been using sex to validate that others are available to you. Pornography and one-night stands are poor substitutes for psychological intimacy, however, and may actually reinforce fears of abandonment.

If you have an avoidant attachment strategy, pornography, one-night stands, voyeurism, exhibitionism, frotteurism, and other behaviors all allow a pseudo-attachment in which you can feel a temporary connection to another without the psychological closeness and intimacy that you find threatening.

 Review your previous journaling about your primary attachment strategy and then respond to the following:

- How does this attachment strategy become a part of your sexuality, including your arousal template?

- In your addiction, did you use sex as a way to deepen psychological intimacy with another or as a way to avoid it?

This is heavy stuff. Ready for some good news? Theorists originally thought that attachment styles were formed in childhood and could not be changed. We now know that, while they are indeed heavily influenced by childhood experiences that cannot be "undone," attachment styles can change in adulthood, primarily through corrective experiences and healing relationships. This process is not a "quick fix" and involves ongoing work and healing through your relationships with others, including family, friends, and God.

While it is beyond our scope in this book to examine all of the work involved in the corrective experiences and healing that you need to become more secure in your attachment with others, we will look at your relationship with God as it relates to this work.

 Respond to the following:

- Review what you journaled in chapter 1 in the Attachment to God section. Based on what you have now learned, is there anything you would add or modify about your attachment to God?

- If you have an insecure attachment to God, is this primarily based on a negative view of yourself or a sense that God is not available to you?

- Consider your attachment to God in a different way by journaling your thoughts and feelings as you reflect on these questions:

  · God, do I matter to you?

  · Are you there for me?

  · Can I trust you?

  · Do you love me?

  · If I need you, will you respond to my needs?

- Reflect on your responses and whether you feel secure in your connection to God.

 Scriptures provide clear answers to these questions.

God, do I matter to you? Do you love me?

For God so loved the world that he gave his one and only Son, that whoever believes in him shall not perish but have eternal life.

JOHN 3:16

Are you there for me?

I waited patiently for the Lord;
he turned to me and heard my cry.
He lifted me out of the slimy pit,

Shadows of the Cross: A Christian Companion to *Facing the Shadow*

out of the mud and mire;
he set my feet on a rock
and gave me a firm place to stand.
He put a new song in my mouth,
a hymn of praise to our God.
PSALM 40:1–3A

Can I trust you?

The Lord is my strength and my shield; my heart trusts in him, and he helps me.
My heart leaps for joy, and with my song I praise him.
PSALM 28:7

May the God of hope fill you with all joy and peace as you trust in him,
so that you may overflow with hope by the power of the Holy Spirit.
ROMANS 15:13

If I need you, will you respond to my needs?

"The Lord will fight for you, and you only have to keep still."
EXODUS 14:14

While scripture provides clear answers to these questions, your acceptance of these truths may be more complicated. If you find yourself struggling to accept that God loves you without condition and that you can rest securely in His care, take time to meditate on the scriptures referenced here.

Feelings behind Addictive Processes

Although there is certainly a thinking component to our attachment strategies, emotions fuel the behaviors that comprise our attachment styles. To better understand how this occurs, consider the following examples:

- John often feared that he was not enough for his wife, Sara (negative view of self). To cope with his fear, he would often withdraw from tense situations, fearing he would say or do the wrong thing. Soon, he was withdrawing from Sara to look at pornography, which calmed his fears in the short term. In the long term, though, he became more withdrawn from Sara and increasingly irritable and angry.

- Carlos experienced high levels of anxiety and fear that his wife, Mariana, was going to leave him for another man. To assuage this fear, he was very controlling, dictating Mariana's every move and "keeping tabs" on what she was doing and to whom she was talking. At the same time, he found that he could calm himself by going to strip clubs and massage parlors, all while drinking heavily. At one point, Carlos accused Mariana of flirting with someone. When Mariana denied this, Carlos hit her. This happened in front of Mariana's parents, and Mariana's father and Carlos then got into a fist fight. Both men ended up with injuries and Mariana filed for divorce soon after. Carlos, devastated that he had lost Mariana, became very angry and resented Mariana for leaving. He was unable to see his role in the demise of his marriage and soon began acting out sexually on a daily basis.

- Haley experienced high levels of anxiety and fear that her husband, Mark, was not there for her. She complained to Mark that he should be home more, but spoke to him with anger and frustration rather than revealing her fears. Mark did not respond well to what he experienced as demands from his wife. Mark worked long hours and traveled a great deal. With two young children to care for, Haley felt unsupported and unloved, believing that she did not matter to Mark. When a man from her church began talking to her, she enjoyed the attention. The two began a texting relationship that started innocently but soon became flirtatious and, within weeks, the two were embroiled in an affair. Mark, whose great fear was of not being good enough for Haley (hence the avoidant behavior), was devastated when he discovered that his wife was cheating on him. Each continued to blame the other and all, including the children, suffered mightily through a contentious divorce.

As a recovering addict, you have emotions that are complex. Your addictive behaviors may have been an escape from painful emotions. If you were raised in a religious community, you may have received messages that it was not okay to feel angry, sad, or afraid. Of course, at times you did feel these things and this may have created a conflict within you. It is possible that you managed this conflict by denying your emotional experiences, isolating yourself in addictive behaviors to cope with feelings that felt unmanageable. Addictive sexual behavior may have become a chronic coping strategy, one that did help manage difficult emotions in the short term, but made things more difficult in the long term, as the emotions of anger, sadness, and fear only increased over time. Addictive sexual behavior, in a way, became your best friend—a friend who helped you cope with your emotions. This may have become part of your addictive cycle as you struggled to manage these increasingly emotional experiences.

In recovery, without the maladaptive coping strategy of sexually acting out at your disposal, you may still be struggling with emotions. There are two common types of struggles in early recovery:

- *Emotional hypo-arousal.* As a result of using addictive sexual behavior to manage emotions, you have "flatlined" emotionally and now experience only minimal emotions. While this means you may not feel much anger, sadness, or fear, you likely also do not experience much joy or peace.
- *Emotional hyper-arousal.* You feel overwhelmed at times by your emotions and are unsure what to do. Experiences of strong emotions may be connected to your impulses to act out, as the addicted brain tells you that you know how not to feel these unpleasant emotions.

In this way, you can think of emotions as water. If you are hypo-aroused emotionally, it is as if there is a massive dam that blocks the flow of the water. If you are hyper-aroused emotionally, it may feel like trying to bathe at the base of Niagara Falls or trying to drink water gushing out of a fire hose. Emotions are meant to flow freely, like a gentle stream or brook. Part of your long-term recovery work involves intentionally increasing (if you are emotionally blocked) or decreasing (if you are emotionally overwhelmed) your emotional experiences.

 Write about your emotional experiences by responding to the following:

1. As you look back at your time in active addiction, can you see ways in which you used addictive sexual behavior to cope with your emotions? If so, what emotions were you working to avoid?
2. How did your addictive sexual behavior affect your emotional life?
3. In recovery, what is your current experience of your emotional life?
4. What beliefs do you hold about anger, sadness, and fear?

Related to emotions, we have two great sources of knowledge: psychology and the life of Jesus. Increasingly, newer psychological models of change are emphasizing the importance of experience, including emotions, and the pitfalls of experiential avoidance. Psychologists tell us that anger, sadness, and fear are nothing compared to what happens when we consciously or unconsciously avoid our experiences and emotions. Emotions that are avoided do not simply go away. Instead, they build up in the body and potentially create great damage.

Perhaps Jesus was the great psychologist who knew this two thousand years earlier. Accounts of his life certainly portray him as peaceful and no one among us would characterize him as angry, sad, or fearful. Yet, at the same time, scripture tells us that, in his human form, Jesus had all of these emotional experiences:

- *Anger* (see John 2:14–16)—John's account of Jesus driving the money changers from the temple courts tells us that he "made a whip out of cords, and drove all from the temple courts." While Jesus was slow to anger in general and, in this instance his anger was wholly justified, he did indeed experience anger.

- *Sadness* (see John 11:35)—The shortest verse in the Bible tells us that "Jesus wept" at the death of Lazarus. Just a few verses prior to this, Jesus told his disciples that he would raise Lazarus from the dead. And a few verses later, he did exactly that. Though he knew that Lazarus would be raised from the dead, he was "greatly disturbed in spirit and deeply moved" (John 11:33) and wept.

- *Fear* (see Mark 14:32–36)—In one of the most striking accounts of how Jesus experienced human emotions, Jesus went to the garden of Gethsemane shortly before his arrest and crucifixion. Scripture tells us that he was "distressed and agitated (v. 33) and that he told Peter, James, and John, "I am deeply grieved, even to death." Although we can scarcely imagine what it would be like to know, as Jesus did, what the next hours were to bring to his human form, he seemed to be overwhelmed with both sadness and fear. His fear is captured again in verse 36 when he prays to God the Father, "Abba, Father, for you all things are possible; remove this cup from me." In his human fear, he asks that circumstances be changed. In the same breath, though, Jesus shows his divinity by saying, "Yet not what I want, but what you want."

Christ is a model of temperance, hope, and courage and, at the same time Jesus the man taught us how to experience our emotions. In these passages, Jesus teaches us how not to avoid our experiences, how to have the "serenity to accept the things [we] cannot change," and, in the end, how to accept God's will.

 With eyes, ears, and heart focused on the emotional experiences that Jesus was having, slowly and prayerfully reread Mark 14:32–36, reflecting on how Jesus did not strive to avoid his emotional experiences and how he spoke of his emotions to a small group of trusted friends (v. 34).

 Reflect on Jesus' emotional experiences. What does this teach you about your own emotional life?

Layers of Emotions ... And the Truth Will Set You Free

Emotions are complicated. As humans, we all struggle to understand our emotional experiences, maintain an ongoing awareness of our emotions, and know what to do when we are emotionally overwhelmed. As noted, Jesus modeled for us the importance of fully experiencing and expressing our emotions and sharing our emotions with others during difficult times.

In recovery, as you work to understand that your emotions are not the enemy, the process becomes even more complicated because our emotions are often multifaceted and layered. Mental health professionals speak of primary and secondary emotions. Simply stated, what we are honestly feeling at our core is our primary emotion. Yet, in our discomfort, we may unconsciously mask the primary emotion with a secondary emotion that feels psychologically safer. Consider the following examples:

- Angelo is driving on a crowded highway in the far right lane. A car comes up beside him quickly and starts to merge into his lane in front of Angelo. Angelo hits his brakes and the car merges in, missing his right front bumper by mere inches. Angelo extends a middle finger at the driver and screams profanities. What is he feeling at this moment? If we slow this scenario down, we can see that at the moment Angelo realizes the car is cutting in front of him, he experiences fear and panic. His heart rate accelerates and he gets a heavy shot of adrenaline into his system to prepare him to respond to the danger that has crossed his path. The primary emotion is fear, yet Angelo moves almost automatically to anger, reacts based on this anger, and may not even be aware of his fear.

- Chris and his wife talked mid-week about how busy they were and how they would find time to spend together over the weekend. Chris assumed this meant they would have sex but didn't communicate this to his wife. They spent some quality time together over the weekend and Chris kept thinking his wife would initiate sex. When she didn't, he became very angry at her and used his anger to justify watching pornography for several hours on Sunday night after she went to bed. Slowing this process down, we see that Chris was feeling fear that his wife didn't really love him and want him physically. As the weekend drew to a close, he also was feeling some sadness that they had not made love. Because these emotions made Chris feel very vulnerable, he moved quickly to resentment and anger at his wife, acted out from this place of anger, and had no awareness of his fear and sadness.

In both of these scenarios, anger is the secondary emotion and fear is the primary emotion. While this is a common pattern, it is important to know that it is not the only pattern. Anger can be a primary emotion, when it is a righteous anger such as Jesus in the temple courts. Similarly, sadness can be a secondary emotion. For example, when a child is abused, he or she may feel a righteous anger about being abused. Unable to express this anger without facing more abuse, however, the child becomes depressed, the sadness becoming a secondary reaction to the anger.

For many addicts, though, irritability, resentment, and anger become the secondary masks put on over their underlying emotions. As discussed earlier, you may struggle with fear of abandonment or fear of being inadequate. You may feel great sadness over things you have done in the past. If you are not watchful, you may lose contact with these deeper emotions and "escape" to a secondary emotion of anger or resentment.

When you are aware only of your secondary emotions and are acting from this awareness, you are not in touch with reality. Working on emotional maturity does not mean being emotionless. Rather, it means having the courage to access and experience your primary emotions. Emotional maturity means putting an end to "the ways of childhood" (I Corinthians 13:11). The reality is that underneath your irritability, anger, or resentment, there is a truth. Part of the emotional work of recovery is slowing down your emotional process so that you can experience the truth of your deeper emotional life.

 Read John 8:32:

"Then you will know the truth, and the truth will set you free."

When you are only conscious of your secondary emotions, you are not free because you do not know the full truth. When you slow down your emotional process, however, and access and experience your primary emotions, you discover a truth that these emotions do not define you and that they can be released and healed. As you do your work of deepening your relationship with your emotions, as it appears that Jesus did, you begin to recognize the following:

- Painful emotions do not last forever.
- If you allow yourself to fully experience emotions of anger and sadness, they can be turned over to God and released.
- You may need support from others to work through emotions.
- At times, you need the support of trusted others to release your primary emotions; without support, you may escape to a secondary emotion.

Shadows of the Cross: A Christian Companion to *Facing the Shadow*

Deepening your relationship with your primary emotions will set you free. You will grow in your ability to experience and express your primary emotions to healthy people in healthy ways and, in so doing, experience healing. Additionally, you cannot surrender to God that to which you still cling through suppression or denial. Just as important, however, accessing and experiencing your primary emotions will give you *vital* information about what you need from others and from God. For example, if Chris had realized that he was feeling sad about not making love to his wife and feeling some fear that she might not want him physically, he could have communicated these things to her. This act, in turn, likely would have drawn her closer, as she would have realized how much Chris loved and wanted her and how his old fear of inadequacy, which stemmed from his difficult childhood, was getting triggered. Such an interaction would have left both Chris and his wife feeling more secure and connected. Because Chris only accessed his secondary emotions of anger and resentment, however, he acted in a way that increased the distance between he and his wife, and only left him feeling more shameful and inadequate.

 Reflect on your own experience of primary and secondary emotions by responding to the following:

- Were there any patterns in your addiction that were similar to what Chris experienced, where you were unable to access, experience, and act from your primary emotions? What did you do instead?

- As you grow in recovery, what are you aware of *right now* about challenges you experience in your emotional life?

 Take time to pray for God's guidance as you grow in your emotional awareness. Specifically

- Pray that God will help you know the truth of your emotional experience and that this truth will set you free.

- Pray that you will access the support you need when you need it, whether from friends, sponsors, therapists, group members, or others.

Spiritual disciplines or practices, while primarily intended to help you communicate with God, also may support you in accessing suppressed emotions (if you struggle more with emotional hypo-arousal) or in calming overwhelming emotions (if you are hyper-aroused emotionally).

Locating Emotions in the Body

One of Jesus' gifts seems to be clarity about what he was feeling in any given moment and how he used this awareness to determine his actions.

Emotions will drive your actions! The only question is whether this will happen at an unconscious or conscious level. If you are aware of your emotional experiences, you can do the following:

- Realize that you are not your emotions.
- Be aware that emotions are temporary.
- Allow yourself to experience your emotions rather than repress and avoid them.
- Make conscious choices about actions rather than allowing emotions to unconsciously drive your response.

Try the following activity:

First, find a comfortable and quiet place where you will not be distracted for the duration of this activity. Position yourself comfortably in a chair that allows you to sit with your spine straight.

Throughout this activity, you will breathe in a way that is slightly more full and deep than your usual breath. This will help you as you "look" into the body to learn about emotions. Also, when distracting thoughts creep in, just take a breath and return your awareness to the experience in your body.

Begin by closing your eyes, breathing deeply, and saying a short prayer asking God to guide your awareness through this activity.

As you continue to breathe deeply, ask God to show you what anger feels like in your body. Stay with this until you get a clear sense of how your body experiences anger, but do not linger. As soon as you are clear about the embodied experience of anger, slow your breath a bit and ask God to help you return to a peaceful state in your body. Take time to breathe in the peace that surpasses all understanding.

Next, continue to breathe deeply, asking God to show you what sadness feels like in your body. Again, stay with this only long enough to get a clear sense of how your body experiences sadness. As soon as you are clear about the embodied sense of sadness, ask God to instill in you a hope for the future that will clear the sadness from your body. Take time to breathe in the hope that comes from God.

Next, continue to breathe deeply, asking God to show you what fear feels like in your body. Do not allow this to grow too much, just enough to be clear of how your body experiences fear. As soon as you are clear about the embodied sense of fear, breathe deeply but slowly, breathing in the love of God whose perfect love casts out fear.

Now, close out this activity by breathing slowly in and out, allowing yourself to rest in the arms of a loving God. Finally, say a prayer of gratitude for anything you learned in this activity.

 Draw an outline of a human body. Now place dots where you felt anger, sadness, and fear. Then, write words, phrases, or images that describe what each of these emotions feels like in your body.

Recognize that as the embodied sensations of anger, sadness, and fear occur, you can consciously breathe in the gift from God that serves to calm that emotion. For anger, you can breathe in peace:

Peace I leave with you; my peace I give you. I do not give to you as the world gives. Do not let your hearts be troubled and do not be afraid.

JOHN 14:27

For sadness, you can breathe in hope:
But those who hope in the Lord will renew their strength.
They will soar on wings like eagles;
they will run and not grow weary, they will walk and not be faint.

ISAIAH 40:31

For fear, you can breathe in love:
There is no fear in love. But perfect love drives out fear,
because fear has to do with punishment.
The one who fears is not made perfect in love.

I JOHN 4:18

Faith and the Addiction Neuropathways

 Before moving on, make sure you have read and reflected on the Addiction Neuropathways section in chapter 7 of *Facing the Shadow*, focusing on the neuropathways that seem most relevant for you.

As a Christian, you are blessed with spiritual neuropathways. If you will accept and practice the principles of the spiritual neuropathways, they will serve to counter and, we believe, heal the addiction neuropathways that have formed. Part of what makes the brain an amazing creation of God is the ability of the brain to reorganize itself by forming new neural connections throughout life.

Arousal

Carnes describes the process through which high arousal becomes a way to deal with pain. Through the spiritual disciplines and activities of this book, you are developing healthy ways to deal with the pain of the past and future pains as they occur.

In time, with a consistent program of recovery and spiritual discipline, you will begin to untangle the fusion of pleasure and danger. You will come to accept that God can and will restore you to a place of sobriety, sanity, and security, a place in which you will be grateful for the simplicity of your life.

The Serenity Prayer can be helpful here. While the first twenty-seven words are usually spoken at Twelve Step meetings, there is guidance for dealing with the arousal neuropathway in the latter part of the full version of the Serenity Prayer:

> *Accepting hardship as the path to peace.*
> *Taking, as He did, this sinful world as it is,*
> *Not as I would have it.*
> *Trusting that He will make all things right*
> *if I surrender to His will.*
> *That I may be reasonably happy in this life,*
> *And supremely happy with Him forever in the next.*

One of the gifts of recovery is accepting life as it comes, which is, of course, not always as you would like it to be. With recovery comes acceptance of "what is" in your life. Rather than seeking the "next hit" of sexual pleasure, you learn to appreciate being "reasonably happy."

Numbing

The addiction pathway here is formed to provide an analgesic experience to the brain—that is, a way to numb the pain. As Carnes described in *Facing the Shadow*, the "hole to be filled, however, is bottomless." We described the God-shaped hole in chapter 1 to explain how your addictive sexual behaviors were your desperate but misguided reaches for God.

Here we can think about the wisdom found in the Twelve Steps: that only God can restore you to sanity but that only occurs when you truly come to believe that it can and then turn your will and your life over to the care of God, followed by working an active program of recovery, seeking communion with God through meditation and prayer, and serving others who struggle.

In the care of a loving God whose love knows no conditions or limits, you can heal the pain from your past. As that pain becomes less palpable, your need to

Shadows of the Cross: A Christian Companion to *Facing the Shadow*

numb out through addictive sexual behavior will lessen as the numbing neuropathways weaken.

Fantasy

When you experience a fantasy of any kind, it is an expression of your soul's deepest longing. Fantasies are symbolic, much like the images and experiences that we have in dreams. When you have a sexual fantasy, then, it usually is not about sex at all. If you have frequent sexual fantasies, you likely are expressing your soul's deepest longing to be more connected to God and to other people in psychologically and spiritually intimate ways. Michael John Cusick referred to the compulsive use of Internet pornography as "surfing for God," supporting the notion that these fantasies are a contaminated expression of healthy longings.[2]

Knowing that sexual fantasies are an expression of a longing for God, you can "be with" your fantasies in a different way. Rather than shaming yourself for another sexual fantasy or snapping a rubber band on your wrist to "punish" yourself for having the fantasy, as a Christian in recovery you can use the fantasy to increase your awareness. When a sexual fantasy occurs, take a few minutes to stop and journal (or reflect in your mind if journaling is not an option in that moment) about what your soul truly desires. You can, of course, practice an awareness of your longing for God without using a sexual fantasy as a portal. At the same time, though, sexual fantasies are "alerts" letting you know that you are feeling disconnected in some way. Remember also that impulses to act out sexually are actually fantasies of a sort and also can serve to heighten your awareness of your longing for God. Over time and with practice, fantasies become less frequent and intense, and when they do occur, you will automatically shift your awareness to your longing for God. There is an adage that "Time heals all wounds." In the case of sexual fantasies, a better adage is "In time, all wounds can be healed." It is the practice of communing with God, with fantasies as the "warning system" or early detection system that you are disconnected, that will bring you into closer communion with God. As you are in closer communion with God, fantasies will decrease, though you likely will experience sexual fantasy intermittently throughout your life.

Deprivation

As a Christian, you need to pay particular attention to the process of deprivation. The following are examples of deprivation:

- Ahmad felt deep shame over his history of addictive sexual behaviors and made an unconscious decision not to have fun. Anytime he began to laugh, enjoy time with friends, or enjoy a healthy experience, he would immediately go into a shame spiral, telling himself, "I don't deserve to be having fun." Then he would remove himself from the pleasant situation.

- Sandy began her recovery by reading through the Twelve Step process. As a Christian, she read about serving others in Step Twelve and thought this was what Jesus wanted for her in recovery. Unfortunately, though, Sandy did not work a thorough program of recovery and started to compulsively serve others in her church. She gave to others to the point that she was exhausted and depleted emotionally and spiritually. She soon relapsed.

- Charlie, early in recovery and struggling through multiple lapses in sobriety, took it upon himself to harshly criticize public figures caught in sex scandals and publicly proclaim the evils of promiscuity in his church. Even as Charlie did these public "purges," he was privately continuing to "binge" on pornography and prostitutes.

As a Christian, you deserve to have fun, to laugh, and to enjoy life. Remember that in John 10:10b, Jesus said:

"I have come that they may have life, and have it to the full."

Similarly, while you are called to help others, both as a Christian and as a recovering person, it also is *critical* that you realize that as a child of God, you *must* take care of yourself, particularly in the early stages of recovery. Some would call this selfish, but this is a false perspective. As a person in recovery, you are becoming increasingly less selfish than when you were active in your addiction. Even so, it is vital that you realize the need for "sacred selfishness," a phrase coined by Bud Harris.[3] Sacred selfishness recognizes that self-care is a critical aspect of being available to serve others. Scripture affords us countless examples of Jesus practicing sacred selfishness, caring for himself by taking time to meditate, pray, and spend time alone with his heavenly Father.

 Reflect on the Addiction Neuropathways information in *Facing the Shadow* and the supplementary material you have just read here. Consider the four addiction neuropathways (arousal, numbing, fantasy, and deprivation). Then respond to the following:

- How do you think these neuropathways influenced you when you were actively in your addiction?

- What changes have you already experienced at this point in your recovery?

- What changes remain works-in-process that need ongoing work and prayer?

Spiritual Disciplines

Continue your daily spiritual practice plan and consider making some additions to it. Following is one spiritual practice that you might find particularly helpful to integrate into your daily plan to support your continued healing.

Breath Prayer

Once again, a breath prayer is a prayer of six to twelve syllables that is repeated. Develop a breath prayer you can use to counter fantasies, euphoric recall, or impulses to act out. Practice this breath prayer before you actually need it.

As you develop your breath prayer, remember that these images and embodied feelings are a misguided attempt to connect to God. Accordingly, make your breath prayer an expression of this longing. We encourage you to develop your own breath prayer but some examples include

1. Lord Jesus Christ, Son of God, have mercy on me (a shortened version of the Jesus prayer).
2. I belong to you, O Lord.
3. Holy Spirit, breathe in me.
4. Speak Lord, your servant is listening.

Chapter Ten

Where is Your Support?

This chapter parallels chapter 8 (Where is Your Support?) in *Facing the Shadow*. Read chapter 8 in Facing the Shadow in its entirety before beginning this chapter.

Early recovery is primarily about coping and community. Although we have already talked about the importance of Twelve Step communities and involving key people in your recovery, the primary emphasis has been on building coping strategies to help you stay sexually sober and on the path to recovery and sexual health. This chapter focuses on Christian-based recovery and support.

Scripture is clear that we are meant to be in healthy communities supporting one another and that we are to be active participants in those communities.

Read the following Bible verses:

And the prayer offered in faith will make the sick person well;
the Lord will raise them up. If they have sinned, they will be forgiven.
Therefore confess your sins to each other and pray for each other so that
you may be healed. The prayer of a righteous person is powerful and effective.
JAMES 5:15–16

Whoever conceals their sins does not prosper,
but the one who confesses and renounces them finds mercy.
PROVERBS 28:13

You, my brothers and sisters, were called to be free. But do not use your
freedom to indulge the flesh; rather, serve one another humbly in love. For the entire law
is fulfilled in keeping this one command: "Love your neighbor as yourself."
GALATIANS 5:13–14

As a Christian, you are called to be in healthy community. Remember that even Jesus traveled with a small group.

A Modern-Day Parable: The Good Samaritan

The Good Samaritan (Luke 10:25–37) is one of the most familiar biblical stories. There are many versions of the Good Samaritan parable and each is written to teach about how to be a good neighbor. The story of the Good Samaritan could be compared to a person in recovery, someone who is working his or her Twelfth Step, which is about ministering and serving others. On the flip side, what of those people who are receiving the help? Are they willing to accept help? Do they recognize help when it comes along? Are they able to set aside negative emotions and reactions toward others, and allow someone to help them unconditionally?

As you read the story of Lisa, consider the following:

- "Who is my 'good neighbor'?"
- "How do I recognize them?"
- "How have I ignored them?"

Lisa lived in the same small town where she grew up. Married to her high school sweetheart, she was raising their two children in the same church she had been a member of since birth. She and her husband sent their children to the same schools they had attended. In the minds of the town's people, Lisa was a pillar of the community, serving in the church, leading women's social groups, and volunteering for school functions. But Lisa had a secret. Her disowned internal sadness and frustrations had carried her into a world of love and sex addiction. She began at first by flirting with other men, but this quickly escalated into a series of emotional and sexual affairs. She knew she needed help so she did the one thing taught to her by her church and parents—she prayed that God would stop these thoughts and behaviors.

But the thoughts and behaviors did not stop; in fact, they became worse. This frustrated Lisa even more until she finally became angry and resentful toward God. "Why are You not fixing me?" she shouted out one day during her prayer time.

Suddenly, the phone rang. Looking at the caller ID, Lisa thought, "Oh no… it's that nosy old lady down the street. She is always asking me over for morning coffee. Doesn't she know how busy I am with the kids' activities, cleaning the house, and running errands for the committees I have joined?"

But Lisa answered the phone and her side of the conversation went like this: "Hello, Mrs. Jones."

"No, I cannot come over for coffee this morning."

Yes, I promise to see you soon."

"Is there anything I can do to help you?"

"No, not really…I am fine."

"I appreciate that you want to pray for me, but there isn't anything I need prayer for right now."

"Yes, see you soon. Take care of yourself."

"Good-bye."

Later in the day, Lisa was at the grocery store. As was the weekly norm, she checked out her groceries at Mary's counter. Mary was always friendly and helpful. She had worked at the grocery store for years, as had Brent. Brent always smiled at Lisa and offered to carry her groceries to the car. His smile was warm and friendly, and he always asked about the family, kept up with Lisa's community involvement, and expressed his gratitude to her for all she did for others. But today, he sensed the sadness in Lisa and he asked if she was okay.

"Why is everyone getting into my business today?" thought Lisa, who was becoming more irritable as the day went along.

"Thank you for asking, Brent, but really I am fine. Just a little tired today," Lisa politely replied.

Driving home, Lisa thought about Mrs. Jones, Mary, and Brent. "How could I ever talk to anyone about my problems? God, please help me! I feel that I am going crazy, but I am trying my best to hold myself together. I cannot let people know my true self. I would be the talk of the town, and the embarrassment of it all would take me and my family down a rough and unforgiving path."

That afternoon, Lisa's children, Tammy and Joe, came running in from school, smiling and anxious to tell their mom about the events of the school day. Lisa listened as she always did, but today she struggled to stay focused on the kids' stories. She fed them snacks of cookies and milk. Tammy finished her snack and her stories, then hurried out to play with her neighbor friends. But seven-year-old Joe stayed behind.

"Mommy," said Joe, "why have you been crying?"

Lisa had no idea Joe had noticed her tears. "Joe, Mommy is okay. Sometimes adults get sad and cry. Please don't worry about me."

Then Joe said, "Mommy, my Sunday School teacher told us that when we are sad or need help, God will send people to help us. Maybe God will send someone to help you."

"From the mouths of babes," Lisa thought. Lisa grabbed Joe and hugged him hard. "Thank you, Joe, for listening to your Sunday School teacher and for teaching Mommy about God's wonderful mercy."

That afternoon, Lisa went to her computer and searched for support groups that could help her. To her surprise, she found a Sex and Love Addiction Anonymous (SLAA) group that met every Tuesday afternoon in a building close to her home. Lisa bowed her head and confessed to God, "I need help. I am guilty of asking You to fix me when I am not doing anything to fix myself. Please give me the courage I need to attend this group, and an open mind to listen for the help."

The next day, Tuesday, Lisa walked into her first SLAA meeting. Shy at first, she suddenly felt peace and calm as she realized she was among friends. There in the circle sat Mrs. Jones, Mary, and Brent, the three people who had asked to help her and whose help she had refused.

And she knew … All along, God had sent her the help she had prayed for, but she was too righteous and proud to recognize it.

Over the next few months, Mrs. Jones became Lisa's sponsor. Mary and Brent continued to provide empathic and compassionate support. With help, Lisa began her recovery and ultimately found the life she longed for, a life of peace, harmony, and balance.

 The moral of the story is we can always trust in God when we commit our lives to Him. However, we must remain open minded to the ways He chooses to help us. Focus on your recovery by responding to the following in your journal:

- Who has offered support to you that you have refused?

- What feelings come up for you when someone asks you about your sadness, anger, frustrations, and problems in your life?

- Where do you believe these feelings come from? Could your shame and guilt over past actions be leading you to resist your emotional experiences and the help and support of others?

- Could you be hanging on to some resistance to change the things in your life that are causing pain and sadness?

The Biggest Lie?

Quite possibly the biggest lie that any addict tells himself or herself is: *I can do this myself.*

 When you were actively in your addiction, did you ever acknowledge that you had a problem, either to yourself or to another person, only to cling to the lie that you could handle your "little problem" by yourself? The scriptures are quite clear that we cannot do "this" without help.

 First, scripture plainly tells us that we need God. Read Proverbs 3:5–6:

Trust in the LORD with all your heart
and lean not on your own understanding;
in all your ways submit to him,
and he will make your paths straight.

In addition to our needing God, scripture tells us we need other people. We are called to gather together and encourage one another in difficult times. Hebrews 10:24–25a says:

And let us consider how we may provoke one another to love and good deeds, not neglect-
ing to meet together, as is the habit of some, but encouraging one another.

Indeed, a community of Christian fellowship and love are vital aspects of growing in Christ, as evidenced in these two verses:

So in Christ we, though many, form one body, and each member belongs to all the others.
ROMANS 12:5

Consequently, you are no longer foreigners and strangers, but fellow citizens with God's
people and also members of his household, built on the foundation of the apostles and
prophets, with Christ Jesus himself as the chief cornerstone.
EPHESIANS 2:19–20

It seems important, then, that you actively participate in a healthy Christian community.

Twelve Step Programs

In *Facing the Shadow*, Carnes delineates the major Twelve Step programs for sex addiction. In addition to these, there are a growing number of Twelve Step programs for sex addiction specifically tailored to Christian men and women in recovery. They include: RSA ministries (rsaministries.org); Overcomers Outreach (overcomersoutreach.org); and Celebrate Recovery (celebraterecovery.com).

You will need to decide whether it is necessary for your Twelve Step group to be a Christian group or whether you can find help in a group that is not explicitly Christian. To some extent, this may be determined by what is available in your area. If both options are nearby, we believe that this is a matter of personal choice. Any healthy Twelve Step group will respect your religious convictions. In short, if a group does not respect your religious beliefs, it is not a healthy group and you should find a different group—quickly!

Twelve Step groups should provide experience, strength, and hope. Within each of the various fellowships mentioned in *Facing the Shadow* and here, there are healthy groups and unhealthy groups. Just as with individual church communities, these are gatherings created by humans; thus, some will be healthier than others.

Furthermore, just as your fellowship should respect your religious convictions, so too should anyone you trust enough to be a sponsor. Be sure that the person you ask to be your sponsor can respect and support your beliefs.

Privacy versus Secrecy

The slogan "You are only as sick as your secrets" is heard often within Twelve Step communities and for good reason: it is a vital truth in recovery. Indeed, it is essential to confess to others your struggles and sins. At the same time, it is critical to be discerning about whom you should confess to. As discussed in chapter 5, we have seen many men and women confess their sexual addiction within their religious communities, either to individuals or to the congregation, with varying results. In some cases, the community has warmly embraced them as children of God who struggle as all children of God do. In other cases, however, individuals and groups in the church have been critical and judgmental, condemning the individual and, in all too many cases, asking the person to leave the religious community.

Such was the case for the alcoholic many years ago, before AA and other groups helped spread the knowledge that alcoholism was more complex than simply a moral issue. Perhaps someday sex addicts will be viewed as alcoholics now are. The reality, though, is that we are not there yet.

For now, it is critical to understand the difference between privacy and secrecy. *Privacy* is about setting healthy boundaries around whom you talk to about your struggles. *Secrecy* is about hiding information from everyone. For example, imagine that you find yourself struggling with an increase in fantasies and recall of previous behaviors but you have thus far been able to avoid any "bottom line" behaviors that would constitute a relapse. What do you do? In this instance, secrecy would involve not telling anyone. By keeping your struggles a secret, you greatly increase your risk for relapse. You are, indeed, only as sick as your secrets. Talking openly and honestly about your struggles in a Twelve Step meeting or to your sponsor or therapist are all healthy behaviors.

Privacy, on the other hand, is not about *whether* to talk to others, but about using good judgment in choosing with whom you talk. For example, many clergy are well equipped to support parishioners who are struggling with addictive sexual behaviors. Unfortunately, others are poorly trained and more likely to respond in unhelpful ways. While it is critical *not* to keep secrets and to have people in your life with whom you can talk, the reality is that you cannot "untell" someone once you have disclosed your addiction. If you are confident that there are individuals in your church, including your clergy, in whom you can confide, consider yourself fortunate and use these resources. On the other hand, if you are not positive that your religious community can support you in your recovery, then rely on your Twelve Step group, therapy group, therapist, and sponsor as your allies in recovery and regard your religious community as your spiritual support group.

 Reflect on the role of secrecy and privacy in your current life. What are healthy choices for you to support your recovery?

A Moral Imperative

While it is imperative that you have support from others, this may or may not come from members of your religious community. The focus on this discussion thus far has been on finding the support you need for your recovery. What about the needs of your religious community, though? Do they have a "right" to know about your addiction? In general, we believe that your addiction is between you, God, and the small group of people (such as your therapist, sponsor, therapy group, and support group) who can support your recovery in healthy ways. At the same time, if you pose *any* risk to the community, you have a moral imperative to protect the needs of the community. For example, if you have had sexual relationships with people in your religious community, you might find someone who can serve as an "on-site accountability partner," keeping you honest while also respecting your privacy. If you have an arousal template that includes children, step down from any work that puts you in close contact with children and adolescents on an ongoing basis and create accountability with a safe person. If you are unsure who is a safe person, talk to your therapist or sponsor. The point here is simple.

 Reflect on any responsibilities you have to your religious community to make changes that will protect the welfare of the community. This is done in the spirit of "an ounce of prevention is worth a pound of cure." If you are unclear, seek wise counsel.

Use the following process to help you make decisions regarding issues of privacy and secrecy:

1. Take some time to pray that God will lead your decisions in this activity.
2. Create four columns in your journal with the headings
    a) Yes, Full Story
    b) Yes, without Details
    c) Unsure
    d) No
3. Under each heading, list the names of people (family, friends, work colleagues, church friends, church staff, and so on) who should hear your full story, people who should know you are struggling with an addiction but without details, people whom you are unsure what you should tell, and people whom you should not tell about your addiction.
4. Make sure that your first list (Yes, Full Story) is inclusive enough to avoid secrets. This list should include your Twelve Step group, therapy group, therapist, and/or sponsor.
5. The second group (Yes, without Details) should include people whom you may wish to know that you have an addiction so they can pray specifically for your recovery. You can choose which people to tell only that you have "an addiction" and which to tell that you have a "sex addiction." If people ask for details, you can tell them that you are not yet ready to talk about the details and ask them to respect your privacy.
6. The third group (Unsure) should include people whom you do not know what to tell or whether you should tell anything. Recognize that you cannot "untell" someone when their reaction is undesirable, choose not to tell those people *until* you are clear which of the other columns they fit in.
7. The fourth group (No) are people who you are clear will not support your recovery.

After completing your list, share it with a therapist or sponsor.

Committing to Use Your Support Network

Having a network that can support you in your spiritual study, disciplines, and recovery is a critical part of your recovery plan. This is only part of the battle, though. You have to use it! People with strong support networks who failed to use them and later relapsed report that:

- "I thought I could handle it myself."
- "It just seemed like a little slip. I thought I could pull it back together."
- "I was ashamed of my slip and isolated myself."
- "By the time I relapsed, I had already isolated myself from my support network for several weeks."

Here are a couple of "tricks" that might help you use your support network when you need it most:

- **Positive practice.** Practice "checking in" with your support network when your recovery is very strong; that is, when you need support the least. Having practiced reaching out to your support network, you will be more likely to use these resources when you are struggling with your sobriety.
- **Accountability around "checking in."** Ask an accountability partner (such as your sponsor, therapy group, or therapist) to hold you accountable for routinely checking in, using a mutually agreed upon plan for frequency of check-ins. In this way, in addition to creating accountability around sobriety, you are creating accountability around recovery-related behaviors.

Spiritual Disciplines

Continue your daily spiritual practice plan. You might find some spiritual practices particularly helpful at this point in your recovery. Integrate these practices into your daily plan as best supports your continued healing.

Eleventh Step Prayer

The Eleventh Step directs you to improve your conscious contact with God through prayer and meditation, praying only for knowledge of God's will for your life and the courage to act in accordance with God's will.

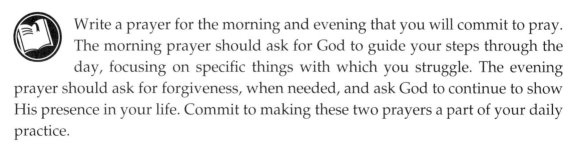 Write a prayer for the morning and evening that you will commit to pray. The morning prayer should ask for God to guide your steps through the day, focusing on specific things with which you struggle. The evening prayer should ask for forgiveness, when needed, and ask God to continue to show His presence in your life. Commit to making these two prayers a part of your daily practice.

Daily Examination of Consciousness

Use the daily examination to reflect on how you used (or did not use) your support network in the day. Use this practice to attend to issues of secrecy and isolation, which may be a red flag for a relapse.

Service

Serving others is a spiritual act. Jesus himself said, "I am among you as one who serves" (Luke 22:27b). Look for ways to serve others in both your recovery community and your religious community.

Submission

Scripture directs you to "Submit yourselves, then, to God" (James 4:7). Jesus' last words before his death on the cross were "Father, into your hands I commit my spirit" (Luke 23:46). When you isolate yourself from others and keep secrets, you are failing to submit to a program of recovery. Develop a daily breath prayer (six to twelve syllables) of submission. Examples include

- God, into your hands I commit my spirit.
- Father, I surrender all to your will.
- Abba, not my will but thine be done.

Chapter Eleven
Where Do I Go from Here?

 This chapter parallels chapter 9 (What Makes for Long-Term Success?) in *Facing the Shadow*. The two chapters should be read and worked through concurrently.

Therefore, with minds that are alert and fully sober, set your hope on the grace to be brought to you when Jesus Christ is revealed at his coming. As obedient children, do not conform to the evil desires you had when you lived in ignorance. But just as he who called you is holy, so be holy in all you do; for it is written: "Be holy, because I am holy."

I PETER 1: 13–16

Thomas Merton said the way we have structured our lives, we spend our whole life climbing up the ladder of supposed success, and when we get to the top of the ladder, we realize it is leaning against the wrong wall—and there is nothing at the top. To return to the place of inherent abundance, you have to let go of all of the false agendas, unreal goals, and images of a false self. It is all about letting go.

In many respects, the Christian spiritual journey is more about unlearning than learning because the deepest you, the part of you in full communion with the Holy Spirit, already knows.

 Read I John 2:20–21:

But you have an anointing from the Holy One, and all of you know the truth. I do not write to you because you do not know the truth, but because you do know it and because no lie comes from the truth.

Reflect on the Bible verse. Specifically

- What does it mean to you that you have an anointing from the Holy One?
- What does John mean when he writes, "all of you know the truth"?
- What does it mean to you that "no lie comes from the truth"?

The focus of this final chapter, then, is on integrating all that you have learned through this book and accessing the "deepest you" who already knows what you need to be sexually healthy.

 Read chapter 9 of *Facing the Shadow* in its entirety. Be sure to read through the lists of tasks and performables, focusing primarily on the first seven tasks.

 Take note of tasks and performables that you feel are solidly complete, those you have done but that need more attention, and those yet to be completed. As Carnes notes, the tasks and performables are tested and true guides to the path of recovery.

Strengthening the Spiritual Life
Modern-Day Parable—The Lost Musician

The following is a modern-day version of Jesus' Parable of the Good Shepherd (Luke 15:3–7). Tiffany loved to sing. "Music quiets my soul," she would say to her therapist, Dr. Duncan, during her weekly individual sessions. She had been going to therapy since her parents caught her using drugs the previous summer. Her shame led her to begin cutting her arms and legs. Dr. Duncan was a good man with a kind voice and a gentle nature. To relate to the musical side of Tiffany, he would refer to the "music behind her words" when he helped her reframe her negative and self-destructive thoughts. Tiffany knew she was getting better, both emotionally and physically.

But Tiffany's world stood still one day. While traveling with her church's youth choir, the bus stopped to get gas and the bus driver allowed the kids to get off the bus. "Everyone is to be back on this bus in fifteen minutes. We have a long trip ahead of us and it appears we are running a bit behind."

Chattering and laughing, everyone got off the bus. Quickly, the gas station attendant behind the counter became overwhelmed with kids buying sodas, candy, gum, and magazines. "How many people are traveling with your group?" the attendant asked. "Oh, we are a church choir group. There are one hundred members traveling to Dallas, TX, for our state championship choir competition," answered Sally, one of Tiffany's friends. She and Sally had been friends since grade school and had gone through many childhood traumas together. Both had parents who divorced when they were very young, both struggled in school, and both feared not fitting in. So, naturally, their friendship held a tight bond not easily broken.

"See you on the bus, Tiffany," said Sally. "I am going on to get our seats. Don't be late. Mr. Thompson said we were leaving in fifteen minutes."

"Yeah, I heard him. I'm coming," said Tiffany. But standing in line to pay for her food, she felt the need to go to the bathroom. "I'll go quickly. Surely the bus will not leave without me," Tiffany thought with confidence.

But the ladies bathroom was small and the line was long. After waiting patiently, Tiffany finally had her turn. "Whew, that took a long time," she thought. Picking up her sack of food, she headed out the door … and stood still. Tears began to flood her eyes. The church bus was *gone*! "This can't be happening to me," she cried. "How could they leave me? What will I do now?"

She sat down on the side of the curb, tucked her knees under her arms, and laid her head down. "Lord, I have tried so hard to do the right thing. But right now, I feel that I am being punished for all my past mistakes: the drugs, cutting, getting bad grades at school. When will the pain stop? When will bad things stop happening to me?" Then, right on schedule, her dark side began to take over her thoughts, creating a storm of negativity inside. "Should I use or should I cut to stop this pain that is driving me mad?" she pondered.

But suddenly, the skills she was learning in therapy rescued her. She knew how to reframe her negative thoughts into positive ones. Dr. Duncan had also instructed her to sing some of her favorite hymns. As she sang, Tiffany felt a peace and calmness flood over her like waves rushing to the shore covering the sand. Closing her eyes and tilting her face to the heavens, she imagined singing to God one of her favorite songs, "I love you Lord and I lift my voice to worship you Lord. Oh my soul, rejoice." She sang over and over until the roar of a motor and screech of the brakes made her stop singing and open her eyes. The bus! They came back. And all the kids were screaming with joy, "We found her—we found Tiffany!"

Mr. Thompson ran over and hugged her. "Girl, you scared us to death! We have been so worried. Can you forgive us for leaving you? Believe me, it was not intentional." Smiling from ear to ear and overcome with emotions, Tiffany could hardly speak but answered by nodding yes. Finally, her words came to her and she whispered to him, "You came back for me." Laughing heartily, Mr. Thompson hugged her again. "Of course we came back. You are part of us. Even though we are 100 strong, without everyone on board, our choir is not complete. You, my dear

Tiffany, are very important to all of us."

Through the help of music and her therapist, Tiffany had learned ways to calm her mind. God had sent people into her life to help her make sense of a confused and senseless world. At the end of the day, she found peace.

Although some question the origin of the statement, C. K. Chesterton is often credited with the following quote:

Every man who knocks on the door of a brothel is looking for God.

Whatever the source, this statement presents a deep Truth. Your sexual addiction is a wayward manifestation of your deepest longing—to know God and to be in full communion with his Presence and his Will for your life.; to know, without a doubt in your mind or your heart, that you are a Child of God.

All of the psychological work that you are doing is vital to your recovery. We have seen many addicts who tried to ignore the psychological work of recovery and make recovery solely a spiritual process. Inevitably, they fail. The term "spiritual bypass" describes this approach. People who are in spiritual bypass overlook the vital psychological work that is part of the healing spiritual journey. They are susceptible to the teachings of charismatic leaders and often avoid the emotional pain of their healing work. While we believe in miracles, we also believe that God calls us to do our part in the recovery process. Expecting deliverance without doing the work of recovery is like expecting to win the lottery without bothering to buy a ticket!

At the same time, we have seen many addicts in recovery who ignore the spiritual aspects of recovery and focus solely on psychological healing. Their work, too, is incomplete. Early recovery is very much about strengthening your coping resources and building a supportive healing community. For *long-term* recovery, though, more is needed. Long-term recovery involves the unfolding of the rest of your life as a recovering addict. While the core principles and practices of recovery remain in place, when you are no longer "white-knuckling" to stay sober, your mind and heart can begin to acknowledge the deeper sustaining work of long-term recovery, of co-creating with God the life you were born to live, and of honoring your deepest longing for God in healthy ways.

Press On

You are a work in progress. It is simply the human condition. The words "whole," "healing," and "holy" all derive from the same root word. This is your path now as a Christian in recovery. To become more whole, to heal what has been broken, and to become more holy are all the same process.

Yet, at the same time, it also is the human condition to lament why we are where we are in the present moment, to negatively judge ourselves for not being more whole, healed, and holy *right now*. We fill our self-talk with *shoulds*, *oughts*, and *musts* to deride ourselves harshly. Scripture calls us to accept that we are, as yet, incomplete and that we can surrender the past and live in the moment, with our eyes and hearts attuned to who God is gently calling us to become in the future. This is particularly evident in a letter Paul wrote to the church at Philippi:

> *Not that I have already obtained all this, or have already arrived at my goal,*
> *but I press on to take hold of that for which Christ Jesus took hold of me.*
> *Brothers and sisters, I do not consider myself yet to have taken hold of it.*
> *But one thing I do:*
> *Forgetting what is behind and straining toward what is ahead,*
> *I press on toward the goal to win the prize*
> *for which God has called me heavenward in Christ Jesus.*
> *All of us, then, who are mature should take such a view of things.*
> *And if on some point you think differently, that too God will make clear to you.*
> *Only let us live up to what we have already attained.*
> PHILIPPIANS 3:12–16

The passage is important as you think about long-term recovery. Paul seems to say of himself, "I am incomplete. I am a work in progress," yet I "press on." While it would be dangerous to deny that you are an addict, Paul encourages you to forget what is behind you, in the sense that God does not wish you to remain trapped in the shame of your past. In fact, He sent his son that you might be "free indeed" (John 8:36). Just as you cannot live in the past, neither can you live in the future. Perhaps Paul emphasized that he has not yet "arrived" to highlight that we must "press on" in the present moment.

 Reflect on the passage above from Paul's letter to the church at Philippi. What does this passage offer you about your own spiritual journey, both in this moment and in the future? Be specific about tasks and performables that remain vital as you "press on."

A Lamp, Not a Flashlight

The psalmist tells us that

> *Your word is a lamp for my feet,*
> *a light on my path.*
>
> PSALM 119:105

In modern times, most people who travel in the dark prefer a flashlight to a lamp because it illuminates the path for a greater distance ahead. If we are honest, we all like to see far ahead on the path. Although the psalmist could not have written, "Your word is a flashlight for my feet" because flashlights were not invented at that time, he could have written, "Your word is like sunshine for me; it lightens all of the darkness and illuminates everything."

But he did not write those words.

Perhaps this is because the psalmist fully understood how God reveals Himself to us through His word. A lamp will only illuminate a short distance around you. Beyond that, there is still darkness and unknown territory. If you are holding a lamp that shines down on the path for two steps in front of you, you must take those steps to see what lies farther ahead. Such is the spiritual journey. If you rely on God's word, it will illuminate your path, but you must have the faith that when you take steps and continue to rely on the light, the next steps will become illuminated.

 Reflect and journal on what this analogy means for you at this point in your recovery and your spiritual journey.

Watch and Pray

As Jesus prayed in the Garden of Gethsemane shortly before his arrest and crucifixion, he admonished his disciples who had fallen asleep. To his beloved disciples, he spoke words more than two thousand years ago that are very relevant for you today as a recovering addict:

> *"Watch and pray so that you will not fall into temptation.*
> *The spirit is willing, but the flesh is weak."*
>
> MATTHEW 26:41

In the days, weeks, months, and years ahead, you will undoubtedly face temptation. In this passage, Jesus is telling the disciples who have fallen asleep to stay awake, watch, and pray. Although they had literally fallen asleep, Jesus also is telling you figuratively not to go back to sleep. One of the greatest enemies of the recovering addict is *complacency*, that voice inside of you who twists your period of sobriety into the lie that a "slippery slope" behavior is not that big of a deal or that you can handle recent triggers without telling anyone. Be clear, this is not the voice of God, but rather the voice of Satan who longs for the "good old days." The part of you that is growing healthier, stronger, and closer to God in both your recovery and your spiritual journey knows that those days were not "good" at all. Discernment comes from staying awake, watching, and praying.

It is important, though, to discern "watching" from hypervigilance. When you are watchful, as Jesus called all of his disciples to be, you are calm, relaxed, and aware. You realize, for example, that a particular commercial on TV is triggering you. Without panicking, you change the channel. If the trigger persists, you call your sponsor. Perhaps you pray a breath prayer to calm your mind, heart, and body. In short, from the watchful place, you recognize the trigger and you take action, calling upon your resources, both divine and human. Hypervigilance, in contrast, is an anxious stance where you remain on high alert at all times. When triggered, you panic. You might get angry at the company that developed the commercial or feel a deep sense of shame that you felt aroused at the images. You have a strong emotional reaction and, in that response, forget to use your recovery tools.

Remember the words of Jesus who seems to call us into a peaceful but watchful place:

> *Peace I leave with you; my peace I give you.*
> *I do not give to you as the world gives.*
> *Do not let your hearts be troubled and do not be afraid.*
> JOHN 14:27

Goal Setting

John Beckley, a successful businessman, is quoted as saying, "Most people don't plan to fail; they fail to plan." At the same time, there is the Yiddish proverb "Man plans and God laughs." These two sayings, taken together, seem to be in contradiction. Should you plan? Should you set goals? Or, is goal setting a fool's folly?

It all depends on the type of goals that you set. If you set detailed content-oriented goals, such as where you will be living, how much money you will be making, or what other people will be doing (or not doing), God is almost assuredly laughing. Such goals squeeze God out of the equation and, in a sense, leave you "playing God" over what needs to happen in your life.

If, however, your goals are more process oriented, such as establishing and sustaining a daily spiritual practice, being faithful to your recovery practices, or growing in your ability to be in healthy community with other believers, you allow space for grace. You invite God into the details of how this plays out in your life in a way that is collaborative, humble, and open.

Write down short-term (over two to three months) and long-term (over three to five years) goals for yourself. Are you setting goals that leave space for grace? Or are you writing goals that squeeze God out of the equation for your future? If you feel unclear, stop and pray for God's guidance before continuing to set goals. If you remain unclear, talk to your trusted counsel about this task.

Spiritual Disciplines

Continue your daily spiritual practice plan. Additionally, you may find other spiritual practices particularly helpful as you continue in your recovery. Integrate these practices into your daily plan as best supports your continued healing.

Prayer of Thanksgiving and Petition

Reflecting on what has been reclaimed through recovery, offer heartfelt expressions of gratitude to God. Then, offer prayers of petition, asking God to help you remain open to His presence in your life and to guide your steps as you continue your recovery journey.

Breath Prayer

Take time to pray the following breath prayer:

I am a child of God

Eleventh Step Prayer

At the conclusion of chapter 10, you developed an Eleventh Step prayer for the morning and one for the evening. Take time to reread and reflect on these prayers.

Below is a prayer you might use as part of ongoing Eleventh Step work for your long-term recovery. Edit as needed to fit your current situation, but maintain an open mind and an open heart as you pray for discernment and courage:

Lord God, have mercy on me, a grateful recovering sex addict.
Help me to calm my mind, heart, and body so that I might hear your voice.
Guide my steps so that I might choose wisely and follow the path you would have me take.
Just for this day, help me to lean into your everlasting arms.
Just for this day, help me to feel your presence.
Help me to know that my deepest longings are always for You.
And grant me the courage, in each moment, to do the next right thing.
Amen

Divine Reading

Use the steps described in chapter 2 to do a contemplative divine reading of the following paraphrase of Jeremiah 29:11, knowing that these are the words of God spoken directly to you:

"I know the plans I have for you (insert your name),
plans to prosper you and not to harm you,
plans to give you a hope and a future."

Conclusion

We are grateful that you are on a healing journey of recovery. As you realize that your deepest thirst is not for anything sexual, but for divine communion with God, you will continue to grow in the knowledge that your addictive behaviors are just the tip of the iceberg and that thoughts, feelings, experiences, and traumas underneath those behaviors will continue to be revealed and healed. God is the great healer. With His guidance, long-term recovery and the reclamation of your life is within your reach. We believe that you can do this. We also believe, based on our experiences, that the road will not always be easy. There will be struggles. There will be temptations. Yet we believe the words of Jesus when he said:

"With man this is impossible, but not with God; all things are possible with God."
MARK 10:27

We close with a few of our favorite passages of scripture and words of inspiration from a poem:

Let love and faithfulness never leave you; bind them around your neck, write them on the
tablet of your heart. Then you will win favor and a good name in the sight of God and
man. Trust in the Lord with all your heart and lean not on your own understanding;

in all your ways submit to him, and he will make your paths straight.

PROVERBS 3:3–6

Peace I leave with you; my peace I give you. I do not give to you as the world gives. Do not let your hearts be troubled and do not be afraid.

JOHN 14:27

You are a child of the universe, no less than the trees and the stars;
you have a right to be here.
And whether or not it is clear to you, no doubt the universe is unfolding as it should.
Therefore be at peace with God, whatever you conceive Him to be,
and whatever your labors and aspirations,
in the noisy confusion of life keep peace with your soul.

MAX EHRMANN, "DESIDERATA"

He has shown you, O mortal, what is good.
And what does the Lord require of you?
To act justly and to love mercy
and to walk humbly with your God.

MICAH 6:8

And this is my prayer: that your love may abound more and more in knowledge and depth of insight, so that you may be able to discern what is best and may be pure and blameless for the day of Christ.

PHILIPPIANS 1:9–10

Blessings to you.

Appendix A

Twelve Steps, Biblical Text, Recovery Principles, and Spiritual Disciplines

Step	Related Biblical Text	Principle	Discipline
One: We admitted we were powerless over the effects of our separation from God—that our lives had become unmanageable.	I know nothing good lives in me, that is, in my sinful nature. For I have the desire to do what is good, but I cannot carry it out. (Romans 7:17)	Acceptance	Submission
Two: Came to believe that a power greater than ourselves could restore us to sanity.	For it is God who works in you to will and to act according to His good purpose. (Phil. 2:13)	Awareness	Conversion
Three: Made a decision to turn our will and our lives over to the care of God *as we understood Him.*	Therefore, I urge you, brothers and sisters, in view of God's mercy, to offer your bodies as a living sacrifice, holy and pleasing to God—this is your true and proper worship. (Rom. 12:1)	Spirituality	Conversion
Four: Made a searching and fearless moral inventory of ourselves.	Let us examine our ways and test them, and let us return to the Lord. (Lam. 3:40)	Responsibility	Confession
Five: Admitted to God, to ourselves, and to another human being the exact nature of our wrongs.	Therefore, confess your sins to each other and pray for each other so that you may be healed. (James 5:16a)	Openness	Confession
Six: Were entirely ready to have God remove all these defects of character.	Humble yourselves before the Lord, and he will lift you up. (James 4:10)	Responsiveness	Repentance

Step	Related Biblical Text	Principle	Discipline
Seven: Humbly asked Him to remove our shortcomings	If we confess our sins, he is faithful and just and will forgive us our sins and purify us from all unrighteousness. (I John 1:9)	Commitment	Repentance
Eight: Made a list of all persons we had harmed and became willing to make amends to them all.	Do to others as you would have them do to you. (Luke 6:31)	Courage	Amends
Nine: Made direct amends to such people wherever possible, except when to do so would injure them or others.	Therefore, if you are offering your gift at the altar and there remember that your brother or sister has something against you, leave your gift there in front of the altar. First go and be reconciled to them; then come and offer your gift. (Matthew 5:23–24)	Honesty	Amends
Ten: Continued to take personal inventory and, when we were wrong, promptly admitted it.	So, if you think you are standing firm, be careful that you don't fall! (1 Cor. 10:12)	Trust	Maintenance
Eleven: Sought through prayer and meditation to improve our conscious contact with God *as we understood Him*, praying only for knowledge of His will for us and the power to carry that out.	Let the word of Christ dwell in you richly. (Col. 3:16a)	Meaning	Prayer
Twelve: Having had a spiritual awakening as the result of these steps, we tried to carry this message to others and to practice these principles in all our affairs.	Brothers and sisters, if someone is caught in a sin, you who live by the Spirit should restore that person gently. But watch yourself, or you also may be tempted. (Gal. 6:1)	Generativity	Ministry

Shadows of the Cross: A Christian Companion to *Facing the Shadow*

Appendix B
First Seven Tasks of the
Thirty Task Recovery Model

Recovery Task	Performables	Life Competency
1. Break through denial	• Creates a problem list • Records a secret list • Completes list of excuses • Completes Consequences Inventory • Learns 14 ways to distort reality • Inventories 14 distortion strategies in personal life • Accountability—Victim Empathy exercise • Makes full disclosure to therapist	• Understands the characteristics of denial and self-delusion • Identifies presence of self-delusion in life • Knows personal preference patterns of thought distortion • Accepts confrontation
2A. Understand the nature of addictive illness	• Completes assigned readings on sex addiction • Learns different ways to define sex addiction • Understands addictive system • Understands deprivation system • Maps out personal addictive system • Understands criteria for addictive illness • Applies criteria to personal behavior • Learns key factors in the genesis of sex addiction	• Knows information on addictive illness • Applies information to personal life

Recovery Task	Performables	Life Competency
2B. Sexual addiction component	• Understands sexual modularity • Understands sexual hierarchy • Knows ten types of behavior • Reviews ten types for personal patterns • Completes and shares sexual history • Completes ideal fantasy list • Completes and shares fantasy contamination exercise	• Understands sexually compulsive patterns • Knows specific stories/scenarios of arousal template
3. Surrenders to process	• Understands context of change, grief, commitment • Understands existential position on change—essence of recovery • Understands principles of anxiety reduction • Completes sexual addiction history • Completes powerless worksheet • Completes unmanageability worksheet • Identifies ten worst moments • Understands guidelines of Step completion • Gives First Step	• Acceptance of addiction in life • Knows personal limitations • Discerns difference between controllable and non-controllable events
4. Limits damage from behavior	• Understands first and second order change • Understands concept of paradigm shift • Records provisional beliefs • Completes damage control plan • Completes a disclosure plan • Writes a "turning it over" letter to Higher Power • Completes and Second and Third Step	• Integrates self-limitation into personal paradigm • Responds to crisis plan fully • Uses boundaries at a minimum level • Has internal skills for anxiety reduction • Develops resolve for change and commitment

Recovery Task	Performables	Life Competency
5. Establish sobriety	• Understands sobriety as boundary problem • Commits to and completes celibacy contract • Writes sobriety statement • Understands relapse process • Writes relapse plan • Establishes a date	• Uses clearly stated boundaries of sobriety • Manages life without dysfunctional sexual behavior
6. Ensure physical integrity	• Learns physical aspects of addiction • Completes physical • Completes psychiatric assessment • Learns neuropathways of addiction • Maps personal neuropathway interactions • Understands arousal template • Maps personal arousal template	• Understands physical aspects of addiction • Identifies neuropathway interaction • Identifies dysfunctional arousal patterns
7. Participate in a culture of support	• Participates in a Twelve Step program • Develops relationship with sponsor • Completes sponsor debriefing • Does service in program • Knows signs of a healthy group • Has a celebration date	• Maintains a healthy support system

Appendix C
The Twelve Steps of Alcoholics Anonymous

1. We admitted we were powerless over alcohol—that our lives had become unmanageable.

2. Came to believe that a Power greater than ourselves could restore us to sanity.

3. Made a decision to turn our will and our lives over to the care of God *as we understood Him*.

4. Made a searching and fearless moral inventory of ourselves.

5. Admitted to God, to ourselves, and to another human being the exact nature of our wrongs.

6. Were entirely ready to have God remove all these defects of character.

7. Humbly asked Him to remove our shortcomings.

8. Made a list of all persons we had harmed, and became willing to make amends to them all.

9. Made direct amends to such people wherever possible, except when to do so would injure them or others.

10. Continued to take personal inventory and when we were wrong promptly admitted it.

11. Sought through prayer and meditation to improve our conscious contact with God *as we understood Him*, praying only for knowledge of His will for us and the power to carry that out.

12. Having had a spiritual awakening as the result of these steps, we tried to carry this message to alcoholics, and to practice these principles in all our affairs.

The Twelve Steps of AA are taken from *Alcoholics Anonymous*, 3d ed., published by AA World Services, Inc., New York, NY, 59–60.

Appendix D
The Twelve Steps of Sexaholics Anonymous

The Twelve Steps of Alcoholics Anonymous Adapted for Sexual Addicts

1. We admitted we were powerless over our sexual addiction—that our lives had become unmanageable.

2. Came to believe a Power greater than ourselves could restore us to sanity.

3. Made a decision to turn our will and our lives over to the care of God, *as we understood Him.*

4. Made a searching and fearless moral inventory of ourselves.

5. Admitted to God, to ourselves, and to another human being the exact nature of our wrongs.

6. Were entirely ready to have God remove all these defects of character.

7. Humbly asked Him to remove our shortcomings.

8. Made a list of all persons we had harmed, and became willing to make amends to them all.

9. Made direct amends to such people wherever possible, except when to do so would injure them or others.

10. Continued to take personal inventory and when we were wrong promptly admitted it.

11. Sought through prayer and meditation to improve our conscious contact with God *as we understood Him*, praying only for knowledge of His will for us and the power to carry that out.

12. Having had a spiritual awakening as the result of these steps, we tried to carry this message to others and to practice these principles in all our affairs.

Adapted from the Twelve Steps of Alcoholics Anonymous.
Reprinted with permission of AA World Services, Inc., New York, NY.

Appendix E
Activity Checklist

Chapter One: Understanding Sex Addiction

- ❑ JOURNAL: Reflect on when you have been immature throughout your active addiction.
- ❑ JOURNAL: Write a list of what maturity will look like for you.
- ❑ PRAYER: Ask God to guide you in becoming more complete and mature.

- ❑ JOURNAL: Reflect on ways to collaborate with God in your recovery.

- ❑ JOURNAL: Reflect on how the Serenity Prayer applies to you.
- ❑ PRAYER: Thank God for what you have learned.

- ❑ BIBLE STUDY: Reflect on John's account of the Samaritan woman at the well (John 4:3-42).
- ❑ JOURNAL: Consider all that Jesus offers you and asks of you.
- ❑ BIBLE STUDY: Read Luke's account of this parable (Luke 15:11–32).

Chapter Two: The Importance of Spiritual Disciplines

- ❑ JOURNAL: Reflect on surrendering to the "still small voice" of God's will.

- ❑ BIBLE STUDY: Read Martha's story (Luke 10:38-42).
- ❑ JOURNAL: Reflect on ways in which you are so distracted by "preparations" that you forget what is most important.

- ❑ JOURNAL: Create a preliminary plan for your spiritual practice.

- ❑ PRAYER: Practice intercessory prayers.
- ❑ JOURNAL: Reflect on your experience of lifting up others in prayer to God.
- ❑ PRAYER: Practice petitionary prayers.
- ❑ JOURNAL: Reflect on your experience of lifting up your petitions to God in prayer.
- ❑ PRAYER: Practice prayers of adoration.
- ❑ JOURNAL: Reflect on your experience of communicating your adoration of God through prayer.
- ❑ PRAYER: Practice prayers of thanksgiving and gratitude.
- ❑ JOURNAL: Reflect on your experience of lifting up your prayers of thanksgiving and gratitude to God.
- ❑ PRAYER: Practice prayers of repentance/forgiveness.
- ❑ JOURNAL: Reflect on whether you feel an unburdening—or are still holding onto your regrets.
- ❑ PRAYER: Practice prayers of deliverance.
- ❑ JOURNAL: Reflect on your experience of praying for deliverance.
- ❑ PRAYER: Repeat the Jesus Prayer.

- ❑ JOURNAL: Reflect on your experience of using the Jesus Prayer.
- ❑ PRAYER: Practice prayers of submission.
- ❑ JOURNAL: Reflect on your experience of offering prayers of submission.
- ❑ JOURNAL: Reflect on the prayer of Saint Francis of Assisi.
- ❑ PRAYER: Ask earnestly for knowledge of God's will and the courage to carry it out.
- ❑ JOURNAL: Reflect on your experience of using the Eleventh Step prayer.
- ❑ JOURNAL: Write six to twelve syllables that will serve as your breath prayer.
- ❑ PRAYER: Spend a few minutes silently speaking your breath prayer.
- ❑ JOURNAL: Reflect on your experience of using the breath prayer.
- ❑ JOURNAL: Ask God to help you discern the best word for your centering prayer.
- ❑ PRAYER: Spend ten minutes in centering prayer.
- ❑ JOURNAL: Reflect on your experience of using your centering prayer.
- ❑ JOURNAL: Reflect on your experience of the examination of consciousness.

- ❑ JOURNAL: Reflect on your experience of using the palms down, palms up meditation.
- ❑ JOURNAL: Reflect on your experience of using the concentration on breathing meditation.
- ❑ JOURNAL: Reflect on your experience of using the seven steps of meditation on scriptures.
- ❑ JOURNAL: List behaviors that might trigger you to relapse.
- ❑ JOURNAL: Reflect on your "slippery slope" behaviors.

- ❑ BIBLE STUDY: Select one of Jesus' Parables.
- ❑ PRAYER: Ask for guidance as you select a parable to study.
- ❑ JOURNAL: Reflect on what you learned by studying the parable.

- ❑ JOURNAL: Develop a list of three ways to simplify your life.

- ❑ JOURNAL: Write down what you did in your addiction that you would like to confess.
- ❑ BIBLE STUDY: Read Psalm 32:5-7.
- ❑ PRAYER: Confess what you wrote in your journal.
- ❑ JOURNAL: Reflect on your experience of using prayers of confession.

- ❑ PRAYER: Integrate brief prayer time into your time of solitude.
- ❑ JOURNAL: After completing your day-long experience of solitude, write about the experience.

- ❑ JOURNAL: Reflect on one specific event connected with one person whom you
59 hope to forgive.

Chapter Three: Jesus and the Twelve Steps

Chapter Four: Who Am I in Christ?

- ❑ JOURNAL: Reflect on Proverbs 14:12.
- ❑ PRAYER: Ask God to help you be "searching and fearless" in your reflections.
- ❑ JOURNAL: Reflect on how you have you failed to trust God and list the fears that affect you the most.
- ❑ JOURNAL: Reflect on how you pretended not to need help, manipulated other people, and hid the light that God placed in your heart.
- ❑ JOURNAL: Reflect on ways that you justified your addictive sexual behavior as something to which you were entitled.
- ❑ JOURNAL: Reflect on how you presented yourself as special in some way to justify addictive sexual behavior and reduce shame; reflect on what it will look like for you to submit to others out of reverence for Christ.
- ❑ PRAYER: Take a few moments to offer a prayer of gratitude.
- ❑ JOURNAL: Reflect on how you've been blessed by the fact that your addiction is no longer a secret; reflect on how you will manifest patience and kindness in your life.
- ❑ FACING THE SHADOW: Read chapter 1 on the consequences of your behavior.
- ❑ JOURNAL: Reflect on how you and one other person been hurt by your addictive sexual behavior, and how you have strayed from the path that God wants you to follow.
- ❑ JOURNAL: Reflect on how you tried to manage your addictive sexual behavior.
- ❑ JOURNAL: Reflect on how you will collaborate with God to live the Serenity Prayer.
- ❑ FACING THE SHADOW: Complete the Problem List (exercise 1.1) in chapter 1.
- ❑ JOURNAL: List the spiritual practices that calm you when your mind, your body, or both are triggered sexually.
- ❑ FACING THE SHADOW: Complete the Secret List (exercise 1.2) in chapter 1.
- ❑ FACING THE SHADOW: Complete the Excuses List (exercise 1.3) in chapter 1.
- ❑ JOURNAL: Reflect on how you made excuses or blamed others to avoid responsibility for your addiction or your recovery.

- ❑ FACING THE SHADOW: Complete the Consequences Inventory (exercise 1.4) in chapter 1.
- ❑ JOURNAL: Describe the spiritual and religious consequences you faced as a result of your addictive sexual behavior.
- ❑ JOURNAL: Describe your own experience of spiritual emptiness and how your addiction affected it.
- ❑ JOURNAL: Reflect on how your addiction left you feeling disconnected from yourself, others, and God.
- ❑ JOURNAL: Describe any experiences of feeling abandoned by God.
- ❑ JOURNAL: Describe any times when you questioned God's existence.
- ❑ JOURNAL: Describe any experiences of being angry with God.
- ❑ JOURNAL: Describe any experiences of feeling sadness, fear, and shame.
- ❑ JOURNAL: Describe any experiences of loss of faith due to your addiction.
- ❑ JOURNAL: Describe any other religious or spiritual consequences you've experienced.

Chapter Five: What Is an Addiction?

- ❑ JOURNAL: Reflect on the images you drew and consider sharing them with another trusted soul, such as a therapist or sponsor.
- ❑ JOURNAL: Review your second drawing again; describe the steps that you are ready, willing, and able to take in realizing the fullness of Christ's love.

- ❑ FACING THE SHADOW: Review the material on sexual anorexia in chapter 2.
- ❑ JOURNAL: Describe your early sexual experiences, the early messages you received about sex, the creation of your sexual "shadow," and any periods of sexual anorexia.

- ❑ JOURNAL: Create a visual image of the "yoke of bondage" you experienced when active in your sex addiction; then draw an image of the "freedom and glory of the children of God" that you experience in recovery.

- ❑ PRAYER: Ask for your continued deliverance from the dark places inside you.
- ❑ PRAYER: "Pour out your heart" to God with on your gratitude for the many spiritual gifts in recovery.
- ❑ PRAYER/JOURNAL: Meditate on how Luke 1:46b–48a calls you to live differently in your daily life.

Chapter Six: What Is a First Step?

- ❑ BIBLE STUDY: Read Matthew 7:24-27, Parable of the Two Houses.
- ❑ JOURNAL: Describe any pieces of your recovery program where you are only pretending to do the work.
- ❑ BIBLE STUDY: Revisit Jeremiah 29:11.
- ❑ JOURNAL: Describe the people in your life who are encouraging and supporting you, even in small ways.
- ❑ JOURNAL: Describe how your negative voice spoke to you during your active addiction and how you reacted as well as how you react now in recovery.
- ❑ BIBLE STUDY/JOURNAL: Reflect on Psalm 6:6–7 and describe your reaction to it.
- ❑ BIBLE STUDY/JOURNAL: Reflect on Deuteronomy 30:19–20 and relate the passage to your own life.
- ❑ BIBLE STUDY: Reflect and review on Mark 4:35–40.
- ❑ JOURNAL: Consider how you would rate your faith in Christ on a scale of 1 to 10.

- ❑ FACING THE SHADOW: Read the introduction to chapter 4, What Is a First Step?
- ❑ JOURNAL: Describe personal examples of denial, minimization, justification, and rationalization.
- ❑ FACING THE SHADOW: Complete the sexual addiction history (exercise 4.1) in chapter 4.
- ❑ JOURNAL: Write a history of your Christian journey, much like you did with your sexual addiction history.

- ❑ JOURNAL: Share any connections between your history of sexual addiction and your spiritual history.
- ❑ FACING THE SHADOW: Complete the Ten Worst Moments exercise (exercise 4.6).
- ❑ JOURNAL: Describe the ten worst moments related to your religious or spiritual life.

- ❑ FACING THE SHADOW: Read the material about sharing your First Step.
- ❑ BIBLE STUDY: Read Ephesians 3:17-19.
- ❑ BIBLE STUDY/JOURNAL: Reflect on what II Corinthians 12:7b–10 reveals about your addiction, your recovery, and the act of telling your story to others.
- ❑ BIBLE STUDY/JOURNAL: Describe what Luke 15:20 means to you at this point in your recovery.
- ❑ BIBLE STUDY: Read and reflect on Psalm 112:4.
- ❑ JOURNAL: Describe any resentments you are harboring and your commitment to be compassionate.
- ❑ BIBLE STUDY/JOURNAL: Reread Matthew 22:37–40 and then describe your personal practice of daily self-compassion.

- ❑ JOURNAL: Reflect on your prayer of petition and what you will need to focus on in the coming days.
- ❑ JOURNAL: Write down the names of people who have been harmed by your addictive sexual behavior.
- ❑ BIBLE STUDY/JOURNAL: Describe your experiences with meditating on Psalm 144:2a.

Chapter Seven: What Damage Has Been Done?

- ❑ BIBLE STUDY: Read Matthew 18:21–35, the Parable of the Unmerciful Servant.
- ❑ JOURNAL: Reflect on the parable of the unmerciful servant from several points of view.

- ❑ FACING THE SHADOW: Complete the Damage Control Worksheets (exercises 5.3-5.10) in chapter 5 of Facing the Shadow.
- ❑ JOURNAL: List "Disconnection from God" as a current problem and describe ways to strengthen or re-establish this connection.

- ❑ JOURNAL: Describe any ways that you might still be in denial, what your emotional life in recovery is like, and your reactions to remembering past behaviors that you had previously forgotten.

- ❑ BIBLE STUDY/JOURNAL: Reflect on Ecclesiastes 3:1–3 and describe how you would characterize your "current" season in recovery and what season you were in as an active sex addict.
- ❑ BIBLE STUDY/JOURNAL: Read John 3:2–4, the story of a Pharisee named Nicodemus, and then describe your own spiritual death and rebirth.
- ❑ JOURNAL: Describe the most important daily behaviors that support your recovery—and the behaviors that need to be uprooted.
- ❑ JOURNAL: Reflect on the relational and individual aspects of a time to kill and a time to heal.
- ❑ JOURNAL: Use the image of a house to describe your active addiction and your engagement in recovery.
- ❑ JOURNAL: Review your two house images and describe the changes that are occurring at a soul level in your recovery.
- ❑ PRAYER: Thank God for changes that are occurring in your life and pray for God to help you continue to build your house of recovery.

- ❑ JOURNAL: Describe some of your common sexual fantasies.

- ❑ BIBLE STUDY: Reread and reflect on Ecclesiastes 3:1-3.

Chapter Eight: What Is Sobriety?

- ❑ BIBLE STUDY: Read and pause to reflect on Job 14:15b.
- ❑ BIBLE STUDY/JOURNAL: Read Philippians 4:8, write down the key words and phrases from this passage and then place a star next to the words that characterize you.

- ❑ JOURNAL: Consider whether this story describes something that has happened to you.
- ❑ BIBLE STUDY: Read Matthew 25:1–13, the Parable of the Wise and Foolish Maidens.
- ❑ JOURNAL: Reflect on the ways you are developing your program of recovery, looking for areas that might need more attention.
- ❑ BIBLE STUDY: Read what the psalmist wrote of endurance in Psalm 119:1-8 and the New Testament scripture which encourages endurance and perseveance Hebrews 12:1-3.
- ❑ JOURNAL: Reflect on what you know about God's path for your life at this point in your recovery, the obstacles you face, and how you will respond to them with recovery tools and spiritual practices.
- ❑ BIBLE STUDY: Read Matthew 25:11–13.
- ❑ JOURNAL: Reflect on how you respond to the triggers, urges, and cravings that occur in recovery.
- ❑ FACING THE SHADOW: Read the opening section of chapter 6 about eight issues that often compound the problem of addiction.

- ❑ JOURNAL: Consider how you are addressing the issues of achievement, self-esteem, accountability, self-care, conscience, self-awareness, relationships, and affect in your life.
- ❑ PRAYER: Thank God for changes that you have already made and pray for guidance in changes yet to come.
- ❑ FACING THE SHADOW: Complete the Three-Circle Method (exercise 6.7).

- ❑ BIBLE STUDY: Read God's response to Micah's question in Micah 6:8.
- ❑ JOURNAL: Reflect on what it looks like for you to act justly, love mercy, and walk humbly with God.
- ❑ PRAYER: Ask God to help you grow in humility, mercy, and just actions.

- ❑ BIBLE STUDY: Read John 14:27, Matthew 11:28-30, and Philippians 4:7.

- ❑ BIBLE STUDY: Read Galatians 5:22–23.
- ❑ JOURNAL: Rate each of the nine fruits and then write about how you can more fully cultivate and nurture the fruits of the spirit: love, joy, peace, forbearance/mercy, kindness, goodness, faithfulness, gentleness, and self-control.
- ❑ PRAYER: Select one of the fruits and take ten minutes to engage in a breath prayer; ask God to increase this fruit in your life.

- ❑ FACING THE SHADOW: Complete the Personal Craziness Index (PCI) (exercises 6.8 and 6.9) and take time to review your results.

- ❑ FACING THE SHADOW: Review the Relapse Scenario Worksheets (exercises 6.3 – 6.5) in chapter 6.
- ❑ JOURNAL: Based on the patterns within your PCI results, consider how you can create more simplicity in your life.

Chapter Nine: What Has Happened to Your Body?

- ❑ BIBLE STUDY/JOURNAL: Read I Corinthians 6:19–20 and then reflect on what it means to honor God with your body.
- ❑ BIBLE STUDY/JOURNAL: Read Matthew 21:12–13 and then reflect on the way that your body is becoming a "house of prayer" and what are you doing to drive out the "money changers" that threaten your recovery.

- ❑ BIBLE STUDY: Read Matthew 13:44, the Parable of the Hidden Treasure.

- ❏ BIBLE STUDY: Read Luke 17:20–21.
- ❏ FACING THE SHADOW: Read about addiction neuropathways in chapter 7. Complete (exercise 7.1) Your Sexual Addiction Matrix, (exercise 7.2) Your Sexual Health Matrix, and (exercise 7.3) Matrix Reflection Questions.
- ❏ JOURNAL: Describe the most important things that you learned from doing the Facing the Shadow exercises.

Thoughts behind Addictive Processes 177
- ❏ JOURNAL: Describe the attachment strategies you most often use.
- ❏ JOURNAL: Reflect on how your attachment strategies affect your close relationships and play a role in your addiction.
- ❏ FACING THE SHADOW: Review the information on the arousal template in chapter 7.
- ❏ FACING THE SHADOW: Complete exercises 7.9 – 7.17, Your Arousal Template Worksheets.
- ❏ JOURNAL: Define your primary attachment strategy and then describe how it became a part of your sexuality; consider whether you use sex as a way to deepen psychological intimacy or to avoid it.
- ❏ JOURNAL: Consider whether there is anything you would change about your attachment to God—and whether you feel secure in your connection to God.
- ❏ BIBLE STUDY: Read John 3:16.

Feelings behind Addictive Processes 183
- ❏ JOURNAL: Describe the relationships between your sexual behavior and your emotions.
- ❏ BIBLE STUDY: Reread Mark 14:32–36, reflecting on how Jesus did not strive to avoid his emotional experiences and how he spoke of his emotions to a small group of trusted friends (v. 34).
- ❏ JOURNAL: Reflect on Jesus' emotional experiences and what they teach you about your own emotional life.
- ❏ BIBLE STUDY: Read John 8:32.
- ❏ JOURNAL: As you become aware of the difference between primary and secondary emotions, describe the current challenges in your emotional life.
- ❏ PRAYER: Ask for God's guidance as you grow in your emotional awareness.
- ❏ JOURNAL: Draw an outline of a human body and then place dots where you feel anger, sadness and fear in your body. Then use words to describe how you experience anger, sadness, and fear in your body.

Faith and the Addiction Neuropathways 191
- ❏ FACING THE SHADOW: Review the addiction neuropathways described in chapter 7 and focus on those that seem most relevant for you.
- ❏ JOURNAL: Consider how the neuropathways influenced your active addiction and how you are changing them in recovery.

Chapter Ten: Where is Your Support?

❏   BIBLE STUDY: Read the following Bible verses: James 5:15-16, Proverbs 28:13, and Galatians 5:13-14.

❏   JOURNAL: Reflect on who has offered to support you, the emotions that you felt, and how you responded.

❏   JOURNAL: Describe times during your active addiction when you believed that you could handle your "little problem" by yourself.
❏   BIBLE STUDY: Read Proverbs 3:5–6.

❏   JOURNAL: Reflect on the role of secrecy and privacy in your current life and the healthy choices that support your recovery.
❏   JOURNAL: Reflect on how you will protect the welfare of your religious community.
❏   JOURNAL: List the names of people who will hear your full story or your story without details; also list people who will not support your recovery in a healthy way and those you're unsure about.

❏   JOURNAL: Write a prayer for the morning to ask for God's guidance during the day; also write an evening prayer asking for God's forgiveness and presence.

Chapter Eleven: Where Do I Go from Here?

❏   BIBLE STUDY/JOURNAL: Read and reflect on I John 2:20–22 and its personal meaning for you.
❏   FACING THE SHADOW: Read chapter 9, focusing on the first seven tasks of recovery.
❏   JOURNAL: List tasks and performables that you feel are solidly complete, those that you have done but which need more attention, and those yet to be completed.

❏   JOURNAL: Reflect on Philippians 3:12–16 and then list specific tasks and performables that remain vital as you "press on" in your recovery.
❏   JOURNAL: Reflect on the description of God's word as a lamp (Psalm 119:105) for your spiritual path and what it means at this point in your recovery.

❏   JOURNAL: Write short-term and long-term goals for your life that leave space for grace.

Endnotes

Chapter 2

1. S. Kierkegaard, S. *Christian Discourses,* trans. Walter Lowie (New York: Oxford University Press, 1940.
2. R. Foster, *Celebration of Discipline: The Path to Spiritual Growth* (London: Hodder and Stoughton, 1978), 14.
3. Ibid.

Chapter 3

1. R. Rohr, *Breathing Under Water: Spirituality and the 12 Steps* (Cincinnati, OH: St. Anthony Messenger Press, 2011).

Chapter 4

1. R. Shapiro, *Recovery: The Sacred Art* (Woodstock, VT: Skylight Paths, 2009).
2. Author unknown, http://www.angelfire.com/mt/theriverofgod/answer.html.

Chapter 5

1. Retrieved April 2014 from http://prodigalsinternational.org/statistics-on-sexual-addiction.html

Chapter 6

1. P. Coelho and M. J. Costa, *Manuscript found in Accra* (New York: Knopf, 2013), 185–86.
2. R. Shapiro, *Recovery—The Sacred Art: The Twelve Steps as Spiritual Practice* (Woodstock, VT: Skylight Paths, 2009), 3.

Chapter 7

1. M. Laaser, "The Role of Fantasy in Addiction," L.I.F.E. Recovery International, accessed August 19, 2013, http://www.freedomeveryday. org/sexual-addiction-articles/viewArticle.php?articleID=62

Chapter 9

1. J. Bowlby, *Attachment and Loss, Vol. 1: Attachment* (New York: Basic Books, 1968).
2. M. J. Cusick, *Surfing for God: Discovering the Divine Desire beneath Sexual Struggle* (Nashville, TN: Thomas Nelson, 2012).
3. B. Harris, *Sacred Selfishness: A Guide to Living a Life of Substance* (Makawao, HI: Inner Ocean Publishing, 2003).

Acknowledgements

Craig S. Cashwell

I want to thank and praise the God of my understanding, from Whom all of my blessings flow. I also wish to thank the most talented and deeply spiritual group that anyone could ask to work with, the faculty in the Department of Counseling and Educational Development at the University of North Carolina at Greensboro. In particular, I want to thank my Department Chair, Dr. J. Scott Young, who wildly encouraged this project from its original conceptualization. Thanks, also, are due to my co-authors Pennie and Pat. What a blessing to know you both, much less work with you! Finally, I have been blessed to share this earthly journey with two amazing women, so I gratefully acknowledge the wisdom of my wife Tammy and my daughter Sam. I learn and grow from and with you each day and love you both more than I will ever have the words to say.

Pennie Johnson

God is amazing. Just when I think I have reached the mountain tops, He raises me up to yet another level of "God sent" journeys showing me pathways toward His plan for me on Earth. I wish to say how grateful I am that Pat saw in me what I was afraid to see. Because of his love and support, I have chosen to accept challenges which have brought awareness of my inner strengths; many that would have other-wise gone unnoticed. I realize now we are more together than we are apart. I have much gratitude to Craig for believing in me and encouraging my process as a new author and mentoring me throughout this journey. I am eternally grateful for the constant love and support I receive from my family, especially the unconditional love of my children, Rebecca, Clinton and his wife, Jennifer. They have served as my anchor throughout our lives together. It is because of my precious grandsons, Bransen and Lucas, that my love of books and short stories enabled me to write the modern day parables in this book. To my friends, Roxana Erickson Klein, Ralph Earle, the Twelve Principles community, the CSAT community, board members of AFAR and staff of IITAP—thank you for believing in me. To each and every one of you, thank you, thank you, thank you, and may God bless you every moment of every day!

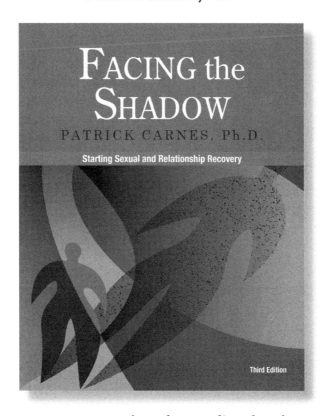

For all addicts, a moment comes when they realize they have a problem. There is sudden clarity—the insight that life has become unmanageable. That moment, however, is fragile. It is easily lost to craving and denial. People struggling with sex addiction find the old refrains creeping back into their thinking: My situation is different…. This will all blow over…. People are over-reacting to my behavior. Or, This is hopeless. I'm just too perverted to change.

"If any of those thoughts occur to you, you are exactly where you should be," notes Dr. Patrick Carnes in the introduction to *Facing the Shadow*. Starting with those gentle words, he guides readers through a series of reflections and exercises that pierce denial and light the path to healing from sex addiction.

Facing the Shadow, used by thousands of therapists with their clients, is based on the thirty-task model of recovery from addiction that forms the basis of Carnes's work. This book takes readers through the first seven of those tasks.

Gentle Path
P R E S S
gentlepath.com